HISTORY OF THE SPANISH REFORMATION

PROGRESS & SUPPRESSION IN THE 16TH CENTURY

THOMAS M'CRIE

FOREWORD BY STEVEN R. MARTINS

HISTORY OF THE SPANISH REFORMATION

PROGRESS & SUPPRESSION IN THE 16TH CENTURY

THOMAS M'CRIE

FOREWORD BY STEVEN R. MARTINS

cántaro
publications

www.cantaroinstitute.org

Published by Cántaro Publications
Cántaro Institute
Jordan Station, Ontario, Canada

Cover design: Steven R. Martins
Copy Editing: Susanna Celso
Interior design and typeset: Steven R. Martins

Library & Archives Canada
ISBN 978-1-990771-22-4

About the Cántaro Institute
Inheriting, Informing, Inspiring

The Cántaro Institute is a confessional evangelical Christian organization established in 2020 that seeks to recover the riches of historic Protestantism for the renewal and edification of the contemporary church and to advance the comprehensive Christian philosophy of life for the religious reformation of the Western and Ibero-American world.

We believe that as the Christian church returns to the fount of Scripture as her ultimate authority for all knowing and living, and wisely applies God's truth to every aspect of life, faithful in spirit to the reformers, her missiological activity will result in not only the renewal of the human person but also the reformation of culture, an inevitable result when the true scope and nature of the gospel is made known and applied.

*This restorative work is dedicated to the executive board
and the supporters of the Cántaro Institute*

CONTENTS

FOREWORD
A Forgotten History

0.1 Reformation Celebration

It was only a few years ago that the Christian church celebrated the 500th anniversary of the protestant reformation, that historic day when the German monk and scholar, Martin Luther, nailed the 95 Theses to the chapel door of Wittenberg castle. What Luther likely thought was an otherwise insignificant event at the time turned out to be the much-needed spark to light an ecclesiastical movement towards reforming all life and thought to the teaching of God's Word alone.

What had prompted this reformation movement to begin with was the fact that the Catholic church had been attempting to synthesize the biblical religious worldview with the antithetical philosophies of man – this was most evident in its development of scholastic thought and its accompanied dualism, a product of ancient Greek philosophy – and what it produced was a 'Christened' form of religious humanism.[1] This is affirmed by William Tyndale,

---

1. For more on how Greek philosophy influenced the development of Catholic theology, vestiges that Protestants are still working today to expunge, read Werner Jaeger, *The Theology of the Early*

the English scholar and protestant, who wrote that:

> In the Universities they have ordained that no man shall look at the scripture, until he be noselled in heathen learning eight or nine years, and armed with false principles; with which he is clean shut out of the understanding of scripture… And then, when they be admitted to study divinity, because the scripture is locked up with such false expositions, and with false principles of natural philosophy, that they cannot enter in, they go about the outside, and dispute all their lives about words and vain opinions…[2]

It wasn't long until the biblical doctrine of soteriology was buried by all the falsehoods and vanities that stem from such a compromised worldview. It was thus a refreshing wind for many faithful Christ-followers when they learned of Luther's disputation against the Catholic church's sale of indulgences, it was a call to repentance, and it became a rallying cry for the church to return to the sole and ultimate authority of Scripture, and to abandon any thought and belief that does not honour Jesus Christ

---

Greek Philosophers: The Gifford Lectures, 1936 (Eugene, OR.: Wipf & Stock Publishers, 2003); Werner Jaeger, "The Greek Ideas of Immortality: The Ingersoll Lecture For 1958", Harvard Theological Review (1959), Vol. 52, Issue 3; and Herman Dooyeweerd, *A New Critique of Theoretical Thought*, 4 Vols. (Jordan Station, ON.: Paideia Press, 2016).

2.   William Tyndale, "Practice of Prelates," in *Expositions and Notes on Sundry Portions of the Holy Scriptures together with the Practice of Prelates*, ed. H. Walker (1849; repr., Cambridge: Cambridge University Press, 1968), 291.

as Lord. As scholar David Robinson writes, in relation to the reformational ministry of Luther and the recovery of the biblical gospel:

> The prophet Hosea cried out to the people of God, "Come, let us return to the LORD, for he has torn us, that he may heal us; he has struck us down, and he will bind us up. After two days he will revive us; on the third day he will raise us up, that we may live before him" (Hos. 6:1-2). Luther was simply repeating this prophetic call. For him, the word of the Gospel breaks us, that it might heal us; it strikes us down, and it will bind us up. By the word of the Gospel, God confronts sinners and executes the Old Adam in us, so that he might revive us and raise us up in the Last Adam. Thus, Luther cried out with Hosea, "Come, let us return to the LORD!" His cry was a call for repentance.[3]

The recovery of the biblical gospel was at the very heart of the protestant reformation, and as the church celebrated its quincentenary, it sought to preserve and advance this biblical gospel by means of new publications, documentaries and films, lectures, sermons and conferences, amongst several other cultural mediums, all emphasizing the significance and relevance of the reformation. However, in spite of the vast wealth of these resources, which to date has been both broad and wide, very little has been made available on the reformation in Ibero-America. Consider,

---

3. David Robinson, "The Sweetest Spectacle: The Cross and God's Justifying Love according to Martin Luther" in *Jubilee: Recovering Biblical Foundations for our Time*, ed., Ryan Eras (Grimsby, ON.: Ezra Institute for Contemporary Christianity, Fall 2017), 10.

for example, how many have heard of John Calvin, Martin Luther, and Ulrich Zwingli. There is no doubt that most have. Compare that then to those who have heard of Casiodoro de Reina, Cipriano de Valera, and Constantino Ponce de la Fuente. You may already be able to discern the great chasm between those familiar with the former and those with the latter. And it is not a chasm that were to shrink by any means if you were to turn to the protestant church in Ibero-America. As a matter of fact, there would not be very much of a difference.

On occasion of the reformation's quincentenary, I had purchased the facsimile reproductions of the *Biblia del Oso* and *Biblia del Cántaro* from the Sociedad Bíblica España, the first two complete Spanish translations of the Bible in the sixteenth century. The first was the result of the work of Reina, and the second contained the revisions introduced by Valera. These are, perhaps, the most treasured out of all my literary possessions. So much so that, whenever my family would have guests over, whether they were church leaders or laymen, I would take the time to showcase these facsimiles in order to teach our guests about the Spanish reformation. Up until the present time, there has not yet been an occasion in which our guests have expressed familiarity with the Spanish reformation, including those who have come from an Iberoamerican background. What might this lack of familiarity indicate? That the Spanish protestant reformation remains to this day forgotten in the shadows of the past.

The same, unfortunately, can be said in regard to the landscape of historical scholarship. As opposed to being a well-known subject, the Spanish reformation is a rather specialized and obscure interest. While it may be true that a list could be produced of numerous publications, unpublished dissertations, theses, and the names of various scholars who have specialized in this field, however long this list might be, it pales in comparison to the studies on the reformation and its influence in other parts of the world, such as that of England, Germany and Switzerland. To better illustrate the disparity, it would be like comparing a puddle of water with the water reservoir of the Hoover Dam.

0.2 Why the Neglect?

Having come from an Iberoamerican heritage myself, and being a reformed protestant, I have often asked myself, *Why has such a significant event been forgotten?* There are several reasons that come to mind. For one, it could be the Old Castilian language that has served as an impediment. Or, it could be the doubt of whether anything good and protestant could come from Catholic Spain. It may also be the scarcity of Spanish reformers, or the lack of historical popularity surrounding their works which has reduced them to obscurity. While these may appear to be plausible, I do not believe that any of these reasons are entirely valid. Firstly, though Old Castilian was not a language ever shared by the Anglosphere, this has not stopped researchers from studying works in Latin, German, French and Dutch. Consider, for example, Miguel Cervantes' *Don Quixote* which has been translated from Old Castilian and is now widely read. Secondly, as to whether anything good or protestant could come from Catholic Spain, this would provoke rather than dissuade curiosity amongst history and religion scholars. And, after all, did not the first Spanish translation of the Bible emerge from Catholic Spain? Is that not good in and of itself? And thirdly, in regard to the scarcity and popularity of the works of the Spanish reformers – though this is a case which I believe could be most convincing – it is often the inaccessible and the rare which has attracted the attention of scholarly research, not necessarily the common.

Where then lies the issue? What has caused this neglect? The mistaken conception that such a reformation movement never happened. In the 1923 publication of the *Enciclopedia Universal Ilustrada*, the reformation in Spain is dismissed as non-existent, stating that:

> (1) its influence was minimal at best due to the Roman ecclesiastical reforms of Cisneros regarding the morality and training of the clergy;

> (2) its efforts were futile because of the deeply-rooted, irrefutable Roman Catholicism of the time; and

> (3) it was extinguished by the Inquisition which stamped out any whiff of Protestantism, including the first two early protestant centres in Seville and Valladolid.[4]

This concept, however, that the reformation never occurred in the history of Spain is erroneous. According to the late scholar Arthur Gordon Kindle, the reformation movement began:

> ...in the 1540s and continued through the 1550s, [although] completely stamped out by the Inquisition in the

---

4.   *Enciclopedia Universal Ilustrada*, L (1923) entry under 'Reforma.'

early 1560s. This movement had its origins both in native currents of evangelical thought and anti-Roman feeling, and also in ideas imported from Erasmus and main-stream Reformers through literary and political contacts with more northerly countries.[5]

The Spanish reformation did come to an end in the early 1560s, if we are referring specifically to the movement within Spanish borders; however, if we are referring to the reformation of God's Spanish-speaking church, which had been exiled from her motherland, this has in fact never come to an end. Instead, faithful to the reformational phrase *Semper Reformanda*, the church has been *always reforming* to the teaching of Scripture. Though it may not be apparent when we look at the Iberoamerican church today (for those who may be familiar with its teachings and culture), there has nonetheless been a faithful remnant of reformed Spanish protestants who have sought this on-going reformation for the church, and it has been only quite recently that the principles of the reformation, those being the five *Solas* (*Sola Scriptura, Sola Fide, Sola Gratia, Solus Christus, Soli Deo Gloria*) are being applied more consistently and faithfully over a much larger ecclesiastical community in Latin America and Spain.[6]

---

5. A. Gordon Kindle, *Casiodoro de Reina: Spanish Reformer of the Sixteenth Century* (London, UK.: Tamesis Books Limited, 1975), xv.

6. Miguel Núñez, "La Reforma Protestante." *Integridad y Sabiduría.* Accessed on February 2, 2018, http://integridadysabiduria.org/la-reforma-protestante/

0.3 The Available Research

Of course, any evaluation of the Iberoamerican church's reformation would require a historical understanding of the reformation's beginnings in Spain. And *this* is precisely what is sorely lacking, not because no research exists, but because the information available to us is not as exhaustive as with other reformation events in Europe, nor as accessible. This, by no means, is to call into question the quality of past and present scholarship, on the contrary, what is available to us today is exemplary, but rather, the problem is that *not enough* research exists. While it is useful to have a biographical study of John Calvin, it is doubly useful to have two, three or more. Like a grand mosaic, it completes the historical picture, for while each work may cover the same ground, one or more scholars may uncover something that had been initially overlooked, and as a result their published research would contribute to the vast body of knowledge we already possess. And while it may be true that what we presently have available to us on the Spanish reformation is far more than we ever did in the past, more work is nonetheless required to recover the treasures of this forgotten movement.

To provide a brief survey of the efforts undertaken to recover this forgotten history, it was in the mid-nineteenth century that the Spaniards Luis de Usoz, Rio and the Englishman Benjamin Baron Wiffen partnered together to publish a twenty-volume work called *Reformistas Antiguos Españoles* (1847-1865), a scholarly publication that to date is difficult to acquire, save for the scattered pieces uploaded onto the internet.[7] This was the first project to "rescue from oblivion the works of Spanish Protestants of the Reformation period," and to redistribute the material with accompanying commentary on the lives and ministries of the reformers.[8]

Initially, it had been Wiffen's intention to provide a more systematic, biographical study of the reformers with bibliographic material. However, due to his passing, much of the burden of that work fell to his colleague Eduard Boehmer, a professor at the University of Strassburg. Boehmer produced a three-volume set entitled *Bibliotheca Wiffeniana* as a memorial to the life and work of his friend.[9] And in addition to this work, he independently published several letters that he discovered by the Spanish reformers.

Sometime later in the late-nineteenth to early-twentieth century, a German scholar, Ernst H.J. Schafer, investigated the Spanish inquisition and its relation to the protestant reformers, culminating in the publication of a three-volume set entitled *Beiträge zur Geschichte des Spanischen Protestantismus* (Gutersloh, 1902), along with sev-

---

7. A facsímile reproduction of the entire set is allegedly available for $1,000 CAD at an online Spanish book distributor site. See REFORMISTAS ANTIGUOS ESPAÑOLES EDICIÓN FACSÍMIL, *Certeza*. Accessed on February 1, 2018, http://www.certeza.com/reformistas-antiguos-espanoles-edicion-facsimil-700-e/

8. Kindle, *Casiodoro de Reina*, xiii.

9. See Eduard Boehmer, *Bibliotheca Wiffeniana* (London/Strassburg, 1883-1904).

eral articles, including one on the early protestant centres of Sevilla and Valladolid.[10]

Also worthy of mention is the contemporary of Schafer, twenty-four-year-old scholar and prodigy Marcelino Menéndez y Pelayo, who studied the preceding work on the Spanish reformation and published in Madrid, from 1880 to 1881, an eight-volume set entitled *Historia de los Heterodoxos Españoles.*

Up until this point, the aforementioned scholars, Luis de Usoz, Rio, Wiffen, Schafer and Menéndez y Pelayo, laid a foundation which, according to Kindle, is to be heavily relied on and referred to for any future studies.[11] We might refer to them as the "Patriarchs of Spanish reformational studies".

Other works that are worth consulting are those by the Frenchman Marcel Bataillon, a professor at the Institut de France, who wrote the two-volume set *Erasme et l'Espagne* (Paris, 1937), the Englishman William MacFadden, who wrote *Antonio del Corro* (Belfast, 1953), and the North-American Paul J. Hauben, who wrote *Three Spanish Heretics* (Geneva, 1967). Also worthy of consideration are the writings of Kindle, who is, in my opinion, to be regarded as one of the top authorities in the field. As a matter of fact, the Cántaro Institute owes part of its inspiration to his work.

---

10. "Sevilla und Valladolid: die evangelischen Gemeinden Spaniens im Reformationzeitalter," in *Schriften des Vereins für Reformationsgeschichte*, Vol. 78 (Halle, 1903).

11. Kindle, *Casiodoro de Reina*, xiv.

0.4 The Contribution of Thomas M'Crie

I have, up until this point, neglected to mention one other name that deserves to be considered alongside the patriarchs of Spanish reformational studies, and that is the name of Thomas M'Crie (1772-1835). As Kindle served as partial inspiration for the Cántaro Institute, M'Crie served as the knowledgeable guide, taking us on a tour throughout the history of the Spanish reformation as it unfolded. I do not know of any other scholar or writer, past or present, who has been able to recount the events of the reformation in Spain with such vividness that defies the general blandness associated with such academic renditions.

M'Crie was a Scottish historian, prolific writer and a reformed minister, born in the town of Duns. He was a vocal advocate for the ongoing reformation of the church, particularly in Scotland, and both his passion for reformational principles and his hostility towards ecclesiastical tyranny spilled into his writings.[12] While some may be inclined to invalidate his work because of his failure to separate his passion and convictions from his scholarship, M'Crie had at heart the best interests of the church, and for this he must be applauded, for instead of divorcing his faith from his scholarship, he rightly discerned that if Christ is Lord over all creation, then scholarship too must pay tribute to His Lordship. It was, therefore, not only a reformation of the institutional church that he advocated for, but a more robust and holistic reformation.

---

12. See Thomas M'Crie the Younger, *The Life of Thomas M'Crie, D. D.* (Philadelphia: William S. Young, 1842).

Some of M'Crie's works, to name a few, are *The Life of John Knox*, *The Life of Patrick Hamilton*, and *The Life of Melville*. Of most interest to us is the two-part publication of *The History of the Progress and Suppression of the Reformation in Italy* and *The History of the Progress and Suppression of the Reformation in Spain in the Sixteenth Century*, the latter of which is herein republished as part of the Cántaro Institute's heritage project.

Faithful to our institutional mandate, we seek to honour the church's inherited protestant tradition by the translation and republication of the forgotten works of the Spanish reformers or works relating to them. M'Crie's *History* of the reformation in Spain, published in 1829, is an invaluable gem of scholarship that deserves wider exposure and distribution, and, in an effort to make it more accessible to modern readership, has been reformatted and retitled to the *History of the Spanish Reformation*. M'Crie's objective was twofold, to contribute towards the history of that reformational movement that affected all of Europe and the New World, and by doing so, rescuing the Spanish reformation from obscurity.

It is our hope that this new edition of the *History of the Spanish Reformation* fosters within you an appreciation for the faith of the saints before us, an admiration for what was accomplished with tears, sweat and blood for the advancement of the biblical gospel and God's kingdom, and that it moves you, inspires you towards fulfilling the church's missional mandate in our day and age for the glory of God. We also anticipate M'Crie's republication of his historic scholarship to challenge a new generation towards investing their time, resources and hard work towards unearthing the protestant heritage of Spain, bringing to light the biblical, reformational teachings of the reformers for our everyday life.

May you benefit from, and enjoy this book, just as much as we have.

Steven R. Martins, MATS
Founding Director
Cántaro Institute

Preface to the Original Edition

THE FOLLOWING WORK is a sequel to that which I lately published on the Reformation in Italy, and completes what I intended as a contribution to the history of that memorable revolution in the sixteenth century which, in a greater or lesser degree, affected all the nations of Europe.

More than twenty years have elapsed since I inserted, in a periodical work, a short account of the introduction of the reformed opinions into Spain, and the means employed to extirpate them. The scanty materials from which that sketch was formed have gradually increased in the course of subsequent reading and research. My earliest authority is Reynaldo Gonzalez de Montes, a Protestant refugee from Spain, who in 1567 published at Heidelberg, in Latin, a Detection of the Arts of the Spanish Inquisition, interspersed with anecdotes of his countrymen who had embraced the Protestant faith, and containing an account of such of them as suffered at Seville. That work was immediately translated into English, and underwent two editions, to the last of which is subjoined an account of Protestant martyrs at Valladolid. Another contemporary authority is Cypriano de Valera, who left Spain for the sake of religion about the same time as De Montes, and has given various notices respecting his Protestant countrymen in his writings, particularly in a book on the Pope and the Mass, of which also an English translation was published during the reign of Elizabeth.

These early works, though well known when they first made their appearance, fell into oblivion for a time, together with the interesting details which they furnish. As a proof of this it is only necessary to mention the fact, that the learned Mosheim translated the meager tract of our countryman Dr. Michael Geddes, entitled, The Spanish Protestant Martyrology, and published it in Germany as the best account of that portion of ecclesiastical history with which he was acquainted.

Additional light has been lately thrown on the fate of Protestantism in Spain by the Critical History of the Spanish Inquisition, compiled by Don Juan Antonio Llorente, formerly secretary to the Inquisition at Madrid. Though confusedly written, that work is very valuable, both on account of the new facts which the official situation of the author enabled him to bring forward, and also because it verifies, in all the leading features, the picture of that odious tribunal drawn by De Montes and other writers, whose representations were exposed to suspicion on account of their presumed want of information, and the prejudices which, as Protestant, they were supposed to entertain. Llorente was in possession of documents from which I might have derived great advantage; and it certainly reflects little honor on Protestants, and especially British Protestants, that he received no encouragement to execute the proposal which he made, to publish at large the trials of those who suffered for the reformed religion in his native country.

The other sources from which I have drawn my information, including many valuable Spanish books lately added to the Advocates Library, will appear in the course of the work itself.

My acknowledgements are due to Dr. Friedrich Bialloblotzky, who kindly furnished me, from the University Library of Göttingen, with copious extracts from the dissertation of Büsching, *De Vestigiis Lutheranismi in Hispania*, a book which I had long sought in vain to procure. For the use of a copy of De Valera's *Dos Tratados, del Papa y la Missa*, now become very rare, as well as of other Spanish books, I am indebted to the politeness of Samuel R. Block, Esquire, London.

The general prevalence, both among Spaniards and others, of the mistaken notion that the Spanish Church was at an early period dependent on the See of Rome, has induced me to enter into minuter details in the preliminary part of this work than I should otherwise have thought necessary.

Edinburgh, 23d October, 1829.

I

Review of the Ecclesiastical History of Spain before the Era of the Reformation

ERRONEOUS OPINIONS as to their early history, originating 1
in vanity, and fostered by ignorance and credulity, have
been common amongst almost every people. These are
often harmless; and while they afford matter of good-hu-
mored raillery to foreigners, excite the more inquisitive
and liberal-minded among themselves to exert their talents in separating truth from fable, by patient research,
and impartial discrimination. But they are sometimes of
a very different character, and have been productive of
the worst consequences. They have been the means of
entailing political and spiritual bondage on a people, of
rearing insurmountable obstacles in the way of their im- 2
provement, of propagating feelings no less hostile to their
domestic comfort than to their national tranquility, and of
making them at once a curse to themselves and a scourge

to all around them.

If the natives of Spain have not advanced those extravagant pretensions to high antiquity which have made the inhabitants of some other countries ridiculous, they have unhappily fallen under the influence of national prejudices equally destitute of truth, and far more pernicious in their tendency. Every true Spaniard is disposed to boast of the purity of his blood, or, in the established language of the country, that he is "an Old Christian, free from all stain of bad descent."[1] The meanest peasant or artisan in Spain looks upon it as a degradation to have in his veins the least mixture of Jewish or Moorish blood, though transmitted by the remotest of his known ancestors, in the male or female line. To have descended from that race, "of which, as concerning the flesh, Christ came," or from Christians who had incurred the censure of a tribunal whose motto is the reverse of his who "came not to destroy men's lives but to save them," is regarded as a greater disgrace than to have sprung from savages or pagans, or from those who had incurred the last sentence of justice for the most unnatural and horrid crimes.

"I verily believe," says a modern Spanish writer who sometimes smiles through tears at the prejudices of his countrymen, "that were St. Peter a Spaniard, he would either deny admittance into heaven to people of tainted blood, or send them into a corner, where they might not

---

1. **Editor's Note:** It is important to consider the date of this writing by M'Crie, this description is not true of a 21st century Spaniard, however, it was an apt description of the 19th century Spaniard.

offend the eyes of the Old Christian."[2] We might go further, and say, that if a Spaniard had the keys of heaven in his keeping, St. Peter, and all the apostles with him, would be "removed into a corner" It is easy to conceive what misery must have been felt by persons and families who have incurred this involuntary infamy in their own estimation, or in that of their neighbors; and what bitter and rancorous feelings must have been generated in the hearts of individuals and races of men living together or contiguously, both in a state of peace and of warfare.

But, when the records of antiquity are consulted, the truth turns out to be, that in no other country of Europe has there been such an intermixture of races as in Spain—Iberian, Celtic, Carthaginian, Roman, Greek, Gothic, Jewish, Saracennic, Syrian, Arabian, and Moorish. With none are the Spaniards more anxious to disclaim all kindred than with the Jews and Moors. Yet anciently their Christian kings did not scruple to form alliances with the Moorish sovereigns of Grenada, to appear at their tournaments, and even to fight under their banners. Down to the middle of the fifteenth century, the Spanish poets and romancers celebrated the chivalry of "the Knights of Grenada, gentlemen though Moors."[3] It was no uncommon 4 occurrence for the Christians in Spain to connect themselves by marriage with Jews and Moors; and the pedigree of many of the grandees and titled nobility has been traced up to these "cankered branches" by the *Tizon de Espana,*

---

2. *Letters of Spain,* by Leucadio Doblado, p. 30.

3. Sismondi, *Hist. Of the Literature of the South,* vol. i. 99, iii. 113, 214.

or Brand of Spain, a book which neither the influence of the government, or the terror of the Inquisition, has been able to suppress.[4] Nor is greater credit due to the opinion which has long been prevalent in the Peninsula, that its inhabitants have uniformly kept themselves free from all stain of heretical depravity, and preserved the purity of the faith inviolate since their first reception into Christianity.

The ancient state of the church in Spain is but little known. Modern writers of that nation have been careful to conceal or to pass lightly over those spots of its history which are calculated to wound the feelings or abate the prejudices of their countrymen. Shut out from access to original documents, or averse to the toil of investigating them, foreigners have generally contented themselves with the information which common books supply. And knowing that the Spaniards have signalized their zeal for the See of Rome and the catholic faith during the last three centuries, the public, as if by general agreement, have come to the hasty conclusion that this was the fact from the beginning. To correct such mistakes, and to furnish materials for an accurate judgment, it may be proper to take a more extensive view of the state of religion in Spain before the Reformation, than would otherwise have been necessary to our undertaking.

The ecclesiastical history of Spain during the three first centuries may be comprised in two facts,—that the Christian religion was early introduced into that country; and that churches were erected in various parts of it, not-

---

4. Llorente, *Hist. Crit. de l'Inquisition*, tom. I pref. p. Xxvi. Doblado's Letters, 30, 31.

withstanding the persecution to which they were exposed
at intervals. All beside this is fable or conjecture. That the
gospel was first preached to their ancestors by St. James,
the son of Zebedee, is an opinion which has been long
so popular among the Spaniards, and so identified with
the national faith, that such of their writers as were most
convinced of the unsound foundation on which it rests
have been forced to join in bearing testimony to its truth.
The ingenuity of the warm partisans of the popedom has
been put to the stretch in managing the obstinate fondness
with which the inhabitants of the Peninsula have clung to
a prepossession so hazardous to the claims of St. Peter and
of Rome. They have alternately exposed the futility of the
arguments produced in its support, and granted that it is
to be received as a probable opinion, resting on tradition.
At one time they have urged that the early martyrdom
of the apostle precludes the idea of such an expedition;
and at another time they have tendered their aid to relieve
the Spaniards from this embarrassment, and to "elude the
objection," by suggesting, with true Italian dexterity, that
the Spirit might have carried the apostle from Palestine 6
to Spain, and after he had performed his task, conveyed
him back with such celerity that he was in time to receive
the martyr's crown at Jerusalem.[5] By such artful manage-

---

5. *"Neque illud sileo, (says Cennius) quod Apostolis veredi non erant
opus, ut terræ ambitum circumirent. Spiritus enim Domini, a
quo Philippum fuisse raptum constat post baptizatum Eunuchum,
etiamsi Jacobum rapuisse in Hispaniam non dictatur, non enim
omnia scriptu sunt, objectionem istam eludit."* In a manner somewhat similar has the benficed Presbyter of the Vatican contrived
to convey the dead body of the Apostle from Jerusalem to Spain.

ments, they succeeded at last in settling the dispute, after the following manner; that, agreeably to the concurring voice of antiquity, the seven first bishops of Spain were ordained by St. Peter, and sent by him into the Peninsula; but that, as is probable, they had been converted to the Christian faith by St. James, who despatched them to Rome to receive holy orders from the prince of the apostles; from which the inference is, that St. James was the first who preached the gospel to the Spaniards, but St. Peter was the founder of the church of Spain.[6] Leaving such

7

(*Cajetani Cenni de Antiquitate Ecclesiæ Hispanæ Dissertationes*, tom. i. p. 35, 36. Romæ, 1741.)

6.   Ibid. Diss. i. cap. 2. A curious specimen of the managements referred to in the text is to be seen in the alterations made on the Roman Calendar. Cardinal Quignoni obtained the following insertion in the Rubric, referring to St. James the elder: "He went to Spain, and preached the Gospel there, according to the authority of St. Isidore." (Breviarium Paul III.) A change more agreeable to the Spaniards was afterwards made: "Having travelled over Spain, and preached the gospel there, he returned to Jerusalem." (Brev. Pii V.) This having given offence to Cardinal Baronius and others at Rome, the following was substituted: "That he visited Spain and made some disciples there, is the tradition of the churches of that province." (Brev. Clementis VIII.) If the former mode of expression gave great offence at Rome, this last gave still greater in Spain. The whole kingdom was thrown into a ferment; and letters and ambassadors were despatched by his Catholic Majesty the Pope, exclaiming against the indignity done to the Spanish nation. At last the following form was agreed upon, which continues to stand in the Calendar: "Having gone to Spain, he made

fabulous accounts, which serve no other purpose than to illustrate human credulity, and the ease with which it is wrought upon by artifice and cunning, we proceed to the period of authentic history.

The facts which we have to bring forward may be arranged under three heads:—the doctrine of the ancient church of Spain; her government; and her worship.

I. Sentiments which by common consent have been regarded as heretical, without as well as within the pale of that church which arrogates to herself the title of catholic, sprang up repeatedly in Spain, and in some instances overran the whole country. In the fourth century, Priscillian, a native of Gallicia, founded a new sect, which united the tenets of the Manichaeans and Gnostics. It made many converts, including persons of the episcopal order, and subsisted in Spain for two hundred years.[7] When they boast of the pure blood of the Goths, the Spaniards appear to forget that their Gothic ancestors were Arians, and that Arianism was the prevailing and established creed of the country for nearly two centuries.[8] Nor did Spain long 8 preserve her faith uncontaminated, after she had adopted the common doctrine under Reccared, who reigned in the close of the sixth century. To pass by the spread of Nestori-

---

some converts to Christ, seven of whom being ordained by St. Peter, were sent to Spain as its first bishops." (Brev. Urbani VIII.)

7. Sulpitius Severus, *Hist. Sacra*, lib. ii. c. 60. Nicol. Antonius, *Bibliotheca Hispana Vetus, curante Franc. Perez Bayerio*, tom. i. p. 168-172. Cenni de Antiq. Eccl. Hisp. Diss. tom. i. p. 212.

8. Gregor. de Turon. *Hist. Franc.* lib. viii. Cap. 46. Nic. Antonius, *ut supra*, p. 294. Cenni Diss. iii. cap. 1 and 2./

anism and some tenets of less note,[9] she gave birth, in the eighth century, to the heresy called adoptionarian, because its disciples held that Christ is the adopted Son of God. This opinion was broached by Elipand, archbishop of Toledo, who was at the head of the Spanish church; it was vigorously defended by Felix, bishop of Urgel, a prelate of great ability; and maintained itself for a considerable time, in spite of the decisions of several councils, supported by the learning of Alcuin and the authority of Charlemagne.[10]

Nor were there wanting in the early ages Spaniards who held some of the leading opinions afterwards avowed by the protestant reformers. Claude, bishop of Turin, who flourished in the ninth century, and distinguished himself by his valuable labors in the illustration of the scriptures, was a native of Spain. His decided condemnation of the worship of images, and of the veneration paid to the relics and sepulchers of the saints, together with his resistance to the ecclesiastical authority which imposed these practices, has exposed the memory of this pious and learned divine to the deadly hatred of all the devotees of superstition and

9

---

9. "*Nequie hi tantum errores in Hispaniis pervagabantur, sed quicquid novæ hæresis emergebat, in easdem admittebatur.*" (Cenni, i. 213.)

10. Rodriguez de Castor, *Bibliotheca Espanola*, tom. ii. p. 406-411. Nic. Antonius, *ut supra*, p. 440-446. Mosheim supposed Felix to be a French bishop, and placed his diocese in Septimania. *(Eccl. Hist. cent.* viii. part ii. chap. v. sect. 3.) Septimania was an ancient province of Gallia Narbonnensis, now called Lenguedoc; but Urgel is a city of Catalonia, and the Counts of Urgel made no small figure in the predatory warfare of the middle ages. (Vaisette. *Hist. Gen. de Languedoc*, tom. iii. p. 108, 145. Preuves, p. 206.)

spiritual despotism.[11] In support of his principal tenet, Claude could plead the authority of one of the most venerable councils of his native church, which ordained that there should be no pictures in churches, and that nothing should be painted on the walls which might be worshiped or adored.[12]

Galindo Prudentio, bishop of Troyes, was a countryman and contemporary of Claude. His learning was superior to that of the age in which he lived; and the comparative purity of his style bears witness to his familiarity with the writings of the ancient classics. Having fixed his residence in France, he enjoyed the confidence of Charlemagne, who employed him in visiting and reforming the monasteries. In the predestinarian controversy which divided the French clergy of that time, he took part with Goteschalcus against Hincmar, archbishop of Rheims, and the noted schoolman, Joannes Scotus, surnamed Erigena. The sentiments which Prudentio held on that subject bear a striking resemblance to those which the church of Rome has since anathematized in the writings of Luther

10

---

11. Nicolas Antonio reckons it necessary to make a formal apology for giving Claude a place in his general biography of Spanish writers, and calls him "pudendum genti nostræ plusquam celebrandum, hominis Hispani nomen." (*Bibl. Hisp. Vet.* tom. i. p. 458.) An exact and full account of Claude's works, both printed and in manuscript, is given by Alb. Fabricius, in his *Bibliotheca Mediæ et Infimæ Aetatis*, tom. i. p. 388.

12. "*Placuit picturas in Ecclesia esse non debere, ne quod colitur vel adoratur, in parietibus pingatur.*" (Concil. *Illiberit.* can. xxxvi. anno 305.)

and Calvin.[13]

II. The Spanish church, at the beginning of the fourth century, acknowledged no other officers than bishops, presbyters, and deacons.[14] She was equally a stranger to the superior orders of metropolitans and archbishops, and to the inferior orders of sub-deacons and lectors. Her discipline was at that time characterized by great strictness and even rigor, of which there was a palpable relaxation when the government of the church came to be formed upon the model of the empire, after Constantine had embraced christianity.[15] This change was, however, introduced more slowly into Spain than into some other countries. The church of Africa was careful to guard the parity of episcopal power against the encroachments of the metropolitans; and the Spanish bishops, who appear from an early period to have paid great deference to her maxims and practices, continued for a considerable time to evince the same jealousy.[16] To the supremacy of the bishops of Rome the

11

---

13. Duchesne, *Hist. Francor. Script.* tom. iii. p. 212. *Barthii Adversaria*, lib. xviii. cap. 11, lib. xliv. cap. 19. The controversial works of Galindus Prudentius remained in MS. until some of them were published, during the Jansenian dispute, by Gilbert Mauguin, in a collection of curious and valuable tracts, under the title: *Veterum Auctorum, qui nono seculo de praedestinatione et gratia scriptserunt, Opera et Fragmenta,* 2 tom. Paris, 1650; a work less known by divines than it ought to be.

14. Concil. *Illiberit.* can. 18, 19; anno 305.

15. Cenni, i. 69; conf. 142-144.

16. "*Ut primæ seids Episcopus non appelletur princeps sacerdotum, aut summus sacerdos, aut aliquid hujusmodi, sed tantum primæ sedis*

ancient church of Spain was a stranger, and there is no good evidence that she acknowledged, during the eight first centuries, their right to interfere authoritatively in her internal affairs.

The titles of pope or father, apostolical bishop, and bishop of the apostolic see, were at first given promiscuously to all who were invested with the episcopal office.[17] After they came to be used in a more restricted sense, they were still applied to a number in common.[18] The bishops of Rome early acquired high consideration among their brethren, founded on the dignity of the city in which they had their residence, the number of the clergy over whom they presided, and the superior sanctity of life by which some of their line had been distinguished; to which must be added the opinion, which soon became general, that

---

Episcopus." (Cod. *African.* can. 39.) To this agrees the language of the fathers of Toledo: "*Statuimus, ut frater, et coepiscopus noster, Montanus, qui in Metropoli est,*" &c. (Concil. *Tolet.* II. can. 5.)

17. Thomassinus, *De Benefic.* part. i. lib. i. cap. 4. Pope Cyprian, pope Augustine, pope Alipius, pope Athanasius, &c. are expressions of frequent recurrence in the writings of the Fathers. Cenni, unable to deny this fact, has recourse to the desperate shift, that those who gave this title to a bishop meant to say, that his merits were such as to entitle him to be advanced to the dignity of supreme pontiff. (*De Antiq. Eccl. Hips.* ii. 53.)

18. The names of καΘολικοι θρονοι, and οικυμενοι θρονοι, catholic thrones, and ecumenical thrones, were given, in the eighth century, to the sees of Rome, Constantinople, Alexandria, Antioch, and Jerusalem. (Theophanes, *apud Salmasii Apparat. de Primatu,* p. 278.)

12 they were the successors of St. Peter. In matters which concerned religion in general, or in difficult questions relating to internal managements, it was a common practice to ask the advice of foreign and even transmarine churches. On these occasions the bishops of Rome were consulted, but not to the exclusion of others. The African bishops, in a council held at Carthage, agreed to take the advice of Siricius, bishop of Rome, and Simplician, bishop of Milan, on the affair of the Donatists; and in a subsequent council, they agreed to consult Anastasius and Venerius, who at that time filled the same sees, on the controversy respecting the validity of the baptism of heretics.[19] With this the practice of the Spanish church agreed.[20] Indeed, the bishops of Rome, in those days, disclaimed the pretentions which they afterwards put forth with such arrogance. Gregory the Great himself, when in danger of being eclipsed by his eastern rival, acknowledged this in the memorable words, which have so much annoyed his successors and their apologists. Speaking of the title of universal patriarch, which the bishop of Constantinople had assumed, he says:—"Far from the hearts of Christians be this name of blasphemy, which takes away the honors of the whole priesthood, while it is madly arrogated by one!—None of

13 my predecessors would ever consent to use this profane word, because if one patriarch is called universal, the rest

---

19. *Salmasii Apparatus ad Libros de Primatu Papæ*, p. 277. Cenni, i. 159.

20. Concil. *Tolet.* i. sent. definit. Constant. Annot. in Epist. 2. Inocent.

are deprived of the name of patriarchs."[21]

But there is positive evidence that the ancient church of Spain maintained its independence, and guarded against the interference of the Roman See, or any other foreign authority. Whatever judgment we form concerning the disputed canon of the council of Sardis, as to the references to the bishop of Rome,[22] it is certain that an African council, which met at Mela in the year 416, decreed that if any of the clergy had a dispute with his bishop, he might bring it before the neighboring bishops; but if he thought proper not to rest in their decision, it should be unlawful for him to make any appeal except to an African council, or to the primates of the African churches.[23] In accordance with the spirit of this canon, with some variation in particulars, the ninth council of Toledo, in the year 655, determined that appeals should lie from a bishop to a metropolitan, and from a metropolitan to the royal audience; a regulation which was confirmed by a subsequent council held in the same city.[24] In the fifth and sixth centuries Arianism was predominant in Spain. During that period the bishops who adhered to the orthodox faith being few in number, discountenanced by the royal authority, 14 and rarely allowed to assemble in provincial councils, were naturally induced to turn their eyes to Rome for counsel

---

21. Gregorii Epp. 32, 36.

22. Council *Sard.* a. 347, can. 3-5. Mosheim, *Cent.* iv. part. ii. chap. ii. § 6. Dupin De Antiq. Discip. diss. ii. chap. i. § 3.

23. Concil. *Millevit*, ii. chap. 22.

24. Concil. *Tolet.* ix. capit. i; xiii. capit. 12: Harduiini Colllect. tom. iii. coll. 973, 1746.

and support; while the popes laid hold of the opportunity which the circumstances afforded them to extend their influence over that country, by holding correspondence with the dissenting clergy, and conferring on some of them the title of apostolical vicars.[25] But, strange as the assertion may appear to some, this intercourse ceased as soon as Spain embraced the catholic faith.

Spain is always spoken of as a catholic country from the time that she renounced Arianism under Reccared; and if we are to believe some of her writers, her monarchs obtained, at that early period, the title of Catholic kings, which they retain to this day, as expressive of their devotion to the faith and authority of the Roman see. But this is a glaring mistake, originating in, or concealed by the equivocal use of a word which was anciently understood in a sense very different from its modern acceptation. It was by adopting the common doctrine received by the church at large, in opposition to the Arian and other errors condemned by the first ecumenical or universal councils, that Spain became catholic, and that her kings, bishops, and people, obtained this designation, and not by conforming to the rites of the church of Rome, or owning the supremacy of its pontiffs. Ecclesiastical affairs were managed in Spain without any interference on the part of the See of Rome, or any reference to it, during the whole of the century which elapsed after the suppression of Arianism. This is so undeniable, that those advocates of the pontifical au-

15

---

25. Concil. *Bracarense*, i. passim. Cenni, i. 194, 200, 214. It is to be observed that in most of these instances we have not the letters of the Spanish bishops, but only those of the popes.

thority who have examined the documents of that age, have been forced to admit the fact, and endeavor to account for it by saying, that such interference and reference was unnecessary during a peaceful state of the church; a concession which goes far to invalidate the whole of their claims.[26] The pall sent from Rome to Leander, bishop of Seville, forms no exception to the remark now made; for, not to mention that it was never received, it was not intended to confer any prerogative upon him, but merely as a testimony of his sanctity, and a mark of personal esteem from pope Gregory, who had contracted a friendship with him when they met at Constantinople. It was of the nature of a badge of honor conferred by a prince on a deserving individual belonging to another kingdom.[27]

There is one piece of history which throws great light on the state of the Spanish church during the seventh century, and which I shall relate at some length, as it has been either passed over or very partially brought forward by later historians. The sixth ecumenical council, held at Constantinople in the year 680, condemned the heresy of the Monothelites, or those who, though they allowed that Christ had two natures, ascribed to him but one will and one operation. In 683, Leo II., bishop of Rome, sent the acts of that council, which he had received from Constantinople, to Spain, requesting the bishops to give them their sanction, and to take measures for having them circulated through their churches. As a council had been held immediately before the arrival of the papal deputa-

16

---

26. Cenni, ii. 67, 69, 154, 155.

27. Cenni, ii. 211-230.

tion, and a heavy fall of snow prevented the re-assembling of the members at that season, it was thought proper to circulate the acts among the bishops, who authorized Julian, archbishop of Toledo, to transmit a rescript to Rome, intimating in general their approbation of the late decision at Constantinople, and stating at considerable length the sentiments of the Spanish church on the controverted point. A council, convened in Toledo during the following year, entered on the formal consideration of this affair, in which they proceeded in such a manner as to evince their determination to preserve at once the purity of the faith and the independence of the Spanish church. They examined the acts of the council at Constantinople, at which it does not appear that they had any representative, and declared that they found them consonant with the decisions of the four preceding canonical councils, particularly that of Chalcedon, of which they appeared to be nearly a transcript. "Whereof (say they) we agree that the acts of the said council be reverenced and received by us, inasmuch as they do not differ from the foresaid councils, or rather as they appear to coincide with them. We allot to them therefore that place in point of order to which their merit entitles them. Let them come after the council of Chalcedon, by whose light they shine." The council next took into consideration the rescript which archbishop Julian had sent to Rome, and pronounced it "a copious and lucid exposition of the truth concerning the double will and operation of Christ;" adding, "wherefore, for the sake of general instruction, and the benefit of ecclesiastical discipline, we confirm and sanction it as entitled to equal honor and reverence, and to have the same permanent au-

17

thority, as the decretal epistles."[28]

The council of Constantinople had condemned pope Honorius I. as an abettor of the Monothelite heresy; a stigma which the advocates of papal infallibility have labored for ages to wipe off. But the Spanish council, on the present occasion, proceeded farther, and advanced a proposition which strikes at the very foundation on which the bishops of Rome rest their claims, by declaring, that the rock on which the church is built is the faith confessed by St. Peter, and not his person or office.[29]

But this was not all that the Spanish clergy did. When the rescript of the archbishop of Seville reached Rome, it met with the disapprobation of Benedict II., who had succeeded Leo in the popedom. Having drawn up certain animadversions upon it, his Holiness gave them to the Spanish deputy to communicate to his constituents, that they might correct those expressions savoring of error which they had been led incautiously to adopt. An answer, not the most agreeable to the pope, was returned by Julian in the mean time; and the subject was afterwards taken up by a national council held in 688 at Toledo. Instead of retracting their former sentiments, or correcting any of the expressions which the pope had blamed, the Spanish prelates drew up and sanctioned a labored vindication

18

---

28. Council. *Tolet.* xiv. capit. 5, 6, 7, 11: Labbe, Collect. Concil. tom. vi. 1280-1284. Harduin, Acta Concil. tom. iii. p. 1754-1756.

29. "*Scientes igitur solam esse fidei confessionem quæ vincat infernum, quæ superat tartarum; de hac enim fide a Domino dictum est, Portæ inferni non prævalebunt contra eam.*" (Ib. capt. 10: Harduin, ut supra, p. 1756.)

of the paper which had given offence to his Holiness, of whom they speak in terms very disrespectful, and even contemptuous. They accuse him of "a careless and cursory perusal" of their rescript, and of having passed over parts of it which were necessary to understand their meaning. He had found fault with them for asserting that there are three substances in Christ,[30] to which they reply: "As we will not be ashamed to defend the truth, so there are perhaps some other persons who will be ashamed at being found ignorant of the truth. For who knows not that in every man there are two substances, namely, soul and body?" After confirming their opinion by quotations from the fathers, they add: "But if any one shall be so shameless as not to acquiesce in these sentiments, and acting the part of a haughty inquirer, shall ask, whence we drew such things, at least he will yield to the words of the gospel, in which Christ declares that he possessed three substances." Having quoted and commented on several passages of the New Testament, the council concludes in these terms: "If, after this statement, and the sentiments of the fathers from which it has been taken, any person shall dissent from us in any thing, we will have no farther dispute with him, but keeping steadily in the plain path, and treading in the footsteps of our predecessors, we are persuaded that our answer will commend itself to the approbation of all lovers

---

30. The same sentiment is expressed in a confession of faith, which a preceding council, held in 675, had drawn up for the use of the Spanish churches.—"*Item, idem Christus in duabus naturis, tribus extat substantiis.*" (Concil. *Tolet.* XI. in Harduini Collect. tom. iii. p. 1022.) The three substances, according to the divines of Spain, were the divine nature of Christ, his human soul, and his body.

of truth who are capable of forming a divine judgment, though we may be charged with obstinacy by the ignorant and envious."[31]

III. The independence of the ancient church of Spain 20 will appear more fully if we attend to its form of worship.

---

31. Concil. *Tolet.* XV. post symbolum: Labbe, VI. 1296-1303. Harduin, III. 1759-1767. Cenni, at a greater expense than that of contradicting himself, labors to do away, or rather to conceal, the indignity offered to the Roman See, and the disregard shown to its authority, by the procedure of the Spanish councils. He allows that the fourteenth council of Toledo "arrogated to itself an unjust authority, and openly departed from obedience to the Holy See;" that "it adopted a new and unheard-of method of approving of the decisions of a general council;" and that, on these accounts, "none of its decrees were admitted to a place in the collection of sacred canons." But he asserts that the fifteenth council of Toledo "manifestly amended their doctrine concerning the three substances;" that "Julian" (as if the decree had been his only, and not that of a national council) "sometimes makes use of words rather too free, though somewhat obscure, against Rome; but that, upon the whole, he changed or explained his former sentiment, agreeably to the admonition of the Roman Pontiff." Yet he grants, or rather pleads, that this "apology", as he calls it, was not approved at Rome; is angry with those writers who speak in its defence; and concludes by saying, that "this blemish on the well-constituted church of Spain should be a perpetual monument to teach the churches of all other nations to revere the one sure, infallible, and supreme judgment of the Holy See, in matters of faith and of manners." (*De Antiq. Eccl. Hispanæ*, tom. ii. p. 55-59.)

All the learned who have directed their attention to ecclesiastical antiquities are now agreed that, although the mode of worship was substantially the same throughout the Christian church, during the fourth, fifth, and sixth centuries, yet different liturgies or forms of celebrating divine service were practiced in different nations, and sometimes in different parts of the same nation. The Ambrosian liturgy, used by the church of Milan, differed from the Roman.[32] It was adopted in many parts of France, and continued in use there until the time of Charlemagne, when it was supplanted by the Roman or Gregorian.[33] So far was the church of Rome from having at first regulated the religious service of other churches by her laws or even by her example, that she did not even preserve her own forms, which were superseded in their most important parts, by the sacramentary or missal which was drawn up by pope Gelasius, corrected finally by Gregory at the close of the sixth century, and imposed gradually, and at distant periods, on the several divisions of the western church.[34] Different offices, or forms of celebrating divine service, were used in Spain down to the year 633, when the fourth council of Toledo passed a decree that one uniform order

21

---

32. Durandus, Rat. Divin. Offic. lib. v. cap. ii.

33. Joannes Diaconus, *Vita Gregorii Magni*, lib. ii. cap. 17. praef. Oper. Gregorii..

34. Gregory, (says the Roman deacon who wrote his life), "after taking away many things from the missal of Gelasius, altering a few things, and adding some things for explaining the evangelical lessons, formed the whole into one book." (Joannes Diaconus, *Vita Gregorii Magni, ut supra.*)

should be observed in all the churches of the Peninsula.[35] This decree led to the adoption of that liturgy which has been called the Gothic, and sometimes the Isidorian, or the Ildefonsian, from St. Isidore and Ildefonso, archbishops of Seville, by whom it was revised and corrected. That this ritual was quite different from the Roman or Gregorian is put beyond all doubt, by the references made to both in the course of the adoptionarian controversy, which raged in the eighth century. The patrons of the adoptionarian tenet in Spain appealed to their national ritual, "compiled by holy men who had gone before them," and quoted passages from it as favorable to their views. To this argument the fathers of the council of Frankfort replied: "It is better to believe the testimony of God the Father concerning his own Son, than that of your Ildefonso, who composed for you such prayers, in the solemn masses, as the universal and holy church of God knows not, and in which we do not think you will be heard. And if your Ildefonso in his prayers called Christ the adopted Son of God, our Gregory, pontiff of the Roman see, and a doctor beloved by the whole world, does not hesitate in his prayers to call him always the only begotten."[36] In like manner Alcuin, after insinuating that they might have taken improper liberties in their quotations, says: "But it matters not much whether these testimonies have been altered or correctly quoted by you; for we wish to be confirmed in the truth of our assertion and faith by Roman rather than Spanish

22

---

35. Concil. *Tolet.* IV. capit. 2.

36. Collect. Concil. tom. vii. p. 1034: Cenni, ii. 346.

authority."[37]

The Gothic or Isidorian office has also been called the Mozarabic or Mixtarabic, probably because it was used and held in great veneration by the Christians in Spain who lived under the dominion of the Arabians or Moors. The identity of these formularies has, indeed, been of late disputed by several learned men.[38] But it is most probable that they were originally the same office, and that alterations were made upon it, both by the Mozarabes and the Montanes, (as those were called who betook themselves to the mountains to escape the yoke of the Moors,) during the period that they lived asunder.

Other instances in which the worship of the ancient church of Spain differed widely from the modern might be produced. We have already mentioned that a national council, in the beginning of the fourth century, prohibited the worship of images, and the use of pictures in church-

---

37. *Alcuin adv. Felicem Urgel.* lib. viii. p. 395: Cenni, ii. 346.—In the beginning of the eighteenth century, cardinal Thomasi published a Gothic Missal, as that of the ancient Spanish church, which was republished by Mabillon from other MSS. But this is supposed not to have been the Spanish Missal, but that of Galli Narbonnensis, or the South of France. (Lebrun, *De Liturg.* tom. ii. diss. 4.) The *Libellus Orationarius,* which Joseph Blanchini prefixed to the first volume of the works of Cardinal Thomasi, has better claims to be considered as an ancient Spanish Liturgy.

38. This is the opinion of Blanchini, in his preface and notes to the Libellus Orat. Gotico-Hispanus, prefixed to the works of cardinal Thomasi; and of Cenni, *De Antiq. Eccl. Hispanæ*, tom. i. p. 28-30. tom. ii. dissert. vii.

es.[39] It may be added, that the first council of Braga, held in the year 561, forbade the use of uninspired hymns, which came afterwards to be tolerated, and were ultimately enjoined under the highest penalties.[40]

Having produced these facts as to the early opinions and usages of the Spanish church, we proceed to state the manner in which she was led to adopt the rites, and submit to the authority of the church of Rome.

In the eleventh century Spain was divided into three kingdoms—the kingdom of Leon and Castile, of Aragon, and of Navarre, of which the two first were by far the most powerful. In the latter part of that century, Alfonso, the sixth of Leon, and first of Castile, after recovering Valentia by the valor of the famous Cid, Ruy Diaz de Bivar, finally obtained possession of Toledo, which had been in the power of the Moors for three centuries and a half. He had married, for his second wife, Constance, a daughter of the royal house of France, who, from attachment to the religious service to which she had been accustomed, or under the influence of the priests who accompanied her, instigated her husband to introduce the Roman liturgy into Castile. Richard, abbot of Marseilles, the papal legate, exerted

24

---

39. See before, p. 9.

40. "*Placuit, ut extra psalmos, vel canonicarum scripturarum novi et veteris Testamenti, nihil poetice compositum in Ecclesia psallatur, sicut et sancti præcipiunt canones.*" (Concil. *Bracarense I*, can. 12: *Harduini Collect.* tom. iii. p. 351.) But another council, held in 633, not only permitted the use of such hymns as those of St. Hilary and St. Ambrose, but threatened all who rejected them with excommunication. (Concil. *Tolet.* iv. capit. 13.)

all his influence in favor of a change so agreeable to the court which he represented. The innovation was warmly opposed by the clergy, nobility, and people at large, but especially by the inhabitants of Toledo and other places which had been under the dominion of the Moors. To determine this controversy, recourse was had, according to the custom of the dark ages, to judicial combat. Two knights, clad in complete armor, appeared before the court and an immense assembly. The champion of the Gothic liturgy prevailed; but the king insisted that the litigated point should undergo another trial, and be submitted to, what was called, the judgment of God. Accordingly, in the presence of another great assembly, a copy of the two rival liturgies was thrown into the fire. The Gothic resisted the flames and was taken out unhurt, while the Roman was consumed. But upon some pretext—apparently the circumstances of the ashes of the Roman liturgy curling on the top of the flames and then leaping out—the king, with the concurrence of Bernard, archbishop of Toledo, who was a Frenchman, gave out that it was the will of God that both offices should be used; and ordained, that the public service should continue to be celebrated according to the Gothic office in the six churches of Toledo which the Christians had enjoyed under the Moors, but that the Roman office should be adopted in all the other churches of the kingdom. The people were displeased with the glaring partiality of this decision, which is said to have given rise to the proverb, The law goes as kings choose.[41] Discountenanced by the court and the superior ecclesiastics, the Gothic liturgy gradually fell into disrepute, until it was

41. *"Alla van leyes, donde quieren Reyes."*

completely superseded by the Roman.[42]

The introduction of the Roman liturgy had been undertaken rather more early in Aragon than in Castile, but was completed in both kingdoms about the same time. 26 The modern inhabitants of the Peninsula please themselves with the idea that they are hearing the self-same mass which has been performed in Spain from the days of the apostles; whereas, the exact day and place in which the modern service began, can be pointed out. The first mass, according to the Roman form, was celebrated in Aragon in the monastery of St. Juan de la Pena, on the 21st of March 1071; and in Castile, in the Grand Mosque of Toledo, on the 25th of October 1086.[43] Gregory VII. commemorates

---

42. Doctor Juan Vergara, apud Quintanilla, p. 115. De Robles, 233-235. Florez, Clave Historial, pp. 129, 130, 202. There is a dissertation on the Mozarabic office in *Espana Sagrada*, tom. iii. Sismondi, who appears to have borrowed part of his information on this controversy from a play of Calderon, entitled "Origen, perdida, y restauracion de la Virgen del Sagrario," is inaccurate in his statement. He says that the king wished to introduce the Ambrosian ceremony, and thinks it fortunate that "the policy of the monarch, and not the jealousy of the priests," was the principal instrument in settling the dispute. (*Hist. of Literature of the South*, vol. iii. p. 196, 197.) Townsend confounds what was done by Alfonso in the end of the eleventh century with what was done by cardinal Ximenes in the beginning of the sixteenth; and praises the decision as indicating a spirit of enlightened toleration. "Cease to persecute, (says he) and all sects will in due time dwindle and decay." (*Travels through Spain*, vol. i. p. 311, 312.)

43. Illescas, *Hist. Pontifical*, tom. i. f. 269. Zurita, Annales de Aragon,

this change, "as the deliverance of Spain from the illusion of the Toledan superstition."[44] His Holiness was more clear-sighted than those moderns, who, looking upon all forms of worship as equal, treat with contempt or indifference the efforts made by a people to defend their religious rights against the encroachments of domestic, or the intrusions of foreign authority. The recognition of the papal authority in Spain followed upon the establishment of the Roman liturgy; nor would the latter have been sought with such eagerness, had it not been with a view to the former. Having once obtained a footing in the Peninsula, the popes pushed their claims, until at last the whole nation, including the highest authorities in it, civil as well as ecclesiastical, acknowledged the supremacy of the Roman see.

It is sufficient to exemplify this statement in the subjugation of the crown and kingdom of Aragon. Don Ramiro I., who died in 1063, was the first Spanish king, according to the testimony of Gregory the Great, who recognized the pope and received the laws of Rome.[45] In 1204, Don Pedro II., eight years after he had ascended the throne, went to Rome, and was crowned by pope Innocent III. On that occasion his Holiness put the crown on his head in the monastery of Pancracio, after Pedro had given his corporal oath that he and all his successors would be faithful to the

27

---

tom. i. f. 25, b.

44 *Zurita*, f. 22, b.

45. "*Fue el primero de los reyes de Epsana, que hizo este reconoscimiento, y encarece mucho el Papa, que como otro Moyses, fue tambien el primero que en su regno recibio las leyes y costumbres Romanas.*" (*Zurita*, tom. i. f. 22, a.)

church of Rome, preserve his kingdom in obedience to it, defend the catholic faith, pursue heretical pravity, and maintain inviolate the liberties and immunities of the holy church. Then going to the chapel of St. Peter, the pope delivered the sword into the hands of the king, who, armed as a cavalier, dedicated all his dominions to St. Peter, the prince of the apostles, and to Innocent and his successors, as a fief of the church; engaging to pay an annual tribute, as a mark of homage and gratitude for his coronation. In return for all this his Holiness granted, as a special favor, that the kings of Aragon, instead of being obliged to come to Rome, should afterwards be crowned in Saragossa, by the archbishop of Tarragona, as papal vicar. This act of submission was highly offensive to the nobility, who protested for their own rights, and to the people at large, who complained that their liberties were sold, and power given to the popes to disturb the peace of the kingdom at their pleasure.[46] It was not long before these fears were realized. The king, having a few years after offended the pope by taking arms in defence of heretics, was laid under the sentence of excommunication, for violating the oath which he had sworn; and his grandson, Pedro the Great, was deprived of his kingdom, as a vassal of the church, which kindled a civil war, and led to the invasion of Aragon by

---

46. *Zurita*, tom. i. f. 90, 91. Mariana, *De Rebus Hispaniae*, lib. xi. cap. xxi. edit. *Schotti Hispania Illustrata*, tom. ii. p. 546. The same oath and homage were given to the pope for Sardinia and Corsica, in 1316, by the ambassadors of James II. of Aragon; which was repeated, in 1337, by Alfonso IV. (*Zurita*, lib. vi. f. 27, 125.)

the French.[47] Attempts to release themselves from this degrading vassalage were made by different monarchs, but these always issued in the renewal of their oaths of fealty to Rome; and they found it too late to throw off a yoke which had by this time been received by all the nations around them, and which they had taught their own subjects to revere and hold sacred.

The history of Spain during the period we are reviewing, furnishes important notices respecting the Waldenses, Vaudois or Albigenses, whom we formerly met with in tracing the progress of the Reformation in Italy. It is well known, that these early reformers had fixed their abode in the southern provinces of France, where they multiplied greatly int he eleventh and twelfth centuries.[48] Various causes contributed to this. The inhabitants of the south of France, though inferior in arms, were superior in civilization, to those of the north. They had addicted themselves to commerce and the arts. Their cities, which were numerous and flourishing, enjoyed privileges favorable to the spirit of liberty, and which raised them nearly to the rank of the Italian republics, with which they had long traded. They possessed a language rich and flexible, which they cultivated both in prose and verse; academies for promoting the Gui Saber, or polite letters, were erected among them; and the Troubadors, as the Provençal poets were called, were received with honor, and listened to with enthusiasm, at the courts of the numerous petty princes

29

---

47. *Zurita*, lib. iv. f. 253-262.

48. *Histoire Generale de Languedoc*, per Le Pere Vaisette, tom. iii. p. 1-4. Usserius, *De Christ. Eccles. Success.* cap. x. sect. 18, p. 154.

among whom the country was divided. A people advanced to this stage of improvement were not disposed to listen with implicit faith to the religious dogmas which the clergy inculcated, or to submit tamely to the superstitious and absurd observances which they sought to impose. Add to this, that the manners of the clergy, both higher and lower, in these provinces, were disorderly and vicious to a proverb. "I would rather be a priest, than have done such a thing!" was a common exclamation among the people on hearing of any unworthy action. With these feelings they were prepared to listen to the reformers, who exposed the errors and corruptions which had defaced the beauty of the primitive church, and whose conduct formed, in point of decency and sobriety, a striking contrast to that of the established clergy. For the last mentioned fact we 30 have the testimony of those monkish writers, who strove to blacken their characters, by alleging that they practiced all kinds of licentiousness in secret. "I will relate (says the abbot of Puy Laurens) what I have heard bishop Fulco tell as to a conversation which he had with Pons Ademar de Rodelia, a prudent knight. 'I cannot bring myself to believe,' said the latter, 'that Rome has sufficient grounds to proceed against these men'—'Are they not unable to answer our arguments?' demanded the bishop. 'I grant it,' said the other. 'Well, then' rejoined the bishop; 'why do you not expel and drive them from your territories?' 'We cannot do it,' replied the knight; 'we have been brought up with them; we have our friends among them; and we see them living honestly.' After relating this anecdote on the authority of the archbishop of Thoulouse, the great adversary of the Albigenses, the historian adds: "Thus it is that falsehood, veiled under the appearance of a spotless life, draws uncautious men from the truth."[49]

The Albigensian barbs, or pastors, enjoying a respite from persecution during the early part of the twelfth century, applied themselves to the study of the scriptures, and devoted their hours of relaxation to the cultivation of poetry. They were held in veneration by the people, who named them in their wills, and left for the support of the new worship those sums which had been formerly bequeathed to the priests or appropriated for the saying of masses for their own souls and those of their departed relations. They had chapels in the principal castles; their religious service was frequented by persons of all ranks; and they numbered among their converts many individuals of noble birth, and who held some of the principal situations in the country. Among their protectors were the powerful counts of Toulouse, Raymond VI. and VII., the counts of Foix and Comenges, the viscounts of Beziers and Bearn, Savary de Mauleon, seneschal of Aquitaine, Guiraud de Minerve, and Olivier de Termes, a cavalier who had distinguished himself greatly in the wars against the infidels in the Holy Land, in Africa and Majorca. Their opinions were avowedly entertained by the wives and sisters of these great lords, as well as by the heads of the noble houses of Mirepoix, Saissac, Lavour, Montreal, St. Michael de Fanjaux, Durfort, Lille-Jourdain, and Montsegur.[50]

---

49. Guil. de Podio-Laur. *Chronic.* cap. viii.

50. *His. Gen. de Languedoc*, tom. iii. pp. 129, 147, 420. Preuves, pp. 58, 392, 435-442. Sismondi, *History of the Crusades against the Albigenses*, pp. 5-8, 63, 73-77, 521, 178. *Hist. of Literature of*

When we have stated these facts, we have said enough to account for the implacable hostility to this sect on the part of the ruling ecclesiastics, and the bloody crusades preached up against it by the monks, and conducted, under the direction of the popes, by Simon de Montfort and Louis VIII. of France, during the early part of the thirteenth century. By means of these the attempted reformation of the church was suppressed, and its disciples nearly exterminated; one of the finest regions of the world was laid waste by countless and successive hordes of barbarous fanatics—its commerce destroyed, its arts annihilated, its literature extinguished; and the progress of the human mind in knowledge and civilization, which had commenced so auspiciously, was arrested and thrown back for ages.[51]

32

South of Europe, vol. i. pp. 217, 219. Mariana, *De Reb. Hisp.* lib. xii. cap. 10.

51. The Provençal poets bewailed the desolation of their country, and inveighed in bitter strains against the crusaders. They were in general friendly to the Albigenses. But one of them, Izarn, a Dominical missionary, sought to inflame the persecution by his poetry, which exhibits the true language of the Inquisition put into rhyme. (Sismondi, *Hist. of the Lit. of the South*, vol. i. p. 227.) Addressing the heretic, whom he failed to convince in a dispute, he says:

As you declare you won't believe, 'tis fit that you should burn,

And as your fellow have been burnt, that you should blaze in turn;

And as you've disobey'd the will of God and of St. Paul,

The intimate connection which subsisted between Spain and the South of France had great influence on the fate of the Albigensian reformers. Provence and Languedoc were at that time more properly Aragonese than French. As count of Provence, the king of Aragon was the immediate liege lord of the viscounts of Narbonne, Beziers, and Carcassone. Avignon and other cities acknowledged him as their baronial superior. The principal lords, though they did homage to the king of France or to the emperor, yielded obedience in reality to the Spanish monarch, lived under his protection, and served in his armies. And several of them, by gifts from the crown, or by marriages, possessed lands in Spain.

33

In consequence of this connection between the two countries, some of the Vaudois had crossed the Pyrenees and established themselves in Spain as early as the middle of the twelfth century.[52] They appear to have enjoyed repose their for some time; but in the year 1194, pope Celestin III. sent the cardinal St. Angelo as legate to attend a council at Lerida, who prevailed on Alfonso II. king of Aragon, to publish an edict, order the Vaudois, or Poor Men of Lyons, and all other heretics, to quit his territories

---

Which nee'r was found within your heart, nor pass'd your teeth at all,

The fire is lit, the pitch is hot, and ready is the stake,

That thro' these tortures, for your sins, your passage you may take.

52. Guil. *Neobrig.* lib. ii. cap. xiii.; apud *His. Gen. de Languedoc*, tom. iii. p. 2.

under severe pains.[53] This edict not having produced any effect, was renewed three years after by Pedro II, in consequence of a decree of a council held at Gironna. With the view of securing the execution of this measure, the subscriptions of all the grandees of Catalonia were procured to the decree; and all governors and judges were required to swear before the bishops, that they would assist in discovering and punishing those infected with heresy, under the penalty of being themselves treated as heretics.[54] Notwithstanding this edict, and the engagements he had contracted at his coronation, Pedro was disposed to be favorable to this sect. He was from the beginning displeased at the crusade which raged on the north of the Pyrenees; and having at last joined his army to those of his brother-in-law Raymond, count of Toulouse, he fell, in the year 1213, fighting in defence of the Albigenses in the battle of Muret.[55]

34

This disaster, together with those that followed it, induced multitudes of the Albigenses to take refuge in Aragon, who gave ample employment to the inquisition after it was established in that country. From the accession of pope Gregory IX. to that of Alexander IV. (that is, from 1227 to 1254,) they had grown to such numbers and cred-

---

53. Llorente, i. 30.

54. Ibid., p. 31, 32. Marca Hisp. apud *Hist. Gen. de Languedoc*, iii. 130.

55. Zurita, *Annales de Aragon*, tom. i. p. 99-101. *Hist. Gen. de Languedoc*, iii. 248-254; Sismondi, *Hist. of Crusades against Albigenses*, p. 98-101. Perrin, ii. 76-92. Usserius, *De Christ. Eccl. Successione et Statu*, cap. x. sect. 37, 38, 39.

it as to have churches in various parts of Catalonia and
Aragon, which were provided with bishops, who boldly
preached their doctrine.[56] Gregory, in a brief which he addressed to the archbishop of Tarragona and his suffragans,
in 1232, complains of the increase of heresy in their dioceses, and exhorts them to make strict inquisition after
it by means of the Dominican monks; and his successor
Alexander repeated the complaint.[57] In 1237, the flames of
persecution were kindled in the viscounty of Cerdagne and
Castlebon, within the diocese of Urgel; forty-five persons
being condemned, of whom fifteen were burnt alive, and
eighteen disinterred bodies cast into the fire.[58] In 1267,
the inquisitors of Barcelona pronounced sentence against
Raymond, count of Forcalquier and Urgel, ordering his
bones, as those of a relapsed heretic, to be taken out of the
grave;[59] and two years after they passed the same sentence
on Arnold, viscount of Castlebon and Cerdagne, and his
daughter Ermesinde, wife of Roger-Bernard II. count of
Foix, surnamed the Great.[60] Both father and daughter had

35

---

56. Mat. Paris, ad. an. 1214. Perrin, part i. p. 246.

57. Llorente, i. 67. Leger, ii. 337.

58. *Hist. de Languedoc*, iii. 412. Preuves, p. 383.

59. Llorente, i. 72.

60. *Hist. Gen. de Languedoc*, iii. 115, 382. In 1207, the bishop of
Ozma, and other preaching missionaries, held a dispute with the
teachers of the Vaudois at Pamiers. On that occasion the count de
Foix entertained both parties alternately in his palace: his countess Ermesinde, and two of his sisters, openly befriended the sectaries. One of the latter, Esclaramonde, married to Joudain II. sieur
de Lille-Jourdain, having said something in their favor during the

been dead upwards of twenty years, yet their bones were ordered to be disinterred, "provided they could be found;" a preposterous and unnatural demonstration of zeal for the faith, which is applauded by the fanatical writers of that age, but was in fact dictated by hatred to the memory of the brave and generous Count de Foix. When summoned in his life-time to appear before the inquisition at Toulouse, that nobleman not only treated their order with contempt, but in his turn summoned the inquisitors of the county of Foix to appear before him as his vassals and subjects. During his exile at the court of his father-in-law, he was excommunicated by the bishop of Urgel as a favorer of heresy; and although the sentence was removed, and 36 he died in the communion of the church, yet the inquisitors never could forgive the disinterested and determined resistance which he had made to their barbarous proceedings. They put one of his servants to the torture, with the view of extorting from him some evidence upon which they might pronounce that his master had died a heretic; and, having failed in that attempt, they now sought to wreck their vengeance on the memory and the ashes of the countess and her father.[61]

It has been said that the Poor Men of Lyons or Waldenses, when they made their first appearance, were looked upon at Rome as an order of monks who wished to revive the decaying fervor of piety among the people,

---

conference, was silenced by one of the missionaries, who rudely ordered her to her distaff. (Ibid. p. 147. Preuves, p. 437.)

61. *Hist. de Languedoc*, iii. 412, 419, 427. Preuves, p. 383-385, 392, 437, 552. Llorente, i. 73, 74.

and to lead a life of superior sanctity among themselves; and that it was seriously proposed at one time to give the pontifical sanctions to their internal regulations.[62]Whatever truth their may be in this statement, it is a curious fact, that, in Spain, some individuals of this sect did obtain a temporary respite from persecution by forming themselves into a new religious fraternity. In consequence of a dispute held at Pamiers in Languedoc, Durando de Huesca, a native of Aragon, with a number of his Albigensian brethren, yielded to the Romish missionaries, and having obtained liberty to retire into Catalonia, formed a religious community under the name of the Society of Poor Catholics. In 1207 Durando went to Rome, where he obtained from Innocent III. the remission of his former heresy, and an approbation of his fraternity, of which he was declared superior. Its members lived on alms, applied themselves to study and the teaching of schools, kept lent twice a-year, and wore a decent habit of white or grey, with shoes open at the top, but distinguished by some particular marks from those of the Poor Men of Lyons, who, from this part of their dress, were sometimes called Insabatati. The new order spread so rapidly, that in a few years it had numerous convents both to the south and north of the Pyrenees. But although the Poor Catholics professed to devote themselves to the conversion of heretics, and their superior wrote some books with that in view, they soon incurred the suspicion of the bishops, who accused them of favoring the Vaudois, and concealing their heretical tenets

37

---

62. Muratori, *Antiq. Ital.* Dissert. 60, tom. v. p. 83. *Abbatis Urspergensis Chronic. ad an. 1212; et auctt. citat. Usserio, de Christ. Eccl. Success. et Statu*, cap. x. sect. 1, p. 146.

under the monastic garb. They had interest to maintain themselves for some time, and even to procure letters from his Holiness, exhorting the bishops to endeavor to gain them by kindness instead of alienating their minds from the church by severe treatment; but their enemies at last prevailed, and within a short time no trace of their establishments was to be found.[63]

The Albigenses were not confined to Aragon and Catalonia. Of the extent to which they spread in the kingdom of Castile and Leon, we may form some judgment from an amusing anecdote, related from personal knowledge, by Lucio, bishop of Tuy, known, as a writer against the Albigenses, by the name of Lucas Tudensis; and which I shall give as nearly in his own words as is consistent with perspicuity. After the death of Roderic, bishop of Leon, (in the year 1237[64]) great dissension arose about the election of his successor. Taking advantage of this circumstance, the heretics flocked from all quarters to that city. In one of the suburbs, where every kind of filth was thrown, lay, along with those of a murderer, the bones of a heretic, named Arnald, who had been buried sixteen years before. Near to this was a fountain, over which they erected an edifice, and having taken up the bones of Arnald, whom they extolled as a martyr, deposited them in it. To this place a number of persons, hired by the hertics, came; and feigning themselves to be blind, lame, and afflicted with other disorders, they drank of the waters of the fountain,

38

---

63. *Antonii Bibl. Hisp. Vetus*, tom. ii. p. 45, 46. Hist. Gen de Languedoc, tom. iii. p. 147, 148.

64. *Antonii Bibl. Hisp. Vet.*, tom. ii. p. 59.

and then went away, saying that they were suddenly and miraculously healed. This being noised abroad, great multitudes flocked to the spot. After they had got a number of the clergy, as well as laity, to give credit to the pretended cures, the heretics disclosed the imposition which they had practiced, and then boasted that all the miracles performed at the tombs of the saints were of the same kind. By this means, they drew many to their heresy. In vain did the Dominican and Franciscan friars attempt to stem the torrent of defection, by exclaiming against the sin of offering sacrilegious prayers in a place defiled by profane bones. They were cried down as heretics and unbelievers. In vain did the adjacent bishops excommunicate those who visited the fountain or worshipped in the temple. The devil had seized upon the minds of the people and fascinated their senses. At last, a deacon, who resided at Rome, hearing of the state of matters in his native city, hastened to Leon, and "in a kind of frenzy," at the risk of his life, upbraided the inhabitants for favoring the heretics, and called on the magistrates to abate the nuisance. For some months before his arrival, the country had been afflicted with a severe drought. This he declared to be a judgment from heaven on account of their sin, but promised that it should be removed within eight days from the time that they pulled down the heretical temple. The magistrates granted him permission, and he razed the building to its foundation. Scarcely was this done, when a fire devoured a great part of the city, and for seven days no symptom of rain appeared; upon which the heretics insulted over the deacon. But on the eighth day the clouds collected, and poured down copious and refreshing showers on all the surrounding country. "After this, the foresaid deacon 40 raised persecution against the heretics, who, being forced to leave the city, were miserably scattered abroad."[65] We are assured, and not without great probability, that the deacon was no other than Lucas Tudensis, whose modesty induced him to suppress his name in relating the prediction and the persecution, in both of which he appears to have equally gloried.[66]

In spite of the occupation given to the clergy by the suppression of the Knights Templars, and the schism of the anti-popes, the persecution of the Albigenses seldom relaxed during the fourteenth century. Scarcely a year passed in which numbers were not barbarously led to the stake.[67] Among those who were condemned for heresy at this period, was Arnaldo of Villanueva in Argaon, a celebrated physician and chemist.[68] He taught, that the whole

---

65. Mariana, de *Rebus Hisp*. lib. xxi. cap. i. in Schotti Hisp. Illustr. tom. ii. p. 556.

66. Florez, *Espana Sagrada*, tom. xxii. p. 108.

67. Llorente, i. 80-85.

68. *Antonii Bibl. Hisp. Vetus*. tom. ii. p. 112-119. Niceron, *Mem. des Hommes Illustres*, tom. xxxiv. p. 82. Arnaldo is celebrated among those who searched for the *Philosopher's Stone* in the following lines of the *Libro del Tesoro*, an ancient poem ascribed to Alfonso X. of Castile, nicknamed The Wise:

> Pero los modernos que le sucedieron,
>> Entre ellos Ranaldo da todos nombrado
>> Camino non dessa, y tan alombrado
>> Que ascuras se veen los que no lo vieron.

Sanchez, *Coleccion de Poesias Castellanas*, tom. i. p. 166.

Christian people had, through the craft of the devil, been led aside from the truth, and retained nothing but the semblance of ecclesiastical worship, which they kept up from the force of custom; that those who lived in cloisters threw themselves out of charity, and that the religious orders in general falsified the doctrine of Christ; that it is not a work of charity to endow chapels for celebrating masses for the dead; and that those who devoted their money to this purpose, instead of providing for the poor, especially the poor belonging to Christ, exposed themselves to damnation; that offices of mercy and medicine are more acceptable to the Deity than the sacrifice of the altar; and that God is praised in the eucharist not by the hands of the priest, but by the mouth of the communicant.[69] Such being his avowed sentiments, we need not wonder that he was doomed to expiate his temerity by suffering the fire, from which he saved himself by flying to his native country, and taking refuge with Ferdinand, king of Sicily.[70] To Arnald we may add a writer of the following century, Raimond de Sebonde, author of a treatise on natural theology, who was charged with heresy for asserting that all saving truths are contained, and clearly proposed, in the sacred scriptures.[71]

41

---

69. *Bulæi Hist. Univ. Paris*, tom. iv. p. 121. MSS. by Arnald in Cottonian Library: Rodriguez de Castro, Bibl. Espan. tom. ii. 743, 474. (sic.)

70. *Antonius, Bibl. Hisp.* Vet. ii. 114.

71. *The Theologia Naturalis of Sebonde* has met with the approbation of Montaigne and Grotius; and, which is not less praise, the censure of the Index Expurgatorius. (Pellicer, *Ensayo*, p. 15-18. Cave,

From 1412 to 1425, a great number of persons who entertained the sentiments of the Vaudois were commit- 42 ted to the flames by the inquisitors of Valentia, Rousillon, and Majorca. It appears, that the followers of Wicliffe had migrated to the Peninsula; for in 1441, the inquisitors of Aragon and Valentia reconciled some of them to the church, and condemned others to the fire as obstinate heretics.[72] If we may trust the monkish annalists, Spain was also visited at this period by the Beghards, a fanatical sect which the corruptions of the church and the ignorance of the times had generated in Germany and other parts of Europe. But this is uncertain, as it was common for the clergy to apply this and similar names to the Vaudois, with the view of exciting odium against them, and justifying their own cruelties. In 1350, we are told, a warm inquisition was commenced in Valentia against the Beghards, whose leader was condemned to perpetual imprisonment, and the bones of many of his disciples dug up and consigned to the flames; and in 1442, it was found they had multiplied at Durango, a town of Biscay, and in the diocese of Calahorra. Alfonso de Mella, a Franciscan, and brother of the bishop of Zamora, who was afterwards invested with the purple, having incurred the suspicion of being at the head of this party, fled along with his companions, to the Moors, among whom "he died miserably at Grenada, being pierced with reeds; an example, (says the biographer of his brother) worthy to be recorded, of 43

Hist. Liter. Append. p. 104.)

72. Dr. Michael Geddes's *Miscellaneous Tracts*, vol. i. p. 559. Llorente, i. 92, 93.

the variety of human affairs, and the opposite dispositions of persons who lay in the same womb."[73] On application to John II. king of Castile, a band of royal musqueteers was sent to scour the mountains of Biscay, and the higher districts of Old Castile, who drove down the heretics like cattle before them, and delivered them to the inquisitors, by whom they were committed to the flames at St. Domingo de la Calzado, and Valladolid.[74] Thus were the Albigenses, after a barbarous and unrelenting persecution of two centuries, exterminated in Spain, with the exception of a few, who contrived to conceal themselves in the more remote and inaccessible parts of the country, and at a subsequent period, furnished occasionally a straggling victim to the familiars of the inquisition, when surfeited with the blood of Jews and Moriscoes.

During these proceedings, Rome succeeded in establishing its empire a second time in Spain, and that in a more durable form than in the days of the Scipios and Augustus. This conquest was achieved chiefly by means of the monks and friars. Anciently the number of convents and of monks in Spain was small; but it multiplied greatly from the twelfth to the fifteenth century. The beginning of that period was marked by the infliction of that scourge of society, and outrage of all decency,—privileged and meritorious mendicity. Of all the orders of mendicant friars, the most devoted to the See of Rome were those founded by St. Dominic and St. Francis, the former the most odi-

44

---

73. *Antonii Bibl. Hisp. Vet.* tom. ii. p. 286. Mariana, lib. xxi. cap. 17.

74. Mariana, lib. xxi. cap. 17. Geddes, *Miscellaneous Tracts*, vol. i. p. 559.

ous, the latter the most frantic, of modern saints. Within a few years after their institution, convents belonging to both these orders were to be found in every part of Spain. Though the Dominicans, owing to the patronage of the court of Rome, or to their founder, being a Spaniard, enjoyed the greatest share of political power, yet the reception given to the Franciscans left them no ground to complain of Spanish inhospitality. An event which happened at the close of the fifteenth century contributed to the still more rapid increase of religious houses. A great part of the wealth which flowed into Spain after the discovery of the New World, found its way to the church. Imitating the Pagan warriors who dedicated the spoils which they had gained to their gods, the Spaniards who enriched themselves by pillaging and murdering the Indians, sought to testify their gratitude or to expiate their crimes by lavishing ornaments on churches, and endowing monasteries. The following examples show the rate at which the regular clergy increased. The first Franciscan missionaries entered Spain in the year 1216; and, in 1400, they had, within the three provinces of Santiago, Castile, and Aragon, including Portugal, twenty-three *custodiae*, composed of a 45 hundred and twenty-one convents.[75] But in the year 1506, the Regular Observantines, who formed only the third division of that order, had a hundred and ninety convents in Spain, excluding Portugal.[76] In the year 1030, the city of Salamanca did not contain a single convent; in 1480, it

---

75. Wadding, *Annales Minorum Ordinum*, cura Jos. Maria Fonseca, tom. i. p. 247-249; conf. tom. ix. p. 206-210.

76. Wadding, tom. xv. p. 342-350.

possessed nine, of which six were for males, and three for females; and in 1518, it could number thirty-nine convents, while its nuns alone amounted to eleven thousand.[77]

The corruption of the monastic institutions kept pace with the increase of their numbers and wealth. The licentiousness of the regular clergy became notorious. They broke through the rules prescribed by their founders, and laid aside that austere mode of living by which they had at first acquired all their reputation.[78] Even those who had vowed the most rigid poverty, such as the Observantines, or third order of St. Francis, procured dispensations from Rome, in virtue of which they possessed rents, and property in houses and lands. By the original regulations of St. Francis, all belonging to his order bound themselves to live purely on alms and were strictly prohibited from receiving any money, on whatever pretext, even as wages for labor performed by them, "unless for the manifest necessity of infirm brethren."[79] The monastic historians are greatly puzzled to account for the glaring departure from this rule of poverty; probably forgetting, or not wishing to have recourse to the well known maxim, that nature abhors a vacuum. Sometimes they wish to account for it by saying that a destructive pestilence, about the beginning of the fourteenth century, thinned the monasteries, which were afterwards filled with novices of a more earthly

46

---

77. Townsend's *Journey through Spain*, vol. ii. p. 84.

78. *Petri Martyris Anglerii Epistolæ*, ep. 163. Alvar. *Gomecius, De rebus gestis Francisci Ximenii*, f. 7. Compluti, 1569. Wadding, *Minor. Ord.* tom. xv. p. 108.

79. Reg. cap. viii. ix; apud Wadding, ut supra, i. 71.

mould.[80] But they are forced to trace the evil to a more remote source, and to impute it to brother Elias,[81] a native of Cortona, and vicar-general of the order of Franciscans, under its founder. As early as 1223, he began to hint to his brethren that the rule prescribed to them was a yoke which neither they nor their successors could bear; but was silenced by the authority of St. Francis. After the death of the saint, he was more successful in gaining proselytes to his opinion, and drew upon himself the sentence of excommunication, from which, however, he was ultimately relieved.[82]

The kings of Spain attempted at different times to correct these abuses, but the monks and friars had always the influence or the address to defeat the measure. When the glaring nature of the evil induced Ferdinand and Isabella to renew the attempt at the close of the fifteenth century, they were obliged to employ force; nor would their united authority have been sufficient to carry the point, had they not availed themselves of the sagacity and firmness of the celebrated cardinal Ximenes, himself a friar, and inflamed with the passion of restoring the order of St. Francis, of which he was then provincial, to all the poverty and rigor of its original institution. Lorenzo Vacca, abbot of the monastery of the Holy Spirit at Segovia, relying on the

---

80. Fernando del Castillo, *Hist. Gen. de Santo Domingo, y de su Orden*, Parte ii. lib. ii. cap. 2, 3. Quintanilla, Vida del Cardenal Ximenes, p. 22.

81. Quintanilla, ut supra.

82. Wadding *Annales. Minor. Ord.* tom. i. p. 62, 216; conf. tom. iii. p. 102.

papal bulls which he had procured, made such resistance to the plans of his provincial, that the government found it necessary to commit him to prison, from which he escaped, and repairing to Rome, exerted himself, through the influence of the Ascanio Sforza and other cardinals, in counteracting the reform of the religious orders in Spain.[83] The Franciscan friars of Toledo carried their resistance so far, that an order was issued to banish them from the kingdom; upon which they left the city in solemn procession, carrying a crucifix before them, and chaunting the psalm which begins, When Israel went up out of Egypt, &c.[84]

48 The biographers of Ximenes represent him as having reformed all the religious institutions in Spain; but it is evident that his success was partial, and chiefly confined to his own order. So far as they proceeded on the rigid principles of monachism, the regulations which he introduced were unnatural and pernicious, and such of them as were favorable to morals were soon swept away by the increasing tide of corruption.

It has been said, that Ximenes abolished a number of superstitious practices which had crept into the worship of the Spanish church during the dark ages; and in proof of this we are told that he revived the Mozarabic office, and appointed it to be used in all the churches of his diocese.[85] But the writers who make this assertion have fallen into a mistake, both as to what was done by the cardinal, and as to the object he had in view. Perceiving that the Mozarabic

---

83. Martyr, et Gomecius, ut supra.

84. De Robles, *Vida del Cardenal Ximenes,* p. 68.

85. Gerdesii *Hist. Reform.* tom. i. p. 15.

service had fallen into desuetude in the six churches of
Toledo, in which its use had been enjoined by an old law,[86]
he was desirous to preserve this venerable relic of antiquity.
With this view he employed Alfonso Ortiz, one of the canons of his cathedral, to collate all the copies of that liturgy
which could be found; and, the Gothic letters in which
they were written being changed into Roman, he caused
the work to be printed.[87] Some years after[88] he erected a
chapel in the cathedral church, with an endowment for 49
thirteen priests, whose duty it was to celebrate the service
according to that liturgy.[89] There is reason to think that he
ordered it to be also used on certain festivals in the church-

---

86. See before, p. 25.

87. *The Mozarabic Missal* was printed at Toledo in the year 1500.
(Mendez, *Typogr. Esp.* p. 307.) *The Breviary* was printed at the
same place in the year 1502. (Quintanilla, p. 116. *Archivo Complutense*, No. 13.)

88. In 1512.

89. Marsollier, *Histoire du Ministère du Cardinal Ximenes*, tom. ii. p.
42-44. *De Robles, del Cardenal Ximenes, y Officio Gotico Muzara-
be*, p. 302. In the *Mozarabic Missal*, as published in 1500, the
words of consecration in the eucharist are taken exactly from the
evangelists. But it was deemed dangerous to practice this mode;
and accordingly the priests were provided with a piece of paper
on the margin, containing the Roman forms of consecration,
which they made use of. (Ib. p. 287, 288.) By degrees the Mozarabic form fell into neglect in the chapel appropriated to it; and
in 1786, when Townsend visited Toledo, there was none present
at the service but himself and the officiating priest. (*Travels*, i.
311, 312.)

es commonly called Mozarabic; but it is certain that the order did not extend to the other churches of his diocese. So far was it from his intention to make any innovation on the existing forms of worship, or to supplant the Roman by the ancient Spanish liturgy, that he interpolated his edition of the latter, in order to render it more conformable to the former; thus destroying its character and use as an ancient document. Among these interpolations are "a prayer for the adoration of the cross," and offices for a number of saints who lived before as well as after the compilation of the liturgy; for the ancient Goths and Mozarabes commemorated none but martyrs in their public service.—Ferdinand de Talavera, archbishop of Granada, endowed, about the same time, a chapel in Salamanca, in which the service continued to be celebrated according to the ritual at the close of the seventeenth century.[90]

50

It might be presumed, from the statements already made, and from what we know of other countries, that the Spanish clergy had sunk very low in point of knowledge, and that the absurdities which one of their countrymen afterwards exposed so wittily in Fray Gerundio, were not less common or less ridiculous before the revival of letters. But on this head we are not left to conjecture. In address to queen Isabella, cardinal Ximenes acknowledges the gross ignorance that prevailed among the priests.[91] This led to the adoption of the most absurd opinions, and the practice of the most extravagant superstitions. Legends and lives of saints formed the favorite reading of the de-

90. Illescas, *Hist. Pontifical*, tom. i. f. 269.

91. Quintanilla, p. 21.

vout, while the vulgar fed on the stories of every-day miracles which the priests and friars ministered fresh to their
credulity. The doctrine of the immaculate conception of
the Virgin met with believers in other countries; but Spain
could boast of an order of nuns consecrated to the honor
of that newly-invented mystery.[92] The doctrine of tran-
substantiation, which many even at that period could not
digest without difficulty, was no trial of faith to a Spaniard. "Do you believe that this wafer is the body of the
Father, Son, and Holy Ghost?" was the question which the
parish priests of Valencia, in the fourteenth century, were 51
accustomed to put to dying persons; and on obtaining an
affirmative answer, they administered the host. Another
attempt to extend the mysterious process a little farther
met with greater opposition. Eimeric, the author of the
celebrated Guide to Inquisitors, wrote against Bonnet
and Mairon, who maintained that St. John the Evangelist
became the real son of the Virgin, in consequence of his
body being transubstantiated into that of Christ, by the
words pronounced on the cross, *Ecce filius tuus*, Behold
thy son.[93]

---

92 Ibid. p. 29-32.

93. *Antonii Bibl. Hisp. Vet.* tom. ii. p. 187, 188.

II

Of the State of Literature in Spain Before the Era of the Reformation

HAVING TAKEN A general survey of the state of religion in Spain before the Reformation, let us look back for a little and trace the restoration of letters, which opened the prospect of a better order of things in that country. The learning of Isidore, archbishop of Seville, who flourished in the seventh century, and next to St. James, is venerated by the Spaniards as a tutelary saint, rests on a better foundation than the encomium of Gregory the Great, who called him a second Daniel. Besides various theological and historical treatises,[1] he composed a work on etymology, which, though disfigured by errors, discovers a considerable portion of philological knowledge, and contributed to check the barbarism which had already invaded every country

---

1. *Antonii Bibl. Hisp. Vet.*tom. i. p. 330—336. Rodriguez de Castro, *Bibl. Espan.* tom. ii. p. 293-344.

53 in Europe. But ages of darkness succeeded, during which, while the name of St. Isidore was held in veneration, his works were disregarded, by an ignorant priesthood, into whose hands the key of knowledge had fallen.

It is not to the credit of Christianity, or at least of those who professed it, that, during the middle ages, letters were preserved from extinction, and even revived from the decline which had seized them, by the exertions of the followers of Mahomet. The tenth century, which has been denominated the leaden age of Europe, was the golden age of Asia. Modern writers have perhaps gone to an extreme on both sides in forming their estimate of the degree in which European literature is indebted to the Arabians. But when we find that this people have left such evident marks of their language upon that of Spain, it seems unreasonable to doubt that they had also great influence upon its literature. Cordova, Granada, and Seville, rivalled one another in the magnificence of their schools and libraries, during the empire of the Saracens, who granted to the Spanish Christians, whom they had subjugated, that protection in their religious rights, which the latter were far from imitating when they in their turn became the conquerors.[2] The

54 two languages were spoken in common.[3] The Christians began to vie with their masters in the pursuit of science,

---

2. Marc. *Hisp.* lib. iii. cap. 2.

3. Alvaro de Cordova, who lived about the year 860, complains that his countrymen "despised the full streams of the church which flowed from Paradise, and, adopting the Arabic, had lost their native tongue, and many of them their faith along with it." (Aldrede, *Origenes de la Lengua Castellana*, lib. i. cap. 22.)

composed commentaries on the scriptures in Arabic, and transfused the beauties of eastern poetry into the Castilian language.[4] It is even said, that a bishop of Seville, at this early period, translated the scriptures into the Arabic tongue.[5]

If the Spanish language was in danger of suffering from the predominance of the Arabians, the evil was counteracted by the cultivation of Provençal poetry. In the twelfth century, Alfonso II. of Aragon, whose name has an honorable place among the Troubadours, zealously patronized those who wrote in the Catalonian or Valencian dialect.[6] In the subsequent century, Alfonso X. of Castile, surnamed the Wise, showed himself equally zealous in encouraging the study of the Castilian tongue, in which he wrote several poems; at the same time that he extracted the knowledge which was to be found in the books of the Arabians; as appears, among other proofs, from the astro- 55

---

4.   Aldrede, ut supra. Casiri, Bibl. Arabico-Hisp. Escurial. tom. i. p. 38. Antonii Bibl. Hisp. Vet. tom. i. p. 483. A more recent Spanish writer, with a national partiality rather glaring, says, that his countrymen carried away all that is good in Arabian literature, while the other nations of Europe took what is bad in it—its dialectic subtleties and sophistry. *"En rsolucion, de lo bueno y malo que contenia la literatura Arabe, los Christianos de Espana tomáron lo bueno y útil, y conserváron el decoro de las disciplinas que aquella no conocia....Los extrangeros, tomando lo malo del saber Arabe, pervertiéndolo mas y mas."* &c. (Juan Pablo Forner, *Oracion Apologetica por la Espana, y su mérito Literario*, p. 62. Madrid, 1786.)

5.   Mar. *Hisp.* lib. iii. cap. 2.

6.   Sanchez, *Coleccion*, tom. i. p. 74.

nomical tables, called from him Alphonsine.[7] The writings of Dante, Checo Dascoli, and Petrarch, gave a new impulse to the literature of Spain. From this period the study of the ancient classics imparted greater purity and elevation to works of imagination; and a taste for poetical compositions in their native tongue began to be felt by the Spanish gentry, who had hitherto found their sole pastime in arms and military tournaments.[8] Among those who distinguished themselves by improving the taste of their countrymen in the first part of the fifteenth century, were two persons of illustrious birth, in whose families the love of learning was long hereditary. Henry of Aragon, marquis of Villena, descended from the royal houses of Aragon and Castile, revived the *Consistorio de la Gaya Sciencia,* an academy situated at Barcelona for the encouragement of poetry, of which he was the president. His superior knowledge, combined perhaps with a portion of that learned credulity of which those who addicted themselves to astronomy and experimental science during the middle ages were often the dupes, brought on him the suspicion of necromancy. In consequence of that, his books were seized after his death, by the orders of Juan II. king of Castile, and sent for examination to Lope de Barrientos, a Dominican monk of considerable learning, and preceptor to the prince of Asturias. "Barrientos," says a contemporary writer, "liking better to walk with the prince than to revise necromancies, committed to the flames upwards of a hundred volumes, without having examined them any more

56

---

7. *Antonii Bibl. Hisp. Vet.* tom. ii. p. 78-87.

8. Zurita, *Annales,* ad an. 1398.

than the king of Morocco, or understood a jot of their contents more than the dean of Ciudad Rodrigo. There are many in the present day," continues he, "who become learned men, by pronouncing others fools and magicians; and what is worse, make themselves saints, by stigmatizing others as sorcerers." This indignity done to the memory of "the ornament of Spain and of the age," was bewailed, both in verse and prose, by writers of that time.[9]

Equally learned as Villena, but more fortunate in preserving his good name and his books, was Inigo Lopez de Mendoza, marquis of Santillana, who, in a treatise, intended as a preface to his countrymen who preceded him in paying court to the muse.[10] The merits of both marquises have been celebrated by the pen of Juan de Mena, unquestionably the first Spanish poet of that age.

It is not unworthy of remark here, that the Jews, while they enjoyed protection in Spain, co-operated with the Christians in the cultivation of polite letters. Rabbi Don Santo, who flourished about the year 1360, makes the following modest and not inelegant apology for taking his place among the poets of the land which had given him birth:— 57

> The rose that twines a thorny sprig,
> Will not the less perfume the earth;

---

9. Sanchez, *Coleccion*, tom. i. p. 5-10. *Ferdinandi Gomesii Epistolæ, apud Antonii Bibl.* ut supra, p. 220-222.

10. Sanchez has given a life of this nobleman, along with his "*Proemio al Condestable de Portugal*," illustrated with learned notes, in the first volume of his collection of ancient Castillian poets.

Good wine, that leaves a creeping twig,
> Is not the worse for humble birth.

The hawk may be of noble kind,
> That from a filthy aiery flew;
And precepts are not less refined,
> Because they issue from a Jew.[11]

58 Long after their expulsion from Spain, the Jews cherished an ardent attachment to the Castilian tongue, in which they continued to compose works both in prose and verse.[12]

---

11. *Por nascer en espino*
La rosa, ya non siento
Que pierde, ni el buen vino
Por salir del sarmiento.

Nin vale el azor menos,
Porque en vil nido siga;
Nin los enxemplos buenos,
Porque Judio los diga.

Rodriguez de Castro supposed Don Santo to have been a converted Jew. (*Bibl. Espanola*, tom. i. p. 198.) But his mistake has been corrected, and its source pointed out, by Sanchez. (*Coleccion de Poesias Castellanas*, tom. iv. p. xii. conf. tom. i. p. 179-184.) Juan Alfonso Baena, a converted Jew, who flourished in the beginning of the fifteenth century, made a very curious collection of the poems of the *Trobadores Espanoles*, including his own, from which Rodriguez de Castro has given copious extracts. (*Bibl. Esp.* tom. i. p. 265-345.)

12. Wolfius has given many examples of this in his *Bibliotheca Hebraea. See also Rodr. de Castro, Escritores Rabinos Espanoles del Siglo*

On looking into the writings of the ancient Spanish poets, we are induced to conclude, that they were not in the habit of using those liberties with the church and clergy which were indulged in by the poets of Italy and the Troubadours of Provence. There is reason however to think, that the absence of these satires is to be accounted for, in no small degree, by the prudence of the editors of their works, and the vigilance of the censors of the press, after the invention of printing. Accordingly, of later years, since the severity of the Inquisition relaxed, and a passion to do justice to their literary antiquities has been felt by the Spaniards, poems have been brought to the light, though still with much caution,[13] which two centuries ago would have earned for their learned editors a perpetual prison. The poems of Juan Ruiz, archpriest of Hita, who flourished in the middle of the fourteenth century, contain severe satires on the avarice and loose manners of the clergy. He represents money as opening the gates of Paradise, purchasing salvation to the people, and benefices to priests; as equally powerful at the court of Rome and elsewhere, with the pope and all orders of the clergy, secular and regular; as converting a lie into the truth, and the truth into a lie.[14] In another poem he is as severe 59

---

xvii. *passim.*

13. See the apologetical notes of Sanchez to his collection of early Castilian poems, particularly tom. iv. p. 76, 119, 199.

14. The following is the description, which Sanchez calls "a false and extravagant satire:"

> *Si toveres dineros, habras consolacion,*
> *Plaser, è alegria, del Papa racion,*

against the manners of the clergy, whom he describes as living avowedly in concubinage. He represents Don Gil de Albornoz, archbishop of Talavera, as having procured a mandate from the pope, ordering all his clergy to put away their wives or concubines whom they kept in their houses, under the pain of excommunication. When this mandate was read to them in a public assembly, it excited a warm opposition; violent speeches were made against it by the dean and others; some of them declared that they would sooner part with their dignities; and it was finally agreed that they should appeal from the pope to the king of Castile.[15]

Compraras paraiso, ganarás salvacion,
Dó son muchos dineros, es mucha benedicion.

   Yo vi en corte de Roma, dó es la santidat,
Que todos al dinero fasen grand homilidat,
Grand honra le fascian con grand solenidat,
Todos à el se homillan como à la magestat.

   Fasie muchos Priores, Obispos, et Abades,
Arzobispos, Doctores, Patriarcas, Potestades,
A muchos Clerigos nescios dábales dinidades,
Fasie de verdat mentiras, et de mentiras verdades.

   Fasia muchos Clerigos e muchos ordenados,
Muchos monges, e monjas, religiosos sagrados,
El dinero los daba por bien exâminados,
A los pobres desian, que non eran letrados.
Coleccion, tom. iv. p. 76, 77.

15. *Cartas eran venidas, que disen en esta manera:*
Que Clerigo nin casado de toda Talavera,
Que non toviese manceba casada nin soltera,

About the middle of the fifteenth century, literature 60
was advanced under the patronage of Alfonso V. of Aragon. The education of this monarch had been neglected,
and the early part of his life was spent in arms; but at fifty
years of age he applied himself to study with such eagerness
that he was soon able to read with ease the Roman classics,
which became his constant companions. He disputed with
the house of Medici the honor of entertaining men of letters, and rescuing the writings of antiquity from oblivion.
When he had taken a town, his soldiers could not do the
prince a greater pleasure than to bring him a book which
they had discovered among the spoils; and Cosmo de'
Medici, by the present of an ancient manuscript, procured
from him a treaty highly favorable to Florence. Anthony
of Palermo, usually styled Panormitanus, who wrote the
history of his life, resided at his court in great honor, and
Laurentius Valla, one of the most profound and elegant
scholars of that age,[16] when persecuted for the freedom of
his opinions, was protected by Alfonso at Naples, where
he opened a school for Greek and Roman eloquence.[17]

Qualquier que la toviese, descomulgado era.

*　　*　　　*　　　*

Pero non alonguemos atanto las rasones,
Apellaron los Clerigos, otro si los Clerisones,
Fesieron luego de mano buenas apelaciones,
Et dende en adelante ciertas procuraciones.
Coleccion, tom. iv. p. 280, 283.

16. *History of the progress and Suppression of the Reformation in Italy,*
   p. 15, 48.

17. Ginguené, *Hist. Lit. d' Italie,* tom. iii. p. 348, 349. *Antonii Bibl.*

61   Alfonso de Palencia, having visited Italy, became acquainted with cardinal Bessarion, and attended the lectures which the learned Greek Trapezuntius delivered on eloquence and his native tongue. On his return to Spain, he was made historiographer to Henry IV. of Castile, and afterwards to queen Isabella; and by his translations from Greek into the Castilian language, as well as by a work on grammar, excited a taste for letters among his countrymen.[18] He was followed by Antonio de Lebrixa, usually styled Nebrissensis, who became to Spain what Valla was to Italy, Erasmus to Germany, and Budé to France. After a residence of ten years in Italy, during which he had stored his mind with various kinds of knowledge, he returned home in 1473, by the advice of the younger Philelphus and Hermolaus Barbarus, with the view of promoting classical learning in his native country. Hitherto the revival of letters in Spain was confined to a few inquisitive individuals, and had not reached the schools and universities, whose teachers continued to teach a barbarous jargon, under the name of Latin, into which they initiated the youth by means of a rude system of grammar, rendered

---

Hisp. Vet. tom. ii. p. 271, 272. From Valla's Dedication of one of his treatises to Alfonso, it appears that they were in the habit of corresponding on classical subjects. (Laur. *Vallae Opera*, p. 438-445.) Valla has also paid a compliment to the early military talents of his patron, in his work *De Rebus Ferdinandi Aragoniæ Rege gestis*; published in the second volume of *Rerum Hispanicarum Scriptores*. Franc. 1509.

18. Pellicer, *Ensayo*, p. 7-13. Antonius, *Bibl. Hisp. Vet.* ii. 333. Mendez, *Typ. Espanola*, p. 173-175, 180-182, 189.

unintelligible, in some instances, by a preposterous intermixture of the most abstruse questions in metaphysics.[19] 62
By the lectures which he read in the universities of Seville,
Salamanca, and Alcala, and by the institutes which he
published on Castilian, Latin, Greek, and Hebrew grammar, Lebrixa contributed in a wonderful degree to expel
barbarism from the seats of education, and to diffuse a
taste for elegant and useful studies among his countrymen.[20] His improvements were warmly opposed by the
monks, who had engrossed the art of teaching, and who
unable to bear the light themselves, wished to prevent all
others from seeing it; but, enjoying the support of persons
of high authority, he disregarded their selfish and ignorant outcries.[21] Lebrixa continued, to an advanced age,
to support the literary reputation of his native country.[22]

---

19. Mayans, *Specimen Bibl. Hisp. Majansianæ*, p. 39.

20. Ib. p. 4. Mendez, p. 233-235, 239, 243, 271, 280. Antonius,
    Bibl. Hisp. Nova, i. 132, 138. Argensola, *Anales de Aragon*, p. 358.
    Among the first scholars trained under Lebrixa were Andres de
    Cerezo, or Gutierez, the author of a Latin grammar, and Fernan-
    do Manzanares Flores, who was regarded as excelling his master
    in purity of style. (Mendez, 275, 278. Ignatius de Asso, *De Libr.
    Hisp. Rar. Disquis.* p. 23, 47. Antonii Bibl. Hisp. Nov. i. 74, 379.)

21. Lebrixa refers to the opposition he had met with, in the dedi-
    catory epistle to the second edition of his *Introductiones Latinæ*,
    printed in 1482.

22. "The cultivation of languages and polite letters has given celeb-
    rity to the university of Alcala, whose principal ornament is that
    illustrious and truly worthy old man, Anthony of Lebrixa, who
    has outstripped many Nestors;" says Erasmus, in a letter to Vives.

63   During his residence at Salamanca, he was joined by three able coadjutors. The first was Arius Barbosa, a Portuguese, who had studied under the elegant Italian scholar, Angelo Politiano, and was equally skilled in Greek as Lebrixa was in Latin.[23] The second was Lucio Marineo, a native of Sicily, who, in 1485, accompanied the grand admiral of Castile into Spain, and began to read lectures on poetry.[24] The third was Peter Martyr of Anghiera, to whose letters we are indebted for some interesting particulars respecting the state of literature in Spain, along with much valuable information on the political transactions of that country, and the affairs of the New World. In 1488, he was persuaded to leave Italy by the conde de Tendilla, who inherited that love of letters which had distinguished his illustrious ancestor, the marquis of Santanillana. Martyr commenced his literary career in Spain, by reading, with great applause, a lecture on one of the satires of Juvenal,

---

Lebrixa, in his old age, was permitted, on account of the failure of his memory, to read his lectures, contrary to the universal custom of that period. After his death, which was caused by apoplexy, the person who preached his funeral sermon ventured to imitate his example, for which he pleaded as an apology the shortness of time allowed him for preparation; but the audience no sooner saw the paper than they burst into expressions of ridicule and disapprobation. "*Parecio tan mal al auditorio esta maniera de predicar por escrito, y con el papel en la mano, que todo fue sonreyr y murmurar.*" (Huarte, Examen de Ingenios, p. 182.)

23. *Martyris Epist.* ep. 68. Anton. ut supra, i. 170. Irving's Memoirs of the Life and Writings of Buchanan, p. 77. 2d edit.

24. Mongitore, *Bibl. Sicula,* ii. 16-18. *Martyris Epist.* ep. 57.

at Salamanca; but he was soon called from that station to an employment of higher responsibility, for which he was eminently qualified. Under the patronage, and at the earnest desire of queen Isabella, who had herself taken lessons from Lebrixa, he undertook to superintend the education 64 of the sons of the principal nobility, with the view of rooting out an opinion almost universally prevalent among persons of that order in Spain, that learning unfitted them for military affairs, in which they placed all their glory. The school was accordingly opened at court, not without a flattering prospect of success. But Spain was destined to exhaust her energies in gratifying the mad ambition for conquest of a succession of princes, and then to sink into inactivity under the benumbing influence of superstition and despotism. Finding the prejudice against education, in the minds of his pupils, more inveterate than he had anticipated, Martyr accepted of a political appointment; and the plan for inspiring the nobility with the love of polite letters, was abandoned soon after it had been begun under such good auspices.[25]

In the mean time, the passion for learning spread from Salamanca to the other universities of the kingdom. In the beginning of the sixteenth century, Francesco Ximenes, at that time archbishop of Toledo, restored and enlarged the university of Alcala de Henares, in which he founded a trilingual college. To acquire celebrity to his favorite institution he procured learned teachers to fill its chairs, among whom were Demetrius Ducas and Nicetas Phaustus, two

---

25. *Martyris Epist.* ep. 102, 103, 113, 115, 205.

natives of Greece,[26] and Fernando Nunez, a descendant of
65 the noble house of Guzman. The latter, who had sacrificed
his prospect of civil honors to the love of study, was inferi-
or to none of his learned countrymen, and has left behind
him a name in the republic of letters.[27]

Living in the midst of Jews and Moors, and frequently engaged in controversy with them on their respective
creeds, the Christians in Spain had better opportunities and a more powerful stimulus to study the oriental
languages, than their brethren in other parts of Europe.
About the middle of the thirteenth century, Raymond de
Pennaforte, general of the Dominicans, persuaded Juan I.

---

26. Gomez, *Vita Ximenii*, f. 37, b. 81, b. *Hodius de Græcis Illustribus*,
   p. 321.

27. *Antonii Bibl. Hisp. Nova*, i. 382. Nunez was of the order of St.
   Iago, and was commonly called, among his countrymen, "the
   Greek commendator." (Argensola, *Anales de Aragon*, p. 352.) His
   notes on the classics are praised by Lipsius, Gronovius, and other critics, who usually cite him by the name of Pincianus, from
   Valladolid, his native city. That he did not confine his attention
   to ancient learning appears from his having published, in 1502,
   an edition of the poems of his countryman Juan de Mena, with
   notes. Cyprian de Valera quotes from a collection of Spanish
   proverbs published by him under the title of *Refranes Espanoles.*
   (*Dos Tratados*, p. 288.) Marineo extols the erudition of Nunez as
   far superior to that of Lebrixa; but, in the first place, he expresses
   this opinion in a letter to the object of his panegyric; and, in the
   second place, he had been involved in a quarrel with Lebrixa, in
   which his countryman, Peter Martyr, was not disposed to take his
   part. (*Martyris Epist.* 3 p. 35.)

king of Aragon, to appropriate funds for the education of young men who might be qualified for entering the lists in argument with Jews and Mahometans.[28] And in 66 1259 it was appointed, at a general chapter of the Dominicans held in Valencia, that the prior of that order in Spain should see to the erection of a school for Arabic, at Barcelona or elsewhere.[29] From this school proceeded several individuals who distinguished themselves as disputants, both orally and by writing. Among the latter was Raymond Martini, the author of Pugio Fidei, or Poignard of the Faith against Jews and Moors; a work which discovers no contemptible acquaintance with the Hebrew language, and with the Rabbinical writings, which it quotes and comments upon in the original.[30] To the attention paid

---

28. Carpzov, *Introd. in Theologiam Judaicam*, p. 91, 97; praefix. Pugioni Fidei H. de Porta, *De Linguis Orient.* p. 60. Juan I. is said to have erected two schools for Arabic; one in the island of Majorca, and the other at Barcelona. (*History of the Expulsion of the Moriscoes from Spain*, in Geddes' *Miscell. Tracts*, vol. i. p. 30.)

29. Simon, *Lettres Choisies*, tom. iii. p. 112. According to another authority, this decree was first made in a chapter held at Toledo in 1250. (Diago, *Cronica Domin. Aragon.* lib. i. cap. 2. lib. ii. cap. 28.)

30. The work was composed in 1278. (*Pugio Fidei*, part. ii. cap. 10. 1. p. 395, edit. Carpzovii.) Its fate is curious. Porchet, a converted Jew in the 14th century, transcribed a great part of it into a work which he composed under the title of *Victoria adversus Hebraeos*, which was printed in 1520. He acknowledged his obligations to Martini; an act of justice which was not done him by Galatinus, who used the same liberties in his *Arcana Catholicae Veritatis*,

to the oriental tongues in Spain may be traced the decree of the council of Vienne, held under Pope Clement V. in the year 1311, which ordained that Hebrew, Chaldee, and Arabic, should be taught in whatever place the pontifical court might be held, and in the universities of Bologna, Paris, Oxford, and Salamanca.[31]

67

The ardor with which these studies were prosecuted, during the fourteenth and fifteenth centuries, led to the publication of the famous Complutensian Polyglot. This chef d'oeuvre of Spanish erudition was executed under the patronage and at the expense of cardinal Ximenes, then archbishop of Toledo; a prelate whose pretensions to learning were slender,[32] but whose ambition prompted him to seek distinction equally in the convent, the academy, the cabinet, and the field. In imitation of the celebrated Origen, he projected an edition of the Bible in various

---

printed in 1513. De Porta says that Galatinus, when he departs from the Pugio, copies almost verbally from the Capistrum or Noose, (another work of Martini,) as he found by consulting a MS. copy of the last-named book in the library of Bologna. (*De Linguis Orient.* p. 62.) The plagiarism of Galatinus was first detected in 1603 by Joseph Scaliger, who however confounded Raymond Martini with Raymond Sebonde. *The Pugio Fidei* was at last published entire in 1651, with learned annotation by Joseph de Voisin, and elegantly reprinted in 1687, under the care of John Benedict Carpzov, who prefixed to it an Introduction to Jewish theology.

31. Clementin. lib. v. tit. i. *De Magistris.*

32. "*Aiunt homines esse virum, (Ximenium) si non literis, morum tamen santitate, egregium.*" (*Martyris Epist.* ep. 160.)

languages, and expended large sums of money in supporting the learned men who were engaged in the undertaking, purchasing manuscripts for their use, and providing
the requisite printers and types. The work commenced in
the year 1502, and the printing was finished in 1517, in
six volumes folio, at the press of Complutum, or Alcala
de Henares.[33] The Old Testament contained the original
Hebrew text, the Vulgate or Latin version of Jerome, and   68
the Greek version of the Septuagint, arranged in three columns; and at the foot of each page of the Pentateuch was
printed the Chaldee paraphrase of Onkelos, accompanied

---

33. Its publication, however, was subsequent to March 22, 1520,
the date of the diploma of Leo X. prefixed to the work. Besides Demetrius Ducas, Lebrixa, and Nunez, already mentioned, the learned men
who took part in this work were Diego Lopes de Zuniga, (better
known by the name of Stunica, in his controversies with Erasmus and
Faver Stapulensis,) Juan de Vergara, Bertolomé de Castro, (called the
Master of Burgos,) Pablo Coronel, Alfoso, a physician of Alcala, and
Alfonso de Zamora. The four persons first named had the charge of
the Greek part of the work, and wrote the interlined Latin version of
the Septuagint. Vergara made some important corrections on the Vulgate version of the books called Sapiential. The three last named were
converted Jews, and skilled in Hebrew. The Latin translation of the
Chalde Paraphrase, and the Hebrew grammar and dictionary, were
the work of Zamora. The cardinal is said to have paid 4000 ducats for
four Hebrew manuscripts; and the whole undertaking is computed to
have cost him upwards of 50,000 ducats. The price of each copy of
the Polyglot was fixed, by the bishop of Avila, at six ducats and a half;
"not judging by the cost of the work, which was infinite, but by its
utility." (Mandat. Franc. *Episcopi Abulensis*, praefix. *Bibl. Complut.* alv.
Gomez, ut infra.)

with a Latin translation. The New Testament contained the original Greek, and the Vulgate Latin version. To the whole were added a grammar and dictionary of the Hebrew language, and a Greek lexicon or vocabulary, with some other explanatory treatises. John Brocar, the son of the printer, was accustomed to relate, that when the last sheet came from the press, he, being then a boy, was sent in his best clothes with a copy of it to the cardinal, who gave thanks to God for sparing him to that day, and turning to his attendants, said that he congratulated himself on the completion of that work more than on any of the acts which had distinguished his administration.[34]

69   Spanish writers have been too lavish of the encomiums on the Polyglot of Alcala. The Hebrew and Greek manuscripts employed by its compilers were neither numerous nor ancient; and instead of correcting the text of the Septuagint from the copies which were in their possession, they made alterations of their own, with the view of adapting it to the Hebrew text. Some of the learned men who labored in this work, must have been ashamed of the following specimen of puerile devotion to the Vulgate, which occurs in one of the prologues written in the name of Ximenes. Speaking of the order in which the matter is disposed in the columns, he says: "We have put the version of St. Jerome between the Hebrew and Septuagint, as between the synagogue and eastern church, which are

---

34. Alvar. Gomez, *Vita Ximenii*, f. 36, 37. Quintanilla, *Vida*, p. 135-139. *Archivo Complutense*, p. 50-55. Le Long, *Bibl. Sac.* edit. Masch, part. i. cap. 3. § 2. Goetz, *Vertheidigung der Complutensischen Bibel*.

like the two thieves, the one on the right and the other on the left hand, and Jesus, that is, the Roman church, in the middle: for this alone, being founded upon a solid rock, remains always immovable in the truth, while the others deviate from the proper sense of scripture."[35] But 70 notwithstanding these defects, when we consider the period at which it was composed, and the example which it held out, we cannot hesitate in affirming that this work reflects great credit on its authors, and on the munificence of the prelate at whose expense it was executed.

The Arabic language was also cultivated at this time by some individuals in Spain.[36] This branch of study was zealously patronized by Fernando de Talavera, who, after the overthrow of the Moorish kingdom, was appointed the first archbishop of Granada. This pious and amiable prelate, being desirous of converting the Moors who resided in his diocese by gentle and rational methods, and

---

35. Many Roman catholic writers are ashamed of this conceit, (as they call it) which, if it has any meaning, implies a severe censure on the whole undertaking. Le Long suppressed it, in his account of the work. Not so Nicolas Ramus, bishop of Cuba, who, in a commentary on the words, informs us that "the Hebrew original represents the bad thief, and the Septuagint version the good thief." Pere Simon appeared at first inclined to make the transatlantic bishop responsible both for the text and the commentary; but he afterwards acknowledges that the former is to be found in the Complutensian prologue to the reader. (*Hist. Crit. du Vieux Test.* p. 350; conf. p. 577.)

36. Nicol. *Clenardi Epist.* p. 278. *Widmanstadii Epist. Dedic. ad Ferdinandum Imp. in Nov. Test. Syriacum.*

consequently of promoting the knowledge of Christianity among them, encouraged the clergy under his charge to make themselves masters of the Arabian tongue. With the view of assisting them in this task, he employed his chaplain, Pedro de Alcala, a Hieronymite monk, to draw up an Arabic grammar, vocabulary, and catechism containing the first rudiments of Christian doctrine, for the use of parish priests and catechists; which were the first books ever printed in that language.[37] In order the more effectually to promote the same object, the archbishop caused the religious service to be performed in their vernacular tongue, to such of the Moors as had submitted to baptism, or were willing to be instructed; and, accordingly, Arabic translations of the collects from the Gospels and Epistles were also made by his orders. It was his intention to have the whole scriptures translated into that language, agreeably to what is said to have been done at an early period of the Moorish dominion in Spain.[38]

These measures, which were applauded by all enlightened men, met with the strenuous opposition of cardinal Ximenes, who, while he wished to be regarded as the patron of learning, was a determined enemy to the progress of knowledge. The archbishop had appealed to the authority of St. Paul, who said, "In the church I had rather speak five words with my understanding, that by my voice

---

37. Schnurrer, *Bibl. Arabica*, p. 16-18. The three tracts were printed at Granada in 1505, in the Arabic language, but in Castilian characters.

38. Cyprian de Valera, *Exhortacion al Christiano Lector*, prefixed to his Spanish translation of the Bible.

I might teach others also, than ten thousand words in an unknown tongue." But the cardinal pleaded that the times were changed, and appealed to St. Peter. To put the sacred oracles into the hands of those who were but newly initiated into our religion, was, in his opinion, to throw pearls before swine. Nor did he think it a whit safer to intrust the old Christians with this treasure; for, (added he, changing the metaphor,) in this old age of the world, when religion is so far degenerated from that purity which prevailed in the time of St. Paul, the vulgar are in danger of wrestling the scriptures to their destruction. Knowing that the common people are inclined to revere what is concealed, and to despise what is known, the wisest nations have always kept 72 them at a distance from the mysteries of religion. Books written by men of approved piety, and calculated, by the examples which they propose, or by the fervor of their style, to raise the dejected, and recall the minds of men from the things of sense to divine contemplation, might be safely circulated in the vulgar tongue;[39] and it was the cardinal's intention, as soon as he found leisure, to publish some works of this description; but the sacred scriptures ought to be exclusively preserved in the three languages in which the inscription on our Saviour's cross was written; and if ever this rule should be neglected, the most

---

39. Flechier includes "catechisms, solid and simple explanations of Christian doctrine, and other writings calculated to enlighten the minds of the people," among the books allowed by the cardinal. (*Histoire du Card. Ximenes*, tom. i. p. 155.) But nothing of the kind is mentioned by Gomez, to whom he refers as his only authority. (*vita Ximenii*, f. 33, a.)

pernicious effects would ensue.[40] This opinion, which is merely a commentary on the favorite maxim of the church of Rome, that ignorance is the mother of devotion, has met with the warm approbation of his biographer, and was afterwards produced as a proof of his prophetic gift, along with his miracles, in the application which the Colegio Mayor de San Ildefonso made to the papal court for his canonization.[41] The arguments of Ximenes were not of a kind to carry conviction to the minds of those who favored enlightened measures; but they were the arguments of a man who, unfortunately for the best interests of Spain, had even then acquired great influence in the councils of government, and continued for many years to have the chief direction of the affairs of the nation, both civil and ecclesiastical. The books which the cardinal had promised as a substitute for the Gospels and Epistles made their appearance, consisting of treatises of mystic or rather monastic devotion, and the lives of some of its most high-flying zealots, both male and female; such as, the Letters of Santa Catalina de Sena, of Santa Angela de Fulgino, and of Santa Matilda, the Degrees of San Juan Climaco, the Instructions of San Vicente Ferrer, and of Santa Clara, the Meditations of the Carthusian Thomas Landulpho, and the Life of St. Thomas a Becket, archbishop of Canterbury.[42]

73

The opposition of Ximenes, and the violent and impolitic measures which the government adopted against

---

40. Gomez, ut supra.

41. Quintanilla, *Vida y Prodigios del S. Card. Ximenes*, p. 225.

42. Quintanilla, p. 141. Gomez, f. 39, a.

the Jews and Moors, checked the cultivation of oriental literature to such a degree, that, in the year 1535, when an enthusiastic scholar visited Spain, he found Hebrew neglected, and could not meet[43] with a single native acquainted with Arabic, except the venerable Nunez, who still recollected the characters of a language to which he had paid some attention in his youth.

A translation of the scriptures into Spanish, of which I shall afterwards speak, had probably little influence in preparing for the introduction of the reformed opinions, as all the copies of it appear to have been destroyed soon after it came from the press. Considerable light was thrown upon the sacred writings by those who studied them in the original languages, at the close of the fifteenth and beginning of the sixteenth century. Pablo de San Maria of Burgos, commonly called Paulus Burgensis, a converted Jew, discovered the same acquaintance with Hebrew which distinguishes the Postilla, or notes on scripture, by Nicolas de Lira, to which he made additions.[44] Alfonso

74

---

43. Nic. *Clenardi Epistolæ*, p. 229, 278-282. What Antonius has stated respecting a treatise on Christian Doctrine in Arabic, by archbishop Ayala, printed at Valencia in 1566, is more than doubtful. (*Bibl. Hisp. Nov.* tom. ii. p. 108.)

44. Simon, *Hist. Crit. du Vieux Test.* liv. iii. chap. 11. p. 464-466. *Colomesii Hispan. Orient.* p. 212-214.—Le Long mentions *"Prophetæ Priores Hebraice cum Commentario R. David Kimchi, Leiriæ in Lusitania, 1494, fol."* (*Bibl. Sac.* edit. Masch, part. i. cap. 1. sect 2. § 37. num. 6.) If this is correct, the work referred to must have been the first Hebrew book, and the only one by a Jew, printed in the Peninsula. None of the Spanish bibliographers

Tostado, bishop of Avila, who wrote commentaries on the historical books of the Old Testament, and on Matthew, had formed correct notions of the literal and proper sense of scripture, and of the duty of an interpreter to adhere to it in opposition to the method of the allegorizing divines; but he swelled his works to an immoderate bulk, by indulging in digressions on common places.[45] Pedro de Osma, professor of theology at Salamanca, employed his talents in correcting the original text of the New Testament, by a critical collation of different manuscripts. He displayed the same freedom of opinion on doctrinal points; and in 1497 was forced to abjure eight propositions relating to the power of the pope, and the sacrament of penance, which were extracted from a book written by him on Confession, and condemned as erroneous by a council held at Alcala.[46] Besides his services in the cause of polite literature, Antonio Lebrixa wrote several works illustrative of the scriptures, for which he was brought before the Inquisition, and would have incurred the same censure as De Osma, had he not been so fortunate as to secure the protection of their Catholic Majesties.[47]

75

---

appears to have seen a copy of it. Mendez reports it incorrectly. (*Typog. Esp.* p. 339.)

45. Tostati Albulensis comment. in Evang. Matthaei, cap. xiii. quaest. 18; conf. cap. ii. quaest. 57. An abridgement of his commentary on Matthew was printed, in two volumes folio, at Seville, in 1491.—(Mendez, p. 179.)

46. Illescas, *Hist. Pontifical*, tom. ii. f. 86, b.

47. *Antonii Nebrissensis Apologia pro seipso; apud Antonii Bibl. Hisp. Vet.* tom. ii. p. 310, 311.

By the labors of these men, together with the writings of their countryman Ludovicus Vives, who had settled in the Low Countries, and of his friend Erasmus, a salutary change was produced on the minds of the youth at the universities. They became disgusted at the barbarism of scholastic theology, read the scriptures for themselves, consulted them in the originals, and from these sources ventured to correct the errors of the Vulgate, and to expose the absurd and puerile interpretations which had so long 76 passed current under the shade of ignorance and credulity.

Having put the reader in possession of the circumstances connected with the state of letters and knowledge which tended to facilitate the introduction of the reformed doctrine into Spain, I shall now take a view of the obstacles with which it had to contend, of which the most formidable by far was the Inquisition.

III

Of the Inquisition, and other Obstacles to the Reformation in Spain

SOON AFTER THE Roman empire became Christian, laws 77
were enacted, subjecting those who propagated erroneous
opinions to punishment, under the false idea that heresy, or error in matters of revelation, was a crime and an
offence against the state. The penalties were in general
moderate, compared with those which were decreed at a
subsequent period. Manicheism, which was considered
as eversive of the principles of natural religion, and dangerous to morals, was the only heresy visited with capital
punishment; a penalty which was afterwards extended to
the Donatists, who were chargeable with exciting tumults
in various parts of the empire. The bishops of that time
were far from soliciting the execution of these penal statutes, which in most instances had passed at their desire,
or with their consent. They flattered themselves that the

78   publication of severe laws, by the terror which it inspired, would repress the hardihood of daring innovators, and induce their deluded followers to listen to instruction, and return to the bosom of the faithful church. When Priscillian was put to death for Manicheism, at Treves in 384, St. Martin, the apostle of the French, remonstrated with the emperor Maximus against the deed, which was regarded with abhorrence by all the bishops of France and Italy.[1] St. Augustine protested to the proconsul of Africa, that, if capital punishment was inflicted on the Donatists, he and his clergy would suffer death at the hands of these turbulent heretics sooner than be instrumental in bringing them before the tribunals.[2] But it is easier to draw than to sheathe the sword of persecution; and the ecclesiastics of a following age were zealous in stimulating reluctant magistrates to execute these laws, and in procuring the application of them to persons who held opinions which their predecessors looked upon as harmless or laudable. In the eleventh century, capital punishment, even in its most dreadful form, that of burning alive, was extended to all who obstinately adhered to opinions differing from the received faith.[3]

---

1.   *Sulpitii Severi Hist. Sacr.* lib. ii. cap. 47, 49.

2.   *S. Augustini Epist.* ep. 127, ad Donatum, Procons. Africæ.

3.   Burning alive was, by a constitution of Constantine, decreed as the punishment of those Jews and Cœlicoli who should offer violence, "*saxis aut alio furoris genere,*", to any who had deserted them, and embraced Christianity. (Cod. lib. i. tit. ix. § 3.) The same punishment was allotted to those who should open the dikes of the Nile, by an edict of Honorius and Theodosius. (Cod.

Historians have not pointed out with precision the pe- 79
riod at which this extension of the penal code took place,
or the grounds on which it proceeded. Instances of the
practice occur previously to the imperial edict of Frederic
II. in 1224, and even to that of Frederic I. in 1184.[4] It appears to me to have been at first introduced by confounding the different sects which arose with the followers of
Manes. Taking advantage of the circumstances, that some
individuals belonging to those who went by the names of
Henricians, Arnoldists, Poor Men of Lyons, and Vaudois,
held the leading tenet of Manicheism, the clergy fixed this
stigma on the whole body, and called on magistrates to
visit them with the penalty decreed against that odious
heresy. In an ignorant age this charge was easily believed.
It was in vain that the victims of persecution protested
against the indiscriminate accusation, or disowned the
sentiments imputed to them. By the time that undeniable facts cleared their innocence, the public mind had
learned to view the severity of their fate with indifference
or approbation; and the punishment of death, under the
general phrase of delivering over to the secular arm, came
to be considered as the common award for all who entertained opinions opposite to those of the church of Rome,
or who presumed to inveigh against the corruptions of the
priesthood.

Other causes, some of which had been long in opera- 80
tion, continued to work, in the course of the eleventh century, a great change on the criminal proceedings against

---

lib. ix. tit. xxxviii.)

4.   Fleury, *Hist. Eccles.* livre lviii. n. 54.

heretics. The sentence of excommunication, which at first only excluded from the privileges of the church, was now considered as inflicting a mark of public infamy on those who incurred it; from which the transition was not difficult, in a superstitious age, to the idea that it deprived them of all the rights, natural or civil, of which they were formerly in possession. The unhappy individuals who were struck with this spiritual thunder, felt all the bonds which connected them with society suddenly dissolved, and were regarded as objects at once of divine execration and human abhorrence. Subjects threw off their allegiance to their legitimate sovereigns; sovereigns gave up their riches and most peaceable provinces to fire and sword; the territories of a vassal became lawful prey to his neighbors; and a man's enemies were those of his own house. The Roman pontiffs, who had extended their authority by affecting an ardent zeal for the honor of the Christian faith, found a powerful engine for accomplishing their ambitious designs, in the crusades, undertaken at their instigation, to deliver the Holy Land, and the sepulchre of Christ, from the pollution of infidels. These mad expeditions, whose indirect influence was ultimately favorable to European civilization, were in the mean time productive of the worst effects. While they weakened the sovereigns who embarked in them, they increased the power of the popes, and placed at their disposal immense armies, which they could direct against all who opposed their measures. They perverted, in the minds of men, the essential principles of religion, justice, and humanity, by cherishing the false idea that it is meritorious to wage war for the glory of the Christian name,—by throwing the veil of sanctity over the

81

greatest enormities of which a licentious soldiery might be guilty,—by conferring the pardon of their sins on all who arrayed themselves under the banners of the cross,—and by holding out the palm of martyrdom to such as should have the honor to fall in fighting against the enemies of the faith. Nor were the popes either dilatory or slack in availing themselves of these prejudices. Finding that their violent measures for suppressing the Albigenses were feebly seconded by the barons of Provence, they proclaimed a crusade against heretics, launched the sentence of excommunication against both superiors and vassals, and carried on a war of extermination in the south of France during a period of twenty years. It was amidst these scenes of blood and horror that the Inquisition arose.

Historians are divided in opinion as to the exact time at which the Inquisition was founded. Inquisitors and informers are mentioned in a law published by the emperor Theodosius against the Manicheans; but these were officers of justice appointed by the prefects, and differed entirely from the persons who became so notorious under these designations many centuries after that period.[5] The fundamental principle of that odious institution was undoubtedly recognized in 1184, by the council of Verona; which however established no separate tribunal for the pursuit of heretics, but left this task entirely in the hands of the bishops. Rainier, Castelnau, and St. Dominic, who were sent into France at different times from 1198 to 1206, had a commission from the pope to search for heretics, and in this sense may be called inquisitors; but they were

82

---

5. Cod. *Theodos.* lib. xvi. tit. v. leg. 9. de hæreticis.

invested with no judicial power to pronounce a definite sentence.[6] The council of the Lateran in 1218 made no innovation on the ancient practice. The council held at Toulouse in 1229, ordained that the bishops should appoint, in each parish of their respective dioceses, "one priest and two or three laics, who should engage upon oath to make a rigorous search after all heretics and their abettors, and for this purpose should visit every house from the garret to the cellar, together with all subterraneous places where they might conceal themselves."[7] But the Inquisition, as a distinct tribunal, was not erected until the year 1233, when pope Gregory IX. took from the bishops the power of discovering and bringing to judgment the heretics who lurked in France, and committed that task to the Dominican friars. In consequence of this the tribunal was immediately set up in Toulouse, and afterwards in the neighboring cities, from which it was introduced into other countries of Europe.[8]

It may be considered as a fact at least somewhat sin-

---

6. *Hist. Gen. de Languedoc,* iii. 130, 134, 558-560.

7. It was by an act of this council that the laity were first prohibited from having the books of the Old and New Testament. (Concil. *Tolos.* can. 14: Labbei Collect. tom. xi. p. 427.)

8. *Hist. Gen. de Languedoc,* tom. iii. p. 131, 383, 394-5. Mosheim, cent. xiii. part ii. chap. v. § 4. Llorente, chap. ii. It appears, however, from a constitution of Frederic II. that the Dominicans in 1229 acted as apostolical inquisitors in Italy, where St. Dominic had erected, under the name of the Militia of Christ, a secular order, whose employment answered to that of those afterwards called *Familiars of the Inquisition. (Llorente, i. 51-54.)*

gular, that in the proceedings of the first Spanish council whose records have reached our time, we find a deeper stigma attached to the character of informers than to that of heretics. The council of Elvira, after limiting the duration of the penance of those who might fall into heresy, decreed that "if a catholic become an informer, and any one be put to death or proscribed in consequence of his denunciation, he shall not receive the communion, even at the hour of death."[9] On a review of criminal proceedings in Spain anterior to the establishment of the court of Inquisition, it appears in general that heretics were more mildly treated there than in other countries. Jews who relapsed, after having been baptized, were subject to whipping and spare diet, according the age of the offenders.[10] Those who apostatized to paganism, if nobles or freemen, were condemned to exile, and if slaves, to whipping and chains.[11] The general law against heretics was, that such as refused to recant, if priests, should be deprived of all their dignities and property, and if laics, that they should, in addition, be condemned to perpetual banishment.[12] Even after the barbarous custom of committing obstinate heretics to the flames had been introduced into other parts of Europe, Spain testified her aversion to sanguinary measures. In 1194, when Alfonso II. of Aragon, at the instigation of the legate of pope Celestine, published an edict, commanding the Vaudois, and all other sectaries, to quit

84

---

9.   Concil. *Illibert.* can. 22, 73.

10.   Concil. *Tolet.* IX. can. 17. Anno 655.

11.   Concil. *Tolet.* XIII. can. 11. Anno 681.

12.   Leg. Goth. lib. xii. tit. ii. de hæret. lex 2.

his dominions, those who remained after the time specified were expressly exempted from suffering either death or the mutilation of their bodies.[13]

No sooner had the Inquisition received the papal sanction, than measures were taken for having it introduced into Spain, where the Dominicans had already established convents of their order. In the course of the thirteenth century, inquisitorial tribunals were permanently erected in the principal towns of the kingdom of Aragon, from which they were extended to Navarre.[14] Though a papal brief was issued in 1236 for the special purpose of introducing the Holy Office into Castile, and Ferdinand III. surnamed the Saint, is said to have carried with his own hand the wood destined for burning of his subjects,—yet it does not appear that there ever was a permanent tribunal in that kingdom under the ancient form of the Inquisition; either because heresy had made little progress among the Castilians, or because they were averse to the new method of extirpating it.[15]

The mode of proceeding in the court of Inquisition, when first erected, was simple, and differed very little from that which was followed in the ordinary courts of justice. In particular, the interrogatories put to persons accused, and to witnesses, were short and direct, evincing merely a desire to ascertain the truth on the subjects of inquiry.[16]

13. Pegna, *Comment. in Direct. Inquis. Nic. Eimerici: Llorente*, i. 31.

14. Llorente, i. 77, 85, 97.

15. Llorente, i. 77, 85, 88, 95.

16. See the *Interrogationes ad Haereticos*, and the extracts from the proceedings of the inquisitors of Carcassone and Avignon, pub-

but this simplicity soon gave place to a system of the most complicated and iniquitous circumvention. Grossly ignorant of judicial matters, the Dominicans modelled their new court after what is called in the Roman church, the Tribunal of Penance. Accustomed, in the confessional, to penetrate into the secrets of conscience, they converted to the destruction of the bodies of men all those arts which a false zeal had taught them to employ for the saving of their souls. Inflamed with a passion for extirpating heresy, and persuading themselves that the end sanctified the means, they not only acted upon, but formally laid down, as a rule for their conduct, maxims founded on the grossest deceit and artifice, according to which they sought in every way 86 to ensnare their victims, and by means of false statements, delusory promises, and a tortuous course of examination, to betray them into confessions which proved fatal to their lives and fortunes.[17] To this mental torture was soon after added the use of bodily tortures, together with the concealment of the names of witnesses.

After this court had subsisted for two centuries and a half, it underwent what its friends have honored with the name of a *reform*; in consequence of which it became

---

lished in *Hist. Gen. de Languedoc*, tom. iii. Preuves, p. 372, 435-441.

17. See two ancient treatises published by the Benedictine fathers, Martene and Durand, in *Thesaur. Nov. Anecdot.* tom. v. p. 1785-1798. Extracts from them are given by Sismondi, who has pointed out the malignant influence which the proceedings of the Inquisition exerted on the criminal jurisprudence of France. (*Hist. of the Crusades against the Albigenses*, p. 220-226.)

a more terrible engine of persecution than before. Under this new form it is usually called the Modern Inquisition, though it may with equal propriety bear the name of the Spanish, as it originated in Spain, and has been confined to that country, including Portugal, and the dominions subject to the two monarchies.

The war of the Albigenses was the pretext used by the popes for the establishment of the ancient Inquisition; the necessity of checking the apostasy of the converts from Judaism was urged as the reason for introducing the modern. While the Spaniards were engaged in continual wars with one another or with the Moors, the Jews, who had been settled for ages in the Peninsula, by addicting themselves to trade and commerce, had, in the fourteenth century, engrossed the wealth of the nation, and attained to great influence in the government both of Castile and Aragon. Those who were indebted to them, and those who envied them on account of the civil offices which they held, united in stirring up the religious prejudices of the populace against them: and in one year five thousand Jews fell a sacrifice to popular fury. With the view of saving their lives, many submitted to baptism, and it is computed that, in the course of a few years, nearly a million of persons renounced the law of Moses and made profession of the Christian faith. The number of converts, as they were called, was increased in the beginning of the fifteenth century, by the zeal of the Dominical missionaries, and especially of St. Vincent Ferrer, to whom the Spanish historians have ascribed more miracles and conversions than were wrought by the apostles.[18] These converts were called *New Christians*, and sometimes *Marranos* from a form of execration then in use among the Jews. As their adoption of the Christian profession proceeded from the fear of death, or a desire to secure secular emoluments, rather than internal persuasion, the greater part repented of having abjured the religion of their fathers, and resumed the practice of its rites in secret, while they publicly conformed to those of the Christians. This forced conformity could not fail to be painful to their minds, and was relaxed in proportion as the fears which they felt for their safety abated. The consequence was, that many of them were discovered by the monks, who cried out that if some severe means were not adopted to repress the evil, the whole body of converted Jews would soon relapse into their former habits, and the faith of the old Christians would be corrupted and over-

88

---

18. Zurita, *Anales*, tom. ii. f. 444; conf. f. 430. *Antonii Bibl. Hisp. Vet.* tom. ii. 205-207. In support of his opinion that the printed sermons of St. Vincent Ferrer were taken from his mouth and translated into Latin by some of his hearers, Nicolas Antonio says: "As he preached, wherever he went, in his own native tongue of Valencia, to English, French, and Italians, all of whom, by a most undoubted miracle, understood him, it is impossible that the same sermons could be conceived and delivered in the vernacular tongue, and turned into Latin, by the same individual, who was so much occupied, and preached to the people extempore and from inspiration rather than premeditation." (*Ut supra*, p. 206.) With all deference to the learned historian, we should think that this reasoning, if to prove anything, proves that the hearers of St. Vincent possessed more miraculous powers than himself, and that they should have been canonized rather than the preacher.

thrown by these concealed apostates with whom they were intermingled.—But, although more immediately intended to guard the fidelity of the New Christians, the modern Inquisition, like the ancient, was charged with the discovery and punishment of all kinds of heresy, and extended its jurisdiction over the Old Christians, as well as Jewish and Moorish converts.

It is proper that the names of those individuals to whom Spain owes this institution should not be forgotten. The most active were Felippe de Barberis, inquisitor of Sicily, and Alfonso de Hoyeda, prior of Seville, both of them Dominicanfriars, assisted by Nicolas Franco, bishop of Treviso, who was at that time nuncio from pope Sixtus IV. to the Spanish court.

89

The whole of Spain was at this period united into one kingdom by the marriage of Ferdinand, king of Aragon, and Isabella, queen of Castile. Ferdinand readily acceded to a proposal which gave him the prospect of filling his coffers by means of confiscations; it was equally agreeable to Sixtus, from its tendency to promote the views of the court of Rome; and they succeeded, by the help of the friars, in overcoming the repugnance which it excited in the humane but superstitious mind of Isabella. The bull for establishing the Inquisition in Castile was issued on the 1st of November 1478, and on the 17th of September 1480, their catholic majesties named the first inquisitors, who commenced their proceedings on the 2d of January 1481, in the Dominican convent of St. Paul at Seville. The tribunal did not however assume a permanent form until two years after, when friar Thomas Torquemada, prior of Santa Cruz in the town of Segovia, was placed at its head, under the designation of inquisitor-general, first of Castile, and afterwards of Aragon.[19] Torquemada proceeded without delay to exercise the high powers with which he was intrusted, by choosing his assessors, and erecting subordinate tribunals in different cities of the united kingdom. Over the whole was placed the *Council of the Supreme*, consisting of the inquisitor-general as president, and three counsellors, two of whom were doctors of law. This regulated and controlled the inferior tribunals; and by its fundamental laws, the counsellors had a deliberative voice in all questions relating to civil law, but a consultative voice only in those which appertained to ecclesiastical law, of which Torquemada was constituted the sole judge by the apostolical bulls. These counsellors appear to have been appointed with the view of preventing encroachments on the secular authorities, and accordingly altercations did sometimes arise between the inquisitors-general and the counsellors of the Supreme; but as the latter were all of the clerical order, and as no clear line of distinction between civil and ecclesiastical affairs was drawn, the questions which came before the court were generally brought under the rules of canon law, or in other words, decided according to the pleasure of the president. Torquemada's next employment was to form a body of laws for the government of his new tribunal. This appeared in 1484; additions were made to it from time to time; and, as a diversity of practice had crept into the subordinate courts, the inquisitor-general Valdes, in 1561, made a revisal of the whole code, which was published in eighty-one articles, and continues, with

90

19. Illescas, *Hist. Pontifical,* tom. ii. f. 101, a. Zurita, *Anales,* lib. xx. sect. 49. Llorente, i. 145, 148-151.

91   the exception of a few slight alterations, to be the law to this day.[20] From these constitutions, as illustrated by the authentic documents connected with the history of the Inquisition which have been lately made public, a correct idea may be formed of the mode of process observed in that dreadful tribunal. Instead however of entering here into details which may be found elsewhere, I shall select such particulars as show that the Inquisition possessed powers which enabled it effectually to arrest the progress of knowledge, and to crush every attempt which might be made for the reformation of religion and the church.

   The first thing which presents itself to our view, is the immense apparatus which the Inquisition possesses for the discovery of heresy, and the apprehension of those who are suspected of having incurred its taint. Deceived by the importance attached to denunciation in the instructions of the Holy Office, some writers would lead us to believe that there is no way in which a process can be commenced before the Inquisition, except by a formal charge preferred by some individual; whereas the truth is, that information, in whatever way it may be obtained, is sufficient for this

92   purpose.[21] The Inquisition is not only a court of justice,

---

20. The editions I have used are the following: "*Copilacion de las Instruciones del Officio de la sancta Inquisicion, hechas por el muy reverendo Senor Fray Thomas de Torquemada,*" &c. Madrid, 1576. "*Copilacion de las Instrucciones del Oficio de la santa Inquisicion, hechas en Toledo, ano de mil y quinientos y sesenta y uno.*" Ibid. 1612.

21. "*Quando los Inquisidores se juntaren a ver las testificaciones que resultan de alguna visita o de otra manera, o que por otra qualquier*

but also, as its name intimates, a body of police, employed in discovering the offenses on which it is afterwards to sit in judgment. Every individual belonging to its tribunals, supreme or subordinate, from the inquisitor-general down to the lowest alguazil or familiar, is charged with this employment. At those periods when its vigilance was aroused by the alarm of heresy, it had its secret spies and authorized agents at every port and pass of the kingdom, as regularly as government had its tide-waiters and custom-house officers, armed with authority to arrest the persons and property of all who incurred their suspicions. In addition to its internal resources, it avails itself of the superstitious prejudices of the people, whom it raises en masse, to drive the poor heretics into the legal toils spread for them in all parts of the country. At any time which it judges proper, but statedly on two Sundays every year during lent, an edict is published in all the churches of the kingdom, requiring everyone who knows any person suspected of heresy to give information to the Inquisition within six days, upon pain of incurring mortal sin and excommunication by their silence. At the same time, the priests in the confessional exert all the influence which they possess over the minds of their penitents to persuade them to comply with this order. In this way the worst and the best, the weak- 93 est and the strongest passions of the human breast are engaged; and persons are induced to become informers from private malice, from pious scruples, and from selfish fears. The father sometimes informs against his own child, the wife against the husband, and the lovesick maiden against the object of her tenderest attachment. Though the holy

causa se huviere recebido," &c. (*Instrucciones de 1561*, art. 1.)

fathers prefer a process by denunciation to one *ex officio*,[22] and in order to encourage informers, conceal their names, yet anonymous informations are received without any scruple, provided they furnish the smallest clue by which the charge may be brought home to the accused. One prosecution is often the means of fastening the suspicion of heresy on a number of individuals; for it is an invariable rule with the inquisitors, not to inform a witness of the particular object for which he is cited, but to commence by desiring him to task his memory and say if he recollects having seen or heard any thing which appeared to be inconsistent with the catholic faith; in consequence of which, he is led to mention names not implicated in the process. If, upon inquiry, the inquisitors are of opinion that they will find it difficult to convict the suspected person, they do not examine him, because this would only serve to put him on his guard; nor do they use any means to recover him from the supposed errors into which he has fallen; but suspending their proceedings, wait until they obtain additional proof to substantiate the charge.[23] If the evidence is deemed sufficient, they issue the order of ar-

94

---

22. *Instruc. de 1561*, art. 19.

23. *Instrucciones de 1561*, art. 4. Llorente appears to have mistaken the latter part of this article, which he translates thus: "*Cette mesure (l'interrogatoire) ne sert qu'à le rendre plus réservé et plus attentif à eviter tout ce qui pourrait aggraver les soupcons ou les preuves acquises contre lui.*" (*Hist. de l'Inquis.* tom. ii. p. 298.) The original words are: "*Semejantes examenes sirven mas de avisar los testificados, que de otro buen efecto: y assi conviene mas aguardar que sobrevenga nueva provança, o nuevos indicios.*"

rest to the alguazil, who, accompanied by the sequestrator and receiver of goods, instantly repairs to the house of the accused; and, provided the latter has absconded, the familiars are furnished, not only with a minute description of his person, but also with his picture, so that it is next to impossible that their prey can escape them.[24]

Nor is it less difficult for a person to escape without condemnation, if he once has had the misfortune to be apprehended. It is only in the way of being able to convict him of heresy, that the inquisitors are entitled to seize on his property; and as it is an established maxim of theirs, that the Holy Office cannot err, they consider it as a reflection on its proceedings, if any individual whom it has apprehended shall clear himself from suspicion. Without acquainting him either with his accuser or the charge brought against him, every art is employed, both by his judges in the repeated examinations to which they subject him, and also by the jailer to whose care he is intrusted, to 95 induce the prisoner to confess that he has been guilty of some offence against the faith. He is strictly interrogated as to his kindred, connections, acquaintances, and manner of life; the records of all the tribunals of the Holy Office are ordered to be searched; and if it is found that any of his ancestors or relations, however remote, either in the male or female line, or any of those with whom he has consorted, were Jews, Moors, or heretics, or had incurred the censures of the Inquisition, this circumstance is regarded as sufficient to fasten on him a legitimate presumption of guilt. Even a failure to repeat the Ave Maria or creed ex-

---

24. Reg. Gonsalv. *Montani Inquis. Hisp. Artes Detectæ*, p. 8, 13, 16.

actly after the manner of the Roman church, is viewed in the same light.[25]

The impenetrable secrecy with which all the proceedings of the Inquisition are shrouded, is at once an instrument of terror, and an encouragement to every species of injustice. Every person who enters its walls is sworn, before he is permitted to depart, to observe the most profound silence as to all that he may have seen, heard, or uttered.[26] The names of the witnesses are carefully concealed from the prisoner; and they are not confronted with him, nor, so far as appears, with one another.[27] No check is imposed

96

---

25. *Instruciones de an. 1488*, art. 9. *Instruc. de an. 1561*, art. 13-15. Montanus, *ut supra*, p. 17-24. Llorente, ii. 302, 303. Frampton's Narrative, in Strype's *Annals*, i. 240, 241.

26. Mr. Townsend relates, that the Dutch consul, with whom he became acquainted during his travels in Spain in 1787, could never be prevailed on to give an account of his imprisonment in the Inquisition at Barcelona, which had happened thirty-five years before, and betrayed the greatest agitation when pressed to say any thing about the treatment he had received. His fellow-prisoner, M. Falconet, who was but a boy, turned gray-headed during his short confinement, and to the day of his death, though retired to Montpellier, observed the most tenacious silence on the subject. He had destroyed a picture of the Virgin; and his friend, the Dutch consul, being present and not turning accuser, was considered as a partner in his guilt. (Townsend's *Journey through Spain*, vol. ii. p. 336.)

27. Llorente, in his abridgement of the constitutions of Valdes, speaks as if the witnesses were confronted with one another; (tom. ii. p. 306.) but I perceive nothing in the original document to warrant

on the infidelity or ignorance of the notaries or clerks who take down the depositions. The accused is not furnished with a copy of the evidence against him, but merely with such garbled extracts as his judges are pleased to order; and, taking advantage of the different modes of expression used by the witnesses in speaking of the same fact, the procurator-fiscal often converts one charge into three or four, by which means the prisoner is thrown into confusion on his defence, and exposed to popular odium, as a person laden with crimes, if he is ultimately brought out in the public auto-da-fe. Every thing which the witnesses in their examination may have said in his favor, or which might be conducive to his exculpation, is studiously and totally suppressed.

The same partial and unjust rules are observed in 97 forming the extracts, both at the commencement and termination of the process, are submitted to certain divines, called qualificators of the Holy Office, whose business it is to say whether the propositions imputed to the accused individual are heretical, or to what degree they subject him to the suspicion of heresy. These individuals, besides, are generally monks or scholastic divines, imbued with false notions, and ready to quality, or stigmatize as heretical, opinions sanctioned by the authority of the most approved doctors of the church, merely because they have not met

this interpretation. (*Instruc. de an. 1561*, art. 26.) The same historian, rather inconsistently, interprets another article as expressly prohibiting that practice; (p. 327.) whereas that article prohibits the confronting of the witnesses with the prisoner. Its title is, "No se careen los testigos con los reos." (*Instruc. de an. 1561*, art. 72.)

with them in the contracted circle of their studies.

It is not easy to conceive a greater mockery of justice than is to be found in the provisions made for the defence of the prisoner. The judges appoint one of their advocates to act as his counsel, who has no means of defending his client, except the garbled extracts from the depositions of the witnesses already mentioned. But the truth is, that his ability is as great as his inclination; for, while nominally the advocate of the prisoner, he is really the agent and proctor of the court, in obedience to whose directions, given at the time of his nomination, he labors in most instances to induce his client to confess and throw himself on the mercy of the judges.[28] Nor is the pretended privilege of challenging the witness less nugatory and insulting to the prisoner. Deprived of every means of knowing the persons who have deponed against him, he can have recourse to conjecture only; malice is the sole ground of exception which he is permitted to urge; he may have been accused

98

28. *Instruc. de an. 1484*, art. 16. *Instruc. de an. 1561*, art. 23.— Llorente, i. 309-312. By the *Instructions of 1484*, the accused was allowed the benefit of a procurator, as well as an advocate; but those of 1561 deprived him of that privilege, "because it had been found to be attended with many inconveniences," (a word frequently used in the regulations of the Inquisition as an excuse for the most glaring violations of justice,)—"*porque la experiencia ha mostrado muchos inconvenientes que dello suelen resultar.*" (*Instruc. de an. 1561*, art. 35.) If the accused is under age, he is allowed a tutor, (ib. art. 25.) but the tutelage is given to the wolf, one of the menials of the Inquisition being often appointed to that office. (Montanus, p. 34, 35.)

from fanaticism, fear, or ignorant scruples; or his personal enemy may have put forward, as the instrument of his malice, an individual whom the prisoner would never think of suspecting; and sometimes the procurator-fiscal takes the precaution of secretly establishing the credibility of his witnesses beforehand, with the view of defeating the challenge. The inquisitors are uniformly disposed to favor the witnesses for the prosecution, and to screen them from punishment, even in cases of perjury.[29] Nor is this evil to be traced to the character of particular judges; it springs from the very genius of the tribunal, which induces all who are connected with it to set at defiance the most essential prin- 99
ciples of justice by which every other court is governed, and even to disregard its own regulations, for the sake of encouraging informations and indulging a morbid jealousy. Of the same illusory nature is the privilege which, in certain cases, they give the prisoner to bring forward exculpatory evidence. For, in the first place, he is restricted in his choice of witnesses. While the testimony of persons of all descriptions—relations, domestics, New Christians, malefactors, infamous characters, children, and even idiots, is admissible against him;[30] he, on the contrary, is directed to name, for his exculpation, only Christians of

---

29. Llorente, i. 314, 315. Montanus, 54-57. False witnesses are either such as falsely accuse a person of heresy, or such as, when interrogated, falsely declare that they know nothing against the person accused. "In the course of my researches," says Llorente, "I have often found witnesses of this second class punished, but seldom or never those of the first." (p. 232.)

30. Llorente, ii. 311. Montanus 41.

ancient race, of unimpeached character, and who are neither his relatives nor domestics. And, in the second place, the tribunal reserves to itself the power of examining such of the prisoner's witnesses only as it shall judge "most fit and worthy of credit."[31]

The injustice of the inquisitorial process can only be equalled by its cruelty. Persons of undoubted veracity, who had the happiness to escape from the secret prisons of the Inquisition during the sixteenth century, have described them as narrow and gloomy cells, which admitted the light only by a small chink,—damp, and resembling graves more than prisons, if they were subterraneous; and if they were situated in the upper part of the building, feeling in summer like heated furnaces.[32] At present, they are described as, in general, good vaulted chambers, well lighted, free of humidity, and of such size as to allow the prisoner to take a little exercise.[33] But even those who give the most favorable description of these abodes admit, that nothing can be conceived more frightful than the situation of the individual who is immured in them, left as he is to conjecture respecting his accuser and the particular crime with which he is charged; kept in ignorance of the state of

100

31. *Instrucciones de an. 1561*, art. 36.

32. Montanus, 105. Frampton's Narrative of his Imprisonment, in Strype's *Annals*, i. 239.

33. Llorente, i. 300. An intelligent native of Spain, who had inspected the secret prisons of the Holy Office at Barcelona, confirmed to me the account given by Llorente; adding, however, that there was one of them below ground, which answered in every respect to the description given by Montanus.

his process; shut out from every kind of intercourse with his friends; denied even the consolation of conversing confidentially with the person to whom his defence has been intrusted; refused all use of books; afraid, if he has a fellow-prisoner with him for a few days, to do more than exchange salutations with him, lest he should be confiding in a spy; threatened if he hum a tune, and especially a sacred one, to relieve his languor; plunged, during the rigor of the winter months, in total darkness for fifteen hours of every day in an abode that never saw the cheerful blaze of a fire; and, in fine, knowing that if ever he should be set free, he must go out to the world lost for ever in public opinion, and loaded with an infamy, heavier than that of the pardoned assassin or parricide, which will attach to his children of the remotest generation. What wonder that 101 such prisoners as are not induced, at an early period of their confinement, to confess guilt, become a prey to dejection, and seek relief from their miseries in death, or else sink into a hopeless and morbid insensibility, from which the rack itself is scarcely sufficient to rouse them?

That part of the process which relates to the torture is a monstrous compound of injustice and barbarity. If, after the evidence is closed, the tribunal find that there is only a demi-proof of guilt against the prisoner, it is warranted, by its instructions, to have recourse to the torture, in order to force him to furnish additional evidence against himself.[34]

---

34. *Instruc. de an. 1484*, art. 15. By this regulation, the prisoner, if he confesses during the torture, and ratifies his confession next day, is held as convicted, and consequently is relaxed, or doomed to the fire. The regulations of Valdes profess to qualify that law, but

He is allowed, indeed, to appeal to the council of the Supreme against the sentence of the inquisitors ordering him to be tortured; but then, by a refinement in cruelty, it is provided that the inquisitors shall be judges of the validity of this appeal, and "if they deem it frivolous, shall proceed to the execution of their sentence without delay."[35] In this case, the appeal of the poor prisoner is as little heard of as are the shrieks which he utters in the subterraneous den to which he is conducted without delay, where every bone is moved from its socket, and the blood is made to start from every vein of his body. But it is not my intention to shock the feelings of the reader by any description of the infernal operation; and, instead of trusting myself to make any reflections of my own on a practice so disgraceful to human nature, I shall merely quote those of the late historian and ex-secretary of the Inquisition. "I do not stop (says he) to describe the several kinds of torture inflicted on the accused by order of the Inquisition; this task having been executed with sufficient exactness by a great many historians. On this head, I declare that none of them can be accused of exaggeration. I have read many processes which have struck and pierced me with horror, and I could regard the inquisitors who had recourse to such methods in no other light than that of cold-blooded barbarians. Suffice it to add, that the council of the Supreme has often been obliged to forbid the repetition of the torture in the same process; but the inquisitors, by an abominable soph-

102

---

still in the way of leaving it to the discretion of the inquisitors to act up to it in all its severity. (Instruc. de an. 1561, art. 53.)

35. *Instruc. de an. 1561*, art. 50.

ism, have found means to render this prohibition almost useless, by giving the name of suspension to that cessation from torture which is imperiously demanded by the imminent danger to which the victim is exposed of dying among their hands. My pen refuses to trace the picture of these horrors, for I know nothing more opposed to the spirit of charity and compassion which Jesus Christ inculcates in the gospel, than this conduct of the inquisitors; and yet, in spite of the scandal which it has given, there is not, after the eighteenth century is closed, any law or decree abolishing the torture."[36]

103

Of the punishments inflicted by the Inquisition, of the san-benito, or coat of infamy, and the auto-da-fe, with all its dread accompaniments, we shall have too much occasion to speak in the sequel.

The principles of the ancient and modern Inquisition were radically the same, but they assumed a more malignant form under the latter than the former. Under the ancient Inquisition, the bishops had always a certain degree of control over its proceedings; the law of secrecy was not so rigidly enforced in practice; greater liberty was allowed to the accused on their defence; and in some countries, as in Aragon, in consequence of the civil rights acquired by the people, the inquisitors were restrained from sequestrating the property of those whom they convicted of heresy.[37] But the leading difference between the two institutions consisted in the organization of the latter into one great independent tribunal, which, extending over the whole

---

36. Llorente, i. 306-309.

37. Ibid. p. 168.

kingdom, was governed by one code of laws, and yielded implicit obedience to one head. The inquisitor-general possessed an authority scarcely inferior to that of the king or the pope; by joining with either of them, he proved an overmatch for the other; and when supported by both, his power was irresistible. The ancient Inquisition was a powerful engine for harassing and rooting out a small body of 104 dissidents; the modern Inquisition stretched its iron arms over a whole nation, upon which it lay like a monstrous incubus, paralysing its exertions, crushing its energies, and extinguishing every other feeling but a sense of weakness and terror.

In the course of the first year in which it was erected, the inquisition of Seville, which then extended over Castile, committed two thousand persons alive to the flames, burnt as many in effigy, and condemned seventeen thousand to different penances.[38] According to a moderate computation, from the same date to 1517, the year in which Luther made his appearance, thirteen thousand persons were burnt alive, eight thousand seven hundred were burnt in effigy, and one hundred and sixty-nine thousand seven hundred and twenty-three were condemned to penances; making in all one hundred and ninety-one thousand four hundred and twenty-three persons condemned by the several tribunals of Spain in the course of thirty-six years.[39] There is reason for thinking that this estimate falls

---

38. Mariana, *Hist. Hisp.* lib. xxiv. cap. 17.

39. Llorente, iv. 251-256. These numbers are taken from the calculation made by Llorente, after he had, with great care and impartiality, lowered his estimates, and corrected some errors into

much below the truth. For, from 1481 to 1520, it is computed that in Andalusia alone thirty thousand persons informed against themselves, from the dread of being accused by others, or in the hope of obtaining a mitigation of their sentence.[40] And down to the commencement of 105 the seventeenth century, the instances of absolution were so rare, that one is scarcely to be found in a thousand cases; the inquisitors making it a point, that, if possible, none should escape without bearing a mark of their censure as at least suspected de levi, or in the lowest degree.[41]

It was to be expected that the inquisitors would exert their power in checking the cultivation of biblical learning. In 1490, many copies of the Hebrew Bible were committed to the flames at Seville by the order of Torquemada; and in an auto-da-fe celebrated soon after at Salamanca, six thousand volumes shared the same fate, under the pretext that they contained judaism, magic, and other illicit arts.[42] Deza, archbishop of Seville, who had

---

which he had fallen in an early part of his work, owing to his not having attended to the exact years in which some of the provincial tribunals were erected. (Tom. i. 272-281, 341, 350.)

40. Puigblanch, *Inquisition Unmasked*, i. 158. According to this author the number of the reconciled and banished in Andalusia, from 1480 to 1520, was a hundred thousand; while forty-five thousand were burnt alive in the archbishopric of Seville. (Ibid. vol. ii. p. 180.)

41. Llorente, i. 319-321. Hence the proverb:
Devant l'Inquisition, quand on vient à jubé,
Si l'on ne sort rôti, l'on sort au moins flambé.

42. Ibid. i. 281, 456.

succeeded Torquemada as inquisitor-general, ordered the papers of Lebrixa to be seized, and passed sentence against him as suspected of heresy, for the corrections which he had made on the text of the Vulgate, and his other labors in elucidation of the scriptures. "The archbishop's object (says Lebrixa, in an apology which he drew up for himself) was to deter me from writing. He wished to extinguish the knowledge of the two languages on which our religion depends; and I was condemned for impiety, because, being no divine but a mere grammarian, I presumed to treat of theological subjects. if a person endeavor to restore the purity of the sacred text, and point out the mistakes which have vitiated it, unless he will retract his opinions, he must be loaded with infamy, excommunicated, and doomed to an ignominious punishment! Is it not enough that I submit my judgment to the will of Christ in the scriptures? must I also reject as false what is as clear and evident as the light of truth itself? What tyranny! To hinder a man, under the most cruel pains, from saying what he thinks, though he express himself with the utmost respect for religion, to forbid him to write in his closet or in the solitude of a prison, to speak to himself, or even to think! On what subject shall we employ our thoughts, if we are prohibited from directing them to those sacred oracles which have been the delight of the pious in every age, and on which they have meditated by day and by night?"[43]

106

Arbitrary as this court was in its principles, and tyrannical and cruel as it has proved in its proceedings, so blind-

---

43. Anton. Nebriss. *Apologia pro seipso: Antonii Bibl. Hisp. Nova*, tom. ii. 138. Llorente, i. 345.

ed did the Spanish nation become as to felicitate herself
on the establishment of the Inquisition. The cities of ancient Greece vied with one another for the honor of having given birth to Homer. The cities of modern Germany   107
have warmly disputed the honor of having invented the
art of printing. Even the credit of having first adopted this
German invention has given rise to an honorable rivalry
among the states of Italy; and the monastery of St. Sub-
iac, in the Campagna di Roma, has endeavored to wrest
the palm from both Milan and Venice.[44] But the cities of
Spain have engaged in a more than inglorious contest for
the credit of having been the first seat of an institution
which, after failing to strangle learning in its birth, has
all along persecuted it with the most unrelenting malice.
The claims of the inhabitants of Seville are engraven on
a monument erected in their city to the memory of this
event. Segovia has contested this honor with Seville, and
its historians are seriously divided on the question, whether the Holy Office held its first sitting in the house of the
marques de Moya, or in that of the majorat de Caceres.[45]

It is but justice, however, to the Spaniards to state,
that this perverted and degrading sentiment was the ef-

---

44. Ginguené, *Hist. Liter. d'Italie*, tom. iii. p. 271.

45. Llorente, i. 151. This is astonishing; but what follows is still more
    so. "During my residence in London (says Llorente) I heard some
    catholics say, that the Inquisition had been useful in Spain by
    preserving the catholic faith; and that it would have been well for
    France if she had had a similar establishment." "An English cath-
    olic priest, in my hearing, made an apology for it." (Ibid. pref. p.
    xxi. and tom. ii. p. 288.)

fect of the Inquisition, and formed no original trait in the national character. The fact is now ascertained beyond all question, that the erection of this tribunal was viewed by the nation with the greatest aversion and alarm.[46] Tala-

108 vera, the excellent archbishop of Granada, resisted its introduction with all his influence. The most enlightened Spaniards of that age spoke of its proceedings with horror and shame. "The losses and misery which the evil ministers of the Inquisition have brought upon my country can never be enough deplored," says the chevalier de Cordova, Gonzalez de Ayora, in a letter to the secretary of king Ferdinand.[47] "O unhappy Spain, mother of so many heroes, how unjustly disgraced by such a horrible scourge!" exclaims Peter Martyr.[48] D'Arbues, the first inquisitor of Aragon, and afterwards canonized as a martyr, was not the only individual who fell a sacrifice to the indignation against the Inquisition, shared by all classes of the

46. Mariana, *Hist. Hisp.* lib. xxiv. cap. 17. Pulgar, *Chronic. de los Reyes Catol.* part. ii. cap. 77. Llorente refers, as witnesses of the fact, to Galindez de Carabajal, historiographer of Ferdinand and Isabella, and to Andres Bernaldez, chaplain of the inquisititor-general Deza. (Tom i. p. 185.) Pulgar, a contemporary writer of great judgment and taste, was not merely an enemy to the Inquisition, but opposed the corporal punishment of heretics, and maintained that they ought to be restrained only by pecuniary mulcts. (*Ferdinandi de Pulgar Epistolæ, a Juliano Magon*, p. 17-19.)

47. This letter, preserved in the Royal Library of Madrid, is not to be found in the edition of Ayora's Letters. (Llorente, i. 349.)

48. *Martyris Epistolæ*, ep. 393. Martyr's Letters, being published out of Spain, escaped the hands of the *expurgatores*.

community. Torquemada, the first inquisitor-general, was obliged to adopt the greatest precautions for his personal safety. In his journeys he was uniformly accompanied by a guard of fifty familiars on horseback, and two hundred on foot; and he had always on his table the tusk of a wild animal, to which he trusted for discovering and neutralizing poisons.[49] In Aragon, where the inhabitants had been accustomed to the old Inquisition for two centuries and a half, the introduction of it in its new form excited tumults in various places, and met with a resistance almost national.[50] No sooner had the inhabitants of Castile felt the yoke, than they sought to throw it off; and the cortes of that kingdom joined with those of Aragon and Catalonia, in representing the grievances which they suffered from the Inquisition, and in demanding a radical reform on its iniquitous and oppressive laws.[51] It is unnecessary to say, that these attempts, which were renewed at intervals during thirty years from the establishment of that tribunal, proved finally abortive.

109

This unfortunate issue was in no small degree owing to cardinal Ximenes, who contributed more than any other individual to rivet the chains of political and spiritual despotism on his native country. Possessed of talents which enabled him to foresee the dire effects which the Inquisition would inevitably produce, he was called to take part in public affairs at a time when these effects had decid-

---

49. Llorente, chap. vi. art. 3; chap. viii. art. 6.

50. Ibid. chap. vi. art. 6.

51. Ibid. chap. x. art. 8; chap. xi. art. 1, 2, 3. *Martyris Epist.* ep 342, 370. Quintanilla, p. 169.

edly appeared. It was in his power to abolish that execrable tribunal altogether as an insufferable nuisance, or at least to impose such checks upon its procedure as would have rendered it comparatively harmless. But he not only allowed himself to be placed at its head, but employed all his influence and address in defeating every attempt to reform its worst and most glaring abuses. In 1512, the New Christians made an offer of six hundred thousand crowns to Ferdinand, to assist him in carrying on the war in Navarre, on condition that a law were passed enjoining the testimonies of the witnesses, in processes before the Inquisition, to be made public. With the view of diverting the king from acceding to this proposal, Ximenes seconded his remonstrances against it by placing a large sum of money at the royal disposal. And, in 1516, when a similar offer was made to the ministers of Charles V., and when the universities and learned men of Spain and Flanders had given their opinion, that the communication of the names and depositions of the witnesses was conformable both to divine and human laws, the cardinal again interposed, and by messengers and letters urged the rejection of the measure, upon the wretched plea that a certain nameless witness had been assassinated, and that the person of the king was put in danger by the admission of converted Jews into the palace.[52] He exerted himself with equal zeal in resisting the applications which the New Christians made to the court of Rome for the same object.[53] During the eleven years that he was at the

---

52. Quintanilla, p. 173. Llorente, i. 365-367.

53. Quintanilla, *ut supra*.

head of this tribunal, fifty-one thousand one hundred and sixty-seven persons were condemned, of whom two thousand five hundred and thirty-six were burnt alive.[54] Not satisfied with perpetuating the Inquisition in his native country, he extended the precious boon to two quarters of the globe, by establishing one tribunal at Oran in Africa, and another at Cuba in America. With the exception of the check which, at the commencement of his ministry, he put on the mad proceedings of the inquisitor Luzero, who, by listening to false accusations, had harassed the good archbishop of Granada, the marquis of Pliego, and many of the most respectable persons of the kingdom,[55] the reforms which the cardinal made on the Inquisition are confined to the substitution of a St. Andrew's cross, in place of the ordinary one, on the san-benito, and the allotment of separate churches for the New Christians. If mankind were to be treated as their foolish admiration of talents merits, they would be left to groan under the rod of oppression. Ximenes has obtained the title of a great man, 112

54. Llorente, iv. 255.

55. *Martyris Epist.* ep. 333, 334, 342, 370, 393. Quintanilla, p. 168, 169. Llorente, i. 345-353. See also the letter of the archbishop to the catholic king, published in Llorente's Appendix, no IX. Martyr speaks of Luzero as condemned; but Quintanilla says he was pronounced innocent, and it is certain he continued his bishopric. After settling that affair, Ximenes held an auto-da-fe, in which fifty Jews were burnt alive; "one of the best *singeings* (says Quintanilla) that had yet been seen;"—"*la mejor chamusquina que se avia visto.*"

from foreigners as well as natives of Spain.[56] But in spite of the eulogiums passed upon him, I cannot help being of opinion, with a modern writer,[57] that Ximenes bore a striking resemblance to Philip II., with this difference, that the cardinal was possessed of higher talents, and that his proceedings were characterized by a certain openness and impartiality, the result of the unlimited confidence which he placed in his own powers. His character was essentially that of a monk, in which the severity of his order was combined with the impetuosity of blood which belongs to the natives of the south.

The cardinal would be still more inexcusable if he were the author of an unpublished work which has been ascribed to him. It is a fictitious composition, after the manner of the Utopia of Sir Thomas More, and treats of the best mode of governing a kingdom. In one part of it, the abuses of the Holy Office are discussed freely and at large in the presence of Prudenciano, monarch of the kingdom of Truth, who, after hearing the inquisitors, decides, with the advice of his counsellors, that all persons accused of heresy shall be put in possession of the names and depositions of the witnesses; that they shall have the same liberty of holding intercourse with their advocates, procurators and friends, which is granted to other prisoners; that they

113

---

56. As an instance of the illusion which a great name throws over the mind of an impartial writer, it may be noticed, that Llorente begins his account of the number of victims who suffered during the time that Ximenes was inquisitor-general, with these words: "Ximenes permitted the condemnation," &c. (Tom. i. p. 360.)

57. Sismondi.

shall not be excluded from the benefit of divine service during their confinement; that New Christians, and the descendants of heretics, shall be admissible to all offices, and exempted from every stigma; that, to prevent ignorant convictions, the tribunals of the inquisition shall be provided with judges well instructed in questions of faith; that the confiscation of the goods of those condemned for heresy shall be limited to the property which they actually possess at the time, and shall not extend to the portions which they had previously given to their married children, nor interfere with the fulfillment of any lawful engagement which they had contracted; and in general, that processes before the Inquisition shall be conducted on the maxims which regulate other courts of criminal judicature.[58] This treatise, drawn up during the minority of Charles V., was intended for the instruction of that young prince, and proves that Spain possessed at that time persons of superior illumination; but we may safely acquit cardinal Ximenes from the suspicion of being the author 114 of a work containing principles of liberal policy and enlightened justice, which there is no reason to think that ghostly statesman ever entertained at any period of his life.

The history of the Inquisition, during the first thirty years after its erection, discloses a series of intrigue, in

---

58. The work is entitled *Del regimento de Principes*, and is preserved in MS. in the library of St. Isidore at Madrid. That part of it which relates to the Inquisition has been published by Llorente, in the appendix to his work, no. x.: and is a most interesting document. Llorente produces no evidence to support his opinion that it was the production of Ximenes.

which it is hard to say whether the court of Rome, the court of Spain, or the Holy Office, acted the most deceitful and unprincipled part. While they combined to oppress and impoverish the people of Spain, each of them sought to overreach the other and to promote its own selfish designs. The court of Rome readily gave its sanction to the establishment of the Inquisition; and Sixtus IV., in a letter to queen Isabella, signified that "he had felt the most lively desire to see it introduced into the kingdom of Castile."[59] Notwithstanding this, the papal court both secretly and openly encouraged the New Christians to appeal to Rome, reversed the sentences which the Inquisition had pronounced against them in Spain, and admitted them to reconciliation in secret. But after it had extorted large sums of money for these favors, no sooner did the Spanish monarch, at the instigation of the inquisitors, reclaim against these proceedings, than it revoked its decisions, suspended the execution of its bulls, and left the victims of its avarice and duplicity to the vengeance of their incensed persecutors.[60] It was evidently on the same avaricious principle that Leo X., in the year 1517, authorized the inquisitors at Rome to judge in complaints of heresy against natives of Spain. On that occasion, Geronimo Vich, the Spanish ambassador, received orders from his court to remonstrate against this decree, as inflicting a stigma on a nation which had testified such zeal for the catholic faith, and to request that the remedy against heresy should be applied equally to those of other countries. To this representation Leo

115

59. Llorente, i. 164.

60. Llorente i., 239-256.

gravely replied, that so far from wishing to inflict a disgrace, he had intended to confer an honor on the Spanish nation; that he had dealt with them as a rich man does with his jewels, which he guards with greater care than the rest of his property; and thought that, as the Spaniards entertained so high an esteem for the Inquisition at home, they would not be offended with it abroad.[61]

The conduct of the Inquisition presented the same glaring contradiction of the avowed principles on which it was founded. Amidst all their professions of zeal for the purity of the faith, the inquisitors carried on the scandalous traffic of commuting canonical censure for pecuniary mulcts. To retain Christians within the sacred enclosure of the catholic church, and in dutiful subjection to its supreme head, was the grand object of the institution of the Holy Office; and the exercise of its powers was delegated to the monks, who were the most devoted supporters of the Roman pontiff, and held that his decrees in matters of faith, when pronounced *ex cathedra*, were infallible. Yet, when the decrees of the holy see were opposite to their own determinations, or interfered with their particular interests, they made no scruple of resisting them, and engaging the government of the country in their quarrel.[62]

It was not to be expected that the conduct of the court of Spain would be less selfish. All are agreed that Ferdinand, in supporting the Inquisition, regarded it, not as a

61. The despatch of the Spanish court on this occasion, and the reply made to the ambassador, are given by Argensola, in his *Anales de Aragon*, p. 373-376.

62. Llorente, i. 240, 247, 392, 395; ii. 81.

means of preserving the purity of religion, but as an instrument of tyranny and extortion. Nor was his grandson Charles V. actuated by higher motives. On assuming the reins of government in Spain, he swore to observe certain equivocal regulations for correcting the abuses of the Inquisition; but he declared, at the same time, in private, that this promise had been extorted from him by the importunity of the representatives of certain cities. Despairing of any relief from this quarter, the cortes of Aragon sent deputies to Rome, and, by the distribution of a sum of money among the cardinals, obtained three briefs reforming the Inquisition, and placing its procedure on the footings of common law. Charles, who wished to employ that formidable tribunal as an engine for suppressing the tumults which his arbitrary measures had excited in various parts of the kingdom, applied to Leo X. for a bull annulling the obnoxious briefs. The negotiation which ensued, and was protracted during three years, is equally disgraceful to both parties. His Holiness told Senor de Belmonte, the Spanish ambassador, that he had been informed by credible persons, that the Inquisition was the cause of terrible mischief in Spain; to which the ambassador bluntly replied, that the persons who gave this information were believed, because they were liberal of their money. At the same time, he advised his master to have recourse to that system of bribery of which he complained. "Cardinal Santiquatro (writes he) can be of great service in this affair, because he draws as much money as possible to his master and himself. It is only on this condition that he is authorized by the pope to act, and he executes his task with great adroitness. The cardinal of Ancona is a learned man, and an enemy to the former. He is minister of justice, and can be useful, as he is well disposed, to serve your majesty; but he is reckoned as great a thief as his colleague." In another missive he says, "Always I am assured that, in what relates to the Inquisition, money is a means of gaining over these cardinals." And after soliciting instructions from his court, he adds, "All this is necessary, and something besides; for money does much here. The pope expects (from Aragon and Catalonia) forty-six or forty-seven thousand ducats." The cardinals were "too wise in their generation" to be deceived by the flattering representations which the ambassador made of his master's disinterestedness, and laughed at the idea of sovereigns supporting the Inquisition "from pure zeal for religion." In vain did Charles himself endeavor to quicken 118 the tardy steps of Leo, by writing that "the world surmised that his Holiness and he understood one another, and wished to squeeze as much money as possible from the bull in question." The crafty pontiff, assuming the tone of justice, threatened, by a decree of the sacred Rota, to annul all the sentences of confiscation pronounced against those Spaniards who had made a voluntary confession of heresy; "and I am told," says the ambassador, "that if this measure pass, as is expected, your majesty will be obliged to restore more than a million of ducats acquired in that way."[63] A few persons, though perversion of judgment, have burnt men alive *for the love of God*, but in the greater number of instances, I apprehend it will be found that this has been done *for the love of money*.

Leo X., having died during this dispute, was succeeded

---

63. Llorente, chap. xi. art. 5.

by Adrian, the preceptor of Charles V., who continued to hold the situation of inquisitor-general of Spain, along with that of supreme pontiff, for nearly two years. This union of offices, in the person of the spiritual adviser of the young monarch, led to measures which extinguished every hope of procuring a reform of the Holy Office. Despairing of relief, the nation submitted to the yoke; habit reconciled them to it; and, making a virtue of necessity, they soon came to congratulate themselves on an institution which they had regarded as an engine of the most intolerable and degrading servitude.

119   Other causes contributed, along with the Inquisition, to rivet the chains of religious bondage on the minds of the Spaniards, and to render the prospect of ecclesiastical reform among them next to hopeless.

One of these causes was the suppression of their civil liberties. Formerly the victims of persecution had often found shelter within the independent domains of the nobles, or the privileged walls of great cities. Cardinal Ximenes, by flattering the commons without adding to their real consequence, had succeeded in breaking the power of the nobility. Charles pursued the line of policy which his minister had begun, by invading the rights of the people. Irritated by the assistance which the latter had given to the attack on their immunities, the nobles either stood aloof from the contest which ensued, or sided with the crown. The consequence was, that the commons, after an enthusiastic resistance, were subdued; the cortes and the chartered towns were stripped of their privileges; and the authority of the sovereign became absolute and despotical throughout the united kingdom.

The great accession of wealth and reputation which Spain acquired by the discovery of the New World, proved no less fatal to her religious than to her personal liberty. Columbus appears to have been at first actuated solely by an enthusiastic passion for nautical discovery; but during the discouragements with which his ardent and unconquerable spirit had to contend, another feeling arose of a no less powerful kind, which was cherished, if not infused, by the monks of La Rabida, among whom he resided for some time, and who zealously assisted him in his applications to the court of Castile, and in his exertions to fit out the fleet with which he entered on his daring enterprise. His imagination was now fired with the idea of not only adding to the boundaries of the known world, but also of enlarging the pale of the catholic church, by converting to the Christian faith the inhabitants of those rich and populous countries with which he hoped to open a communication, by stretching across the waters of the western ocean. Similar views, but associated with baser feelings, were adopted by the successors of Columbus. As the see of Rome, in virtue of the universal authority which it arrogated, had granted to Spain all the countries which she might discover beyond the Atlantic, the conquerors of America looked upon themselves as the servants of the church as much as of the sovereigns from whom they immediately received their commission; their cupidity was inflamed by fanaticism; and the consideration that every battle which they won was subservient to the spread of the catholic faith, atoned for and sanctified, in their eyes, the unheard-of cruelties which they inflicted on the intimidated and unoffending natives of the New World. Sanc-

120

tioned as they were by the government and clergy, these views were easily diffused through the nation. Astonished
121 at the intelligence which they received from their country-men who had visited the newly-discovered regions, elated by the splendid success which had crowned their under-takings, and flushed with the hopes of the inexhaustible riches which would continue to flow in upon them, the Spaniards were thrown into a feverish intoxication, which, meeting with other causes, produced an important change on their sentiments and character. New feelings sprung up in their breasts; and late transactions were seen by them in a light different from that in which they had formerly viewed them. Reflecting that they had expelled the Jews, the hereditary and inveterate enemies of Christianity, from their coasts, overturned the Mahomedan empire which had been established for ages in the Peninsula, and planted the standard of the cross among pagans on a new continent of incalculable extent, they began to consider themselves as the favorites of heaven, destined to propa-gate and defend the truth faith, and bound, by national honor as well as duty, to preserve their sacred soil from being polluted by the slightest taint of heretical pravity.

To these causes must be added the vast increase of strength which the Spanish monarchy received by the suc-cession of its youthful sovereign to his paternal dominions in the Low Countries, Austria, Bohemia, and Hungary; and by his elevation to the imperial throne of Germany, under the name of Charles V. The chief obstacle which this presented to the spread of the reformed opinions in Spain, did not lie in the ease with which it enabled him to crush the least symptom of revolt from the established faith. In-

dependently of all personal convictions, Charles, in seek-   122
ing to realize his towering projects of universal empire,
must have seen it in his interest to cultivate the friendship
of the court of Rome; and although he was involved in
contests with particular pontiffs, and held one of them for
some time a prisoner in his own castle, yet he uniformly
testified the warmest regard for the catholic faith, and the
honor of the popedom. In the forcible measures to which
he had recourse for suppressing the Reformation in Germany, he relied chiefly on the troops which he drew from
Spain, whose detestation of heresy was heightened by
the hostilities which they waged against its professors. To
their countrymen at home, who already regarded them as
champions of the faith, they transmitted the most hateful
representation of the protestants, whom they described as
at once the pest of the church, and the great obstacle to the
execution of the splendid schemes of their beloved monarch. Thus the glory of the Spanish arms became associated with the extirpation of heresy. And when the protestant
cause ultimately triumphed over the policy and power of
the emperor, the mortification felt by the Spaniards settled
into a deadly antipathy to every thing which proceeded
from Germany, and a jealous dread lest the heresy with
which it was infected should secretly find its way into their
own country.

IV

Introduction of the Reformed Doctrine into Spain

THE BOLDNESS with which Luther attacked, first the abus- 123
es, and afterwards the authority of the Roman see, soon
attracted general attention throughout Christendom. Nor
could his opinions remain long unknown in Spain, especially after the intercourse between that country and Germany became frequent, in consequence of the advancement of the Spanish monarch to the imperial throne.

So early as the beginning of the year 1519, John
Froben, a celebrated printer at Basle, sent to Spain a quantity of a collection of tracts by Luther, which he had lately
reprinted.[1] These were in Latin, and consequently were

---

1. This is stated in a letter from Froben to Luther, dated 14 Feb.
    1519; Luther's *Sämtliche Schriften*, edit. Walch, tom. sv. p. 1631,
    1632.) and in a letter from Wolfg. Fabricius Capito to the same,
    dated 12 calend. Martii, 1519. (*Fabricii Centifolium Lutheranum*,
    tom. i. p. 318.) From Froben's letter it appears that he had also
    sent copies of the book to England.

124 confined to the learned. But, in the course of the following year, the reformer's commentary on the Galatians, a
work which exhibited the doctrinal sentiments on the
most important points, was translated into Spanish.[2] This
was followed by translations into the same language of his
treatise on Christian liberty, and his reply to Erasmus on
free-will.[3] These books appear to have been translated and
printed at Antwerp, a place of great trade within the paternal dominions of Charles V., from which the Spanish merchants, who were at the expense of the publication, could
most easily get copies conveyed to their native country.[4]

Alfonso Vales, a young man of talents who accompanied Charles V., as secretary, to his coronation in 1520,
sent to Spain, at the request of Peter Martyr, a particular
account of the religious dispute in Germany, from the first
declaration of Luther against indulgences to his burning
of the pontifical decrees at Wittenberg. In another letter,
written during the following year, he continued his account to the close of the diet of Worms. His narrative is
in general correct; and although he expresses great horror at the boldness with which the reformer attacked the
125 papal authority, he acknowledges the necessity of reform,
and ascribes the continuance of the evil to the aversion
of the pope to a general council, and "his preferring his

2. Beausobre, *Hist. of the Reform.* vol. i. p. 262.

3. Gerdesii *Hist. Reform.* tom. iii. 168, not. g.

4. Pallavicini, Istor. Concil. Trent. p. 33. The cardinal says, that
the persons who procured these works "must have sprung from
Moorish blood; for who would suspect the Old Christians of
Spain of such an action?"

private interest to the public good." "While he tenacious-
ly adheres to his rights," says he, "and shutting his ears,
under the influence of a pious feeling perhaps, wishes to
have Luther devoted to the flames, the whole Christian
commonwealth is going to ruin, if God interpose not."[5]
Martyr, who seems to have felt in the same way with his
correspondent, imparted these letters to his friends; but
it may be mentioned, as a proof of the state of feeling in
Spain, that he declined giving them any account of Luther's opinions, referring them for this to the writings of
his opponents, "which they could easily procure, if they
wished them, and in which they would find the antidote
along with the poison."[6]

Another Spaniard of greater authority, who was in
Germany at the same time, felt somewhat differently from
Valdes. Francisco de Angelis, provincial of the religious
order called Angeli in Spain, had been present at the coronation of the emperor, by whom he was despatched, after
the diet of Worms, to assist in quelling the revolt which
had broken out in Castile. On his way home he stopped at
Basle, where he had a long conversation with Conrad Pel-   126
lican on the opinions of Luther, with whom he professed
to agree upon most points.[7]

Who would have thought of the Spanish ambassador

---

5. Valdes's first letter is dated from Brussels, prid. cal. Sept. 1520;
    and his second from Worms, 3 id. Maii, 1521. (*Martyris Epist.*
    ep. 689, 722.) There is some reason to think that the first of these
    letters was printed at the time. (Ukert, *Luther's Leben*, ii. 100.)

6. *Martyris Epist.* p. 412.

7. *Vita Pellicani: Melch. Adami Vitæ Germ. Theol.* p. 288.

at Rome writing home in favor of Luther? We have already adverted to the difficulty which Charles found in procuring the recall of certain briefs which the pope had issued for the reform of the Inquisition. It occurred to Don Juan de Manuel, as a stroke of policy, that his master should give countenance to another species of reform which his Holiness dreaded. Accordingly, in a letter dated 10 May 1520, he advises his majesty "to undertake a journey to Germany, and to appear to show a little favor to a certain friar, Martin Luther, at the court of Saxony, who gives great uneasiness to the sovereign pontiff, by certain things which he preaches and publishes against the papal authority. This monk (adds the ambassador) is said to be very learned, and creates great embarrassment to the pope." Nor was this a mere passing thought; for he recurs to the subject in a subsequent letter. "As to the affair of Liege, the pope appears much more discontented, because it has been told him that the bishop favours friar Martin Luther, who condemns the pontifical power in Germany. He is also displeased with Erasmus in Holland, and for the same reason. I say, they complain here of the bishop of Liege in the affair of Luther, who gives them more distress than they could wish."[8]

127   On the 20th of March 1521, Leo X. issued two briefs, one addressed to the constable and the other to the admiral of Castile, who governed the kingdom in the absence of Charles V., requiring them to adopt measures for preventing the introduction of the books of Luther and his defenders into Spain. In the course of the following

---

8.   Llorente, i. 398.

month, cardinal Adrian charged the inquisitors to seize all books of this description; and this charge was reiterated by him in the year 1523, after he had ascended the papal throne, on which occasion he required the corregidor of Guipuscoa to furnish the officers of the Inquisition with every assistance which they might require in the execution of this duty.[9]

These were not measures of mere precaution, or intended only for the purpose of display; for the works of Luther were read and approved of in Spain. The report of this fact drew from Erasmus the sarcasm which gave great offence to the duke of Alva, "that the Spaniards favored Luther, in order that they might be thought Christians."[10] So eager were the inquisitors in their search after the disciples of the new doctrine, that they fixed their suspicions on the venerable Juan de Avila, commonly called the apostle of Andalusia. In his preaching, which was recommended by the exemplary piety and charity of his life, he kept 128 to the simplicity of scripture rejecting the abstruse and foolish questions of the schools. Irritated by his reproofs, and envious of his fame, the monks, in 1525, denounced to the Inquisition some propositions advanced by him, as Lutheran, or savoring of Lutheranism and the doctrine of the illuminati. He was thrown into prison, and would have been condemned, had not Manrique, one of the mildest of the inquisitors-general, who felt a high respect for his character, extended to him the shield of his powerful pro-

---

9. Ibid., i. 419, 457.

10. Vives Erasmo, 19 Jan. 1522: Epistolæ Thomæ Mori et Lud. Vives, col. 91.

tection, which did not however prevent his works from being afterwards put into the list of prohibited books.[11]

The Spanish monks were diverted for a time from searching after the writings of Luther, by their anxiety to suppress those of Erasmus, from which they dreaded more immediate danger. This learned man, to whom the name of the forerunner of Luther has not unjustly been given, had many friends in Spain, who were so confident in their strength, as to write him that they expected to be victorious in the contest. They were mistaken; for his adversaries outnumbered them in an ecclesiastical junta held at Madrid in the year 1527; and in consequence of this, his Colloquies, his Praise of Folly, and his Paraphrase 129 of the New Testament, were censured, and prohibited to be explained in schools, or to be sold or read.[12] "How I

---

11. Llorente, ii. 6, 7, 423. Vives, in a letter to Erasmus, intimates that Manrique wished to restrain the fury of the Inquisition. (*Epistolæ*, ut. supra. col. 109.)

12. Erasmi Epistolæ, ep. 884, 907, 910. Burscheri Spicilegia Autogr. Erasm. Spic. v. p. 12, 20, 24. Llorente, i. 459-462. A Spanish translation of the *Enchiridion of Erasmus* was printed in 1517, and met with such encouragement that it was intended to publish his Paraphrase in the same language. (*Epistolæ T. Mori et L. Vives*, col. 107; conf. Schlegel, *Vita Spalatini*, p. 111, not. 1.) John Maldonat, counsellor to Charles V., in a letter, dated Burgos, 3 cal. Dec. 1527, after mentioning a certain Dominican who had been active in inflaming the minds of his brethren against Erasmus, adds, "He has acted in the same way with certain intermeddlling nuns, and with some noble women, who in this country have great influence over their husbands in what

am to be pitied!" exclaims he; "the Lutherans attack me as a convicted papist, and the Catholics run me down as a friend of Luther."

The patrons of ignorance resolved to pursue their victory, and prosecutions of heresy were immediately commenced against some of the most learned men in the kingdom. Pedro de Lerma, professor of divinity and chancellor of the university of Alcala, was denounced to the inquisition of Toledo, as suspected of the Lutheran opinions, and fled to Paris. His nephew and successor, Luis de Cadena, soon fell under the same suspicion, and followed his example.[13] Juan de Vergara, one of the editors of the Polyglot, and his brother Bernardin Tobar, were less fortunate; for, being seized by the orders of the inquisitors of Toledo, they were not permitted to leave the dungeons of the Holy Office, until they had abjured the heresy of Luther as persons slightly suspected, received absolution *ad cautelam, and submitted to certain penances.*[14]   130

Two events which happened at this time had considerable influence in turning the attention of the Spaniards

---

relates to religion." (*Burscheri Spicil.* ut supra, p. 24.)

13. Llorente, ii. 430, 454. *Antonii Bibl. Hisp. Nova,* ii. 29. Gomez, while he eulogizes the talents and services of Lerma and Cadena, passes over the cause of their disgrace. (*Vita Ximenii,* p. 79, 83, 224, 225.)

14. Ibid., ii. 7, 8. Vives, in a letter to Erasmus, 10 May 1534, says, "We live in difficult times, in which one can neither speak nor be silent without danger. Vergara and his brother Tovar, with some other learned men in Spain, have been apprehended." (*Epistolæ T. Mori et L. Vives,* col. 114.)

to the cause of Luther, and giving them a more favorable impression of his opinions. The first was the dispute between Charles V. and pope Clement VII., which led, in 1527, to the sack of Rome and imprisonment of the pontiff. Though Charles, on that occasion, ordered the public rejoicings for the birth of his son Philip to be suspended, as a mark of his sorrow for so untoward an occurrence, yet it was regarded as a triumph by the nation, and gave occasion to satirical ballads against the pope and see of Rome.[15]

---

15. The following is a specimen of one of the poems composed at that time in Spain:

> La gran sobervia de Roma
> Agora Espana la refrena
> Por la culpa del pastor
> El ganado se condena.
>
> *   *   *
>
> El governalle quitado
> La aguja se desgovierna,
> Gran agua coge la bomba,
> Menester tiene carena,
> Por la culpa del piloto
> Que la rege y la govierna.

Depping, *Sammlung der besten alten Spanischen Romanzen*, p. 447.

We have mentioned elsewhere the ridicule with which the Germans in the imperial army treated Clement VII. during his imprisonment. (*Hist. of the Reformation in Italy*, p. 59-61.) It appears that the Spaniards took part in the scene. They composed a new pater-noster in verse, with which they serenaded his Holiness. The following is one of the coplas, alluding to his claims on

The other event was the presenting, in 1530, of the prot- 131
estant confession of faith to the imperial diet of Augsburg,
at which Charles was present, attended by a great body of
Spanish nobles and clergy.[16] This had no inconsiderable
effect in dissipating the false idea of the opinions of Luther which had hitherto been industriously propagated.
At the diet of Worms in 1521, the Spanish attendants of
the emperor, instead of admiring the heroism displayed
by Luther, treated him with insult as he retired from the
court-room to his lodgings.[17] But there was a marked difference in their behavior on the present occasion. Persons
of note, including the emperor's confessor, who was a native of Spain, acknowledged that they had hitherto been
deceived.[18] When Charles asked the advice of the Spanish nobility who were present, they replied, after perusing
the confession in a French translation, that if his majesty
found it contrary to the articles of faith, he ought to suppress the Lutherans; but if it merely required the abolition
of certain ceremonies and such like things, he ought not to 132

Milan:

> Padre nuestro en quanto Papa,
> > Soys Clemeynte, sin que os quadre:
> Mas reniego yo del Padre,
> > Que al hijo quita la capa.

Dos Tratados, p. 216.

16 Buschingii Comment. de Vestigiis Lutheranismi in Hispania. §
2. not. (d.) Goetting. 1755.

17. Luther's *Samtliche Schriften*, tom. xv. p. 2309.

18. Christ. Aug.Salig, *Historie der Augspurgischen Confession*, tom. i.
p. 225.

have recourse to violent measures against them; and they gave it as their advice, that the litigated points should be submitted to some pious persons who were addicted to neither party.[19] Alfonso Valdes, the emperor's secretary, of whom we have already spoken,[20] had several friendly and confidential interviews with Melanchthon at this important crisis. He read the Augsburg Confession before it was presented to the diet; and the only objection which he appears to have made to it was, that its language was rather too severe for its opponents.[21] In one of the conversations between these two learned men, held in the presence of Cornelius Scepper, an agent of the king of Denmark, Melanchthon lamented the strong prejudices which the natives of Spain had conceived against the reformers, and said, that he had frequently endeavored, both by word of mouth and by letters, to convince them of the misconceptions under which they labored, but with very little success. Valdes acknowledged that it was a common opinion among his countrymen, that Luther and his followers

133

---

19. This is the advice of which Melanchthon speaks with satisfaction, in a letter to Luther; (*Epist. Melanch.* lib. i. ep. 5.) and which is highly praised by Spalatinus. (*Annales*, p. 143, 144.) "But where were these pious impartial persons to be found?" says Salig. (*Historie*, ut supra, p. 227.)

20. See above, p. 124.

21. *Melanchthonis Epist.* lib. iv. ep. 95; conf. lib. i. ep. 2, lib. iv. ep. 99. Valdes translated the Augsburg Confession into Spanish. (Salig, i. 224.) The same task was afterwards performed by Sancoval. (*Fabricii Centif. Lutheran.* i. 111.) But it is probable that neither of these translations was printed. (Ukert, *Luther's Leben*, i. 279.)

believed neither in God nor the Trinity, in Christ nor the Virgin; and that in Spain it was thought as meritorious an action to strangle a Lutheran as to shoot a Turk.[22] He added, that his influence had been exerted to relieve the mind of the emperor from such false impressions; and that, at a late interview, he had received it in charge to say, that his majesty wished Melanchthon to draw up a clear summary of the opinion of the Lutherans, contrasted, article by article, with those of their opponents. The reformer readily complied with this request, and the result of his labors was communicated by Valdes to Campegio, the papal legate.[23]

These proceedings did not escape the vigilant eye of

---

22. The following is a specimen of the manner in which the Spanish poets were accustomed to couple the reformers with the worst heretics and greatest enemies of religion:

> *El Germano Martin la despedaza:*
> *Arrio, Sabelio, helvidio & Justiniano*
> *Sieguen de Cristo la homicida caza,*
> *Calvino con Pelagio y el Nestoriano*
> *Como tras fiera van tras El á caza:*
> *Quien toma pierna o pie, quien brazo o mano:*
> *Denuncia guerra Acab contra Miquea,*
> *Y Malco á Dios de nuevo abofetea.*

Francisco de Aldan, *Obras: Floresta de Rimas Antiguas Casellanas,* vol. i. p. 180.

23. Salig. i. 186, 187. Schlegel, Vita Spalatini, p. 121, 122. Coelestin has inserted what he considers as the paper referred to, consisting of 17 articles. (*Hist. Aug. Comit.* tom. i. f. 94.) But Seckendorf is of opinion that it is not the work of Melanchthon. (*Hist. Lutheranismi,* lib. ii. p. 166.)

the Inquisition. When Vales returned soon after to his native country, he was accused before the Holy Office, and condemned as a suspected Lutheran; a censure which he incurred by his exertions to promise polite letters in his native country, as well as by the familiarity which he had cultivated with the reformers of Germany.[24] Alfonso de Virves met with the same treatment as his friend Valdes, and for the same reasons. This learned Benedictine was chaplain to Charles V. who had taken him along with him in his late visits to Germany, and was so fond of him that, on his return to Spain, he would hear no other preacher. Virves had favored, though with much reserve, the writings of Erasmus, and was known to have conversed with some of the principal reformers.[25] On these grounds his conduct was watched, and he soon found himself in the hands of the inquisitors at Seville. In vain did he appeal to a work against Melanchthon which he had prepared for the press; and, what is more singular, in vain did the emperor interpose to stop the process, banish the inquisitor-general from Seville, and signify his displeasure against the other members of the council of the Supreme. Virves was kept in the secret prisons for four years, during which,

---

24. Llorente, ii. 280, 281. Burscheri Spicil. V. p. 17, 20.

25 In a letter, dated Valeoleti, 13 kal. Jun. 1527, Virves blames Erasmus for taking freedoms in his writings which were offensive to himself and others of his friends. In another letter to him, dated Ratispona, 15 April 1532, he says, "In the mean time I am busy with preaching, having this for my object, that if I cannot reclaim the German from error, I may at least preserve the Spaniards from infection." (*Burscheri Spicil.* v. p. 12-14, 16.)

to use his own words, "he was occupied, without breathing 135
or respite, with charges, replies, rejoinders, depositions,
defences, arguments, acts, (words, the very utterance of
which made him shudder) errors, heresies, schisms, blasphemies, anathemas." At last, in 1537, a definitive sentence was pronounced, condemning him, as suspected of
holding the errors of Luther, to make a formal abjuration,
to be absolved ad cautelam, to be confined in a monastery
for two years, and to be prohibited from preaching for other two years. He was accordingly obliged to abjure, on the
day of his auto-da-fe in the metropolitan church of Seville,
all the heresies of Luther in general, and those in particular
which he was suspected of entertaining. The emperor procured a brief from the pope, absolving his favorite preacher from the remaining pains of censure; but when he afterwards presented him to the bishopric of the Canaries, it
was with the utmost reluctance that his Holiness granted
the bull of confirmation to a man who had incurred the
suspicion of heresy in the eyes of the Inquisition.[26] "Many
have adopted the maxim," says Virves, speaking of the
proper manner of converting heretics, "that it is lawful to
abuse a heretic by word and writing, when they have it
not in their power to kill or torture him. If they get a poor
man, whom they can persecute with impunity, into their
hands, they subject him to a disgraceful sentence; so that,
though he prove himself innocent and obtain an acquit-
tal, he is stigmatized for life as a criminal. If, on the other 136
hand, the unhappy person has fallen into error through
inadvertence, or the conversation of those with whom he
associated, his judges do not labor to undeceive him by

---

26. Llorente, ii. 8-14.

explaining the doctrine of scripture, soft persuasion, and paternal advice, but, in spite of the character of fathers to which they lay claim, have recourse to the prison, the torture, chains, and the axe. And what is the effect of these horrible means? All these torments inflicted on the body can produce no change whatever on the dispositions of the mind, which can be brought back to the truth only by the word of God, which is quick, powerful, and sharper than a two-edged sword."[27]

These reflections are so excellent in themselves, and so refreshing as coming from the pen of a Spanish catholic of the sixteenth century, that, in reading them, we feel disposed to rejoice, instead of grieving at that imprisonment which, if it did not suggest them, must have served to deepen their impression on his mind. No thanks, however, to the persecutors. Some writers have expressed their surprise that the proceedings against Virves and others did not open the eyes of Charles V. to the iniquity of the Inquisition; and they think he continued to be its protector from horror at Lutheranism.[28] But Charles was instructed 137 in the nature of that court, and had given it his decided support, before the name of Luther became formidable. A despotical monarch may be displeased at the procedure of a tribunal of terror when it happens to touch one of his favorites, and may choose to check its encroachments on his own authority, without feeling the slightest wish to weaken its power as an engine for enslaving and oppressing his subjects.

---

27. Virves, *Philippicæ Disputationes, apud Llorente*. ii. 15.

28. Llorente, ii. 13.

In the mean time every method was taken to prevent the spread of Lutheran books and opinions. The council of the Supreme, in 1530, addressed a circular letter to the inquisitors dispersed over the kingdom, informing them that the writings of Luther had made their way into the country under fictitious names, and that his errors were introduced in the form of notes appended to the works of catholic authors; and therefore requiring them to add to the annual edict of denunciation a clause relating to such books, and to examine all public libraries with the view of discovering them. This led to the domiciliary visits which the familiars of the Inquisition were accustomed, at a subsequent period, to pay to private houses. During the following year the inquisitors were authorized to strike with the sentence of excommunication all who hindered them in the discharge of their duty, and all who read or kept such books, or who did not denounce those whom they knew to be guilty of that offence. The same penalty was extended to the parish priests who did not publish the edict in every city, town, and village; and all prelates 138 of the regular orders, confessors, and preachers, were laid under an obligation to urge their hearers and penitents, under the pain of incurring mortal sin, to inform against themselves and others. The edict enumerated the different articles of the Lutheran heresy, down to the slightest deviation from the ceremonies of the church, and required the informers to declare "if they knew or had heard it said, that any person had taught, maintained, or entertained in his thoughts, any of these opinions."[29]

---

29. Llorente, i. 457-459; ii. 1, 2.

Hitherto we have not met with a single Spaniard who avowed the reformed tenets, or who was convicted on good grounds of holding them. We have every reason, however, to think that there were persons of this description in Spain, though their names have not come down to us. If this had not been the case, the inquisitors would have been guilty of the grossest indiscretion, in exposing the ears of the people to the risk of infection by publishing, with such particularity, the opinions of the German heretic in every parish church of the kingdom. Yet it must be acknowledged that, in their eagerness to discover what did not exist, and to aggravate the slightest deviation from the received faith into a dangerous error, they were sometimes instrumental in propagating what they sought to extirpate. A simple countryman was brought before the inquisitors in Seville, accused of having said among friends, that he did not think there was any purgatory but the blood of Christ. He confessed that he had thought so, but, understanding that it was offensive to the holy fathers, declared himself ready to retract the sentiment. This was by no means satisfactory to the inquisitors, who told him, that by adopting that one error he had involved himself in a multitude; for, if there was no purgatory, then the pope, who had decreed the contrary, was not infallible, then general councils had erred, then justification was by faith; and so on. In vain did the poor man protest that such ideas had never once entered into his mind; he was remanded to prison until he should be prepared to retract them. The consequence was, that he was led seriously to think on these topics, and came out of the Inquisition a confirmed Lutheran.[30]

The study of polite letters had been communicated from Spain to Portugal,[31] and the knowledge of the reformed opinions proceeded in the same course. As early as 1521, Emanuel, the Portuguese monarch, addressed a letter to the elector of Saxony, urging him to punish Luther, and extirpate his pernicious tenets, before they should spread farther in Germany and penetrate into other Christian countries.[32] In 1534, pope Clement VII, being informed that the reformed opinions were daily making progress in Portugal, appointed Diego de Silva as inquisitor of that kingdom; and in the following year, we find the king representing to the court of Rome that a number of the converted Jews had become protestants.[33]

It has been conjectured that the first converts to the reformed doctrine in Spain belonged to the religious fraternity of Franciscans, because the pope, in 1526, grant-

140

---

30. Reginaldus Gonsalvius Montanus, *Inquisitionis Hispanicæ Artes Detectæ*, p. 31-33. Heydelbergæ, 1567, 8vo.

31. An accurate account of the state of learning in Portugal during the first part of the sixteenth century is given by Dr. Irving in his *Memoirs of Buchanan*, p. 75-88. Diego Sigea is said by Vassaeus, in his *Chronicle of Spain*, to have been the first or among the first restorers of polite letters in Portugal. He was the father of two learned females, Luisa and Angela, the former of whom was skilled in Hebrew, Syriac, and Arabic, as well as in Latin and Greek. (*Colomesii Italia et Hispania Orientalis*, p. 236, 237. *Antonii Bibl. Hisp. Nov.* tom. ii. p. 71, 72.)

32. *Fabricii Centifol. Luth.* tom. i. p. 85-88.

33. Llorente, ii. 100.

ed power to the general and provincials of that order to absolve such of their brethren as had imbibed the new opinions, and were willing to abjure them.[34] But this is rather to be viewed in the light of a privilege, craved by the Franciscans to exempt them from the jurisdiction of the inquisitors, who were at first chosen from the rival order of Dominicans. Few of those who afterwards became protestants belonged to the brotherhood of St. Francis.

Juan Valdes, with whom we have met elsewhere,[35] was the first person, so far as I can discover, who embraced and was active in spreading the reformed opinions in Spain. He was of a good family, and had received a liberal education. If we may judge from those with whom he was on terms of intimacy, he had studied at the university of Alcala. Having attached himself to the court, he quitted Spain about the year 1535 in the company of Charles V, who sent him to Naples to act as secretary to the viceroy.[36] The common opinion has been that he became a convert to the Lutheran creed in Germany, but the fact is, that his mind was imbued with its leading tenets before he left his native country. This appears from a treatise drawn up by him under the title of Advice on the Interpreters of

---

34. Llorente, ii. 4.

35. *History of the Reformation in Italy*, p. 16, 121, 122.

36. Llorente is disposed to identify him with Alfonso Valdes, whom we have already mentioned, and to call him Juan Alfonso Valdes. (ii. 478; iii. 221.) But they were evidently different persons. The latter was a priest; (see *Burscheri Spicil.* v. p. 17.) the former was a knight: the latter is styled secretary to Charles V.; the former, papal secretary at Naples.

sacred scripture, which was circulated privately among his acquaintance. It was originally sent in the form of a letter to his friend Bartolomé Carranza, who afterwards became archbishop of Toledo, but had early incurred the suspicions of the Holy Office by the freedom of his opinions.[37] This tract was found among the papers of the primate when he was subsequently seized by the order of the Inquisition, and formed one of the gravest articles of charge against that distinguished and long-persecuted prelate. The Advice contained the following propositions, among others: first, that in order to understand the sacred scriptures, we must not rely on the interpretations of the fathers; second, that we are justified by a lively faith in the passion and death of our Saviour; and third, that we may attain to certainty concerning our justification. The agreement between these and the leading sentiments maintained by Luther, renders it highly probable that Valdes had read the writings of that reformer or of some of his adherents. At the same time we are told that the principal things in this tract were taken from the Christian institutes of Tauler.[38] This fact throws light on the sentiments of Valdes, and the peculiar cast of his writings. John Tauler was a distinguished German preacher of the fourteenth century, and one of those writers in the church of Rome who have obtained the name of mystics. They were disgusted with the intricate and jejune theology of the scholastic divines, and with the routine of exterior services which constituted the whole practice of piety in the convents; but, being

142

---

37. Llorente, iii. 185-187.

38. Llorente, ii. 478; iii. 221, 244, 245.

imperfectly instructed in the doctrine of the gospel, in fly-ing from the vice of their age they fell into the opposite extreme. They resolved religion almost entirely into con-templation and meditation; their discourses, consisting of soliloquies on the love of God and the sufferings of Christ, were chiefly calculated to stimulate the passions; and they occasionally made use of extravagant and hyperbolical ex-pressions, which implied that the soul of the devotee was absorbed in the divine essence, and, when favored with supernatural visitations, was rendered independent upon and superior to external means and ordinances. The Exer-cises, or meditations, on the Life of Christ by Tauler bear a strong resemblance to the better-known work of Thomas à Kempis on the Imitation of Christ. They have the same ex-cellencies and the same faults; breathe the same rich odor of spiritual devotion, and labor under the same deficiency of clear and distinct views of divine truth.[39] Those who are well grounded in the doctrines of Christianity may reap great advantage from a perusal of them; candidates for the ministry will find in them an excellent supplement to a

143

39. Marco Antonio Flaminio, in a letter to Carlo Gualteruccio, has given a just character of the work of Thomas à Kempis. After recommending it highly, he says, "One fault I find with this book; I do not approve of the way of fear which he recommends. Not that I would set aside every kind of fear, but merely penal fear, which proceeds either from unbelief or weak faith." The whole letter is excellent. Cardinal Quirini produced it with the view of showing that the writer was not a protestant, whereas there cannot be a stronger proof to the contrary, so far as doctrine is concerned. (*Quirini Præfat.* p. 69, 70. ad *Collect. Epist. Poli,* vol. iii.)

course of systematic divinity; but in minds warm and un-informed they are apt to foster a self-righteous and servile disposition, and to give rise to enthusiastic notions.[40]

The mystic theology had its votaries in Spain. A Span- 144 ish translation of the Imitation of Christ, and of an earlier work of the same character, entitled the Ladder of Paradise, were published at the close of the fifteenth century.[41] Juan de Avila, Luis de Granada, confessor to the queen regent of Portugal, and St. Francis de Borgia, duke of Gandia, and third general of the order of Jesuits, were the authors of works, for which they were persecuted before the Inquisition as mystics and illuminati.[42] Several of the protestants, who were afterwards brought to the stake at Valladolid, appealed to the writings of the two last-named individuals as containing sentiments similar to those which they held on the head of justification.[43]

Valdes may have become acquainted with the writings of Tauler through the recommendation of Luther, who, at

---

40. The most distinguished of the mystic authors of the middle ages besides A Kempis and Tauler, were Ruysbrok and Harph. Those who wish information respecting this class of writers, will find it in *Gottf. Arnoldi Historia Theologiæ Mysticæ Veteris et Novae*; in *Andr. de Saussay de Mysticis Galliæ Scriptoribus*; and in the Preface to the edition to Tauler's works by Philip James Spener.

41. Pellicer, *Ensayo*, p. 124-134.

42. Llorente, iii. 103-107, 123. The illuminati of Spain in the 16th century, if we may judge from the accounts of the inquisitors, resembled the quakers, rather more than the quietists of France. (Ib. ii. 3.)

43. Ibid. iii. p. 106, 123.

one period of his life, was enamored with them, and republished, with a commendatory preface, a work written
in the same strain, but more liable to exception, under the
title of German Theology. In a letter to his friend Spalatin,
the reformer says, "If you wish to read in your own language the ancient and pure divinity, procure Tauler's sermons, of which I now send you an abstract; for nowhere,
either in Latin or German, have I met with a theology
145 more wholesome and accordant to the gospel."[44] The doctrines of justification by faith in Christ, and of regeneration by the agency of the Spirit, form the groundwork in
the writings of Valdes, and so far his creed is Lutheran or
protestant; but we can trace in them the influence of the
transcendental divinity which he had caught from Tauler.
More intellectual and speculative than the mystic divines,
he exhibits in his works the rationale of their creed rather than an exemplification of their mode of writing, and
hazards some sentiments which gave just offence to several
of the principal reformers.[45] It is amusing to observe his

---

44. Luther's *Sämtliche Schriften*, tom. xxi. p. 566. Philip Marnix,
    Sieur de St. Aldegonde, had a less favorable opinion of Tauler,
    whom he calls "*delirus monachus.*" He was afraid of certain en-
    thusiasts in the Low Countries, who sought to gain credit to their
    cause by the name of that preacher, while they taught that God
    was the soul of the universe, and deified not only men, but brutes
    and vegetables. (*Scrinium Antiquarium*, tom. iv. p. 544, 545.)

45. Beza was chiefly offended with Valdes for leading his readers from
    the scriptures to revelations of the Spirit. That he had good rea-
    sons, must appear to any one who reads the sixty-third chapter
    of the *Divine Considerations*. Its title is, "By seven conformities is

natural inquisitiveness contending with and overcoming that principle in his creed which led him to condemn as sinful all curious inquiries into matters of religion, or indeed into any other matter.

Valdes left his native country at an early period, but 146 he contributed greatly to the spread of the reformed opinions in it by his writings, several of which were published in Spanish.[46] Though he had remained, his personal pres-

---

shewed that the Holy Scripture is like a candle in a dark place, and that the Holy Spirit is like the sun." To the English translation of the work, printed in 1646, George Herbert added notes, qualifying the most exceptionable passages.

46. His commentary on the Epistle to the Romans was published in Spanish at Venice in 1556, with a dedication, by his countryman Juan Perez, to Julia Gonzaga. (Gerdesii Italia Reformata, p. 344.) The following is the title of another of his commentaries: "*Commentario breve, ò declaracion compendiosa, y familiar, sobre la primera epistola de San Pablo à los Corinthios, muy util para todos los amadores de la piedad Christiana.*" In the Spanish *Index Expurg.* this work is mentioned both with and without the author's name. (*Bayle, Dict. v. Valdes.*) Schelhorn promised to "produce not a few testimonies to the truth" from a work by the same author, of which two editions were published in Italy, translated from Spanish, and entitled, "*Due Dialoghi: l'uno de Mercurio et Caronte; Paltro di Lattantio et di uno Archidiacono.*" (*Amœn. Hist. Eccl. et Lit.* tom. ii. p. 51.) He elsewhere ascribes to him a work entitled, "*Modo di tenere, nell'insegnar et nel predicar, al principio della Religion Christiana.*" (*Ergötzlichkeiten,* tom. ii. p. 31.) Both these works are in the *Index Libr. Prohib. a. 1559.* Llorente makes Valdes the author of another work, which he calls

ence would most probably have produced little effect. It required a person of less caution and more adventurous spirit to burst the terrible barrier which opposed the entrance of the gospel into Spain, and to raise the standard of truth within sight of the flames of the Inquisition. Such a person was found in the man of whom I am now to speak.

Rodrigo de Valer, a native of Lebrixa, distant about thirty miles from Seville, had spent his youth in those idle and dissipated habits which were common among the nobility and gentry of Spain. The love of dress, and of horses and sports, engrossed his attention; and in Seville, which was his favorite residence, he shone in the first rank among the young men of fashion in every scene of amusement and feat of gallantry. All of a sudden he disappeared from those places of entertainment of which he had been the life and ornament. He was in good health, and his fortune had sustained no injury. But his mind had undergone a complete change; his splendid equipage was laid aside; he became negligent of his dress; and, shut up in his closet, he devoted himself entirely to reading and meditation on religion. Had he become unexpectedly pious, and immured himself in a convent, his conduct would not have excited general surprise among his countrymen; but to retire from the world, and yet to shun those consecrated abodes, the choice of which was viewed as the great and almost exclusive mark of superior sanctity, appeared to them unaccountable on any other supposition than that of mental derangement. Valer had acquired a slight acquaintance with the Latin language in his youth. He now procured a

147

Acharo. (ii. 478.)

copy of the Vulgate, the only translation of the Bible permitted in Spain; and having by dint of application, by day and by night, made himself master of the language, he, in a short time, became so well acquainted with the contents of the scriptures, that he could repeat almost any passage in them from memory, and explain it with wonderful promptitude and intelligence. Whether he had any other means of instruction, or what these were, must remain a secret; but it is certain that he was led to form a system of 148 doctrine not different from that of the reformers in Germany, and to lay the foundations of a church in Seville which was Lutheran in all the main articles of its belief.

When Valer had informed and satisfied his mind as to the truths of religion, he left off that solitary life which had been chosen by him as an instrument, and not as an end. He now returned to company, but with a very different spirit and intention. His great desire was now to impart to others those impressions of divine truth which had been made on his own mind. With this view, he courted the society of the clergy and monks, with whom he dealt, first by argument and persuasion, and afterwards in the severer style of reproof. He set before them the general defection, among all classes, from primitive Christianity, both as to faith and practice; the corruptions of their own order, which had contributed to spread infection over the whole Christian community; and the sacred obligations which they were under to apply a speedy and thorough remedy to the evil before it should become altogether incurable. These representations were uniformly accompanied with an appeal to the sacred writings as the supreme standard in religion, and with an exhibition of the principal doctrines which they taught. When the clergy, weary of the ungrateful theme, shunned his company, he threw himself in their way, and did not hesitate to introduce his favorite but dangerous topics in the public walks and other places 149 of concourse. His exhortations were not entirely without success; but in most instances their effects were such as might have been anticipated from the situation and character of those to whom they were addressed. The surprised excited by his first address gave place to indignation and disdain. It was not to be borne that a layman, and one who had no pretensions to learning, should presume to instruct his teachers, and inveigh against doctrines and institutions which were held in reverence by the universal church, and sanctioned by its highest authority. Whence had he his pretended knowledge of the scriptures? Who gave him a right to teach? And what were the signs and proof of his mission? To these questions Valer replied with candor, but with firmness. That it was true he had been brought up in ignorance of divine things; he had derived his knowledge, not from the polluted streams of tradition and human inventions, but from the pure fountain of revealed truth, through the teaching of that Spirit by whose influence living waters are made to flow from the hearts of those who believe in Christ; there was no good reason for supposing that these influences were confined to persons of the ecclesiastical order, especially when it was so deeply depraved as at present; private and illiterate men had convicted a learned sanhedrim of blindness, and called a whole world to the knowledge of salvation; he had the authority of Christ for warning them of their errors and 150 vices; and none would require a sign from him but a spurious and degenerate race, whose eyes could not bear the brightness of that pure light which laid open and reproved their works of darkness.

It was not to be expected that he would be long permitted to continue in this offensive course. He was brought before the inquisitors, with whom he maintained a keen dispute on the church, the marks by which it is distinguished, justification, and similar points. On that occasion, some individuals of considerable authority, who had secretly imbibed his sentiments, exerted themselves in his favor. Their influence, joined to the purity of his descent, the station which he held in society, and the circumstances that the judges either believed or wished it to be believed that he was insane, procured for him a milder sentence than that jealous and inexorable tribunal was accustomed to pronounce. He was dismissed with the loss of his property. But neither confiscation of goods, nor the fear of a severer punishment, could induce Valer to alter his conduct. He yielded so far to the importunities of his friends as to abstain from a public declaration of his sentiments for a short time, during which he explained to them in private the Epistle to the Romans.[47] But his zeal soon burst through his restraint. He considered himself in the light of a soldier sent on the forlorn hope, and resolved to fall in the breach, trusting that others, animated by his example, would press forward and secure the victory. Resuming his 151 former reproofs of the reigning errors and superstition, he was a second time denounced to the Holy Office, which condemned him to wear a san-benito, and to be impris-

---

47. Montanus, p. 268.

oned for life. When conducted, along with other penitents, to the church of St. Salvador in Seville, to attend
public service on festival days, instead of exhibiting the
marks of sorrow exacted from persons in his situation, he
scrupled not to address the audience after sermon, and to
warn them against the erroneous doctrine which they had
heard from the preacher, whenever he thought it contrary
to the word of God. This of itself would have been reckoned sufficient cause for adjudging him to the flames; but
the reasons already mentioned had influence to save him
from that fate. To rid themselves in the most quiet way of
so troublesome a penitent, the inquisitors came to the resolution of confining him in a monastery belonging to the
town of San Lucar, near the mouth of the Guadalquivir,
where, secluded from all society, he died about the age of
fifty. His san-benito, which was hung up in the metropolitan church of Sevilla, long attracted curiosity by its extraordinary size, and the inscription which it bore,—"Rodrigo Valer, a citizen of Lebrixa and Seville, an apostate,
and false apostle who pretended to be sent of God."[48]

48. Cypriano de Valera has given an account of Rodrigo de Valer
    in his *Dos Tratados:—del Papa, y de la Missa*, p. 242-246. The
    second edition of this work was printed, *"En casa de Ricardo del
    Campo, ano de 1599."* An English translation of it appeared un-
    der the title of *"Two Treatises: the first, of the Lives of the Popes, and
    their doctrine; the second, of the Masse, &c. The second edition in
    Spanish, augmented by the author himself, M. Cyprian Valera, and
    translated into English by John Golburne."* London 1600, 4to. But
    both Cypriano de Valera, and Llorente (ii. 147-149.) have bor-
    rowed their accounts from that of Reynaldo Gonzalez de Mon-
    tes, (or Montanus) in his *Inquisitionis Hispanicæ Artes Detectæ*, p.

It was about the year 1541 that the final sentence was   152
pronounced on Valer.[49] The most distinguished of his converts was Juan Gil, commonly called Dr. Egidius. He was
born at Olvera in Aragon, and educated at the university
of Alcala, where he distinguished himself by his skill in
scholastic theology, the only science then valued in Spain,
except among a few individuals who, by addicting themselves to the study of scripture in the original languages,
were derisively named Biblists. After obtaining the highest
academical honors, he was appointed professor of divinity
at Siguenza. Such was his celebrity, that when the office
of canon-magistral, or preacher, in the cathedral church
of Seville became vacant, he was chosen to fill it by the
unanimous vote of the chapter, without being required
to undergo the comparative trial prescribed in such cases.
But how well versed soever in the writings of Lombard,
Aquinas, and Scotus, he proved an unpopular preacher;
and not being indifferent to his reputation and usefulness,
he felt, after continuing for some years, nearly as anxious   153
to relinquish his situation as the people were to get rid of
him. In this state of mind he was accosted by Valer, who
had the penetration to discover his feelings, and to perceive the good dispositions, as well as talents, with which
he was endowed. He pointed out the defects of his mode
of preaching, and exhorted him, as the sure remedy, to give

259-264. The narrative of De Montes is original and authentic,
as he received the particulars from the mouth of Valer's disciple,
Dr. Juan Gil, (or Egidius) with whom he was intimate at Seville.

49. Montanus, ut supra, p. 259. Cypriano de Valera says, "*cerca del
ano 1545.*" (*Dos Tratados*, p. 246.)

himself to the diligent and serious perusal of the word of God. This advice, frequently repeated, produced at last the desired effect. He took the course pointed out to him, and his "profiting appeared to all." He soon became the most acceptable preacher who had appeared in Seville. Instead of the dry, abstruse, and unprofitable discussions which he had formerly pursued, he brought forward the great truths of the Bible; and the frigid manner in which he had been accustomed to acquit himself in public was succeeded by powerful appeals to the consciences, and affectionate addresses to the hearts of his auditors. Their attention was aroused; deep convictions of the necessity and suitableness of that salvation which the gospel reveals were made on their minds; and they were prepared for receiving those new views of divine truth which the preacher presented to them, as they were gradually unfolded to himself, and with a caution which regard to the weakness of the people, as well as to his own perilous situation, seemed to warrant

154 and require.[50] In this manner, by a zeal more tempered with prudence than that of his revered instructor, he was honored not only to make converts to Christ, but to train up martyrs for the truth. "Among the other gifts divinely bestowed on this holy man," says one who owed his soul to him, "was the singular faculty which he had of kindling in the breasts of those who listened to his instructions a sacred flame which animated them in all the exercises of piety, internal and external, and made them not only willing to take up the cross, but cheerful in the prospect of the sufferings of which they stood in jeopardy every hour; a clear proof that the master whom he served was present

---

50. Montanus, p. 256-259, 265.

with him, by his Spirit engraving the doctrine which he taught on the hearts of his hearers.[51]

Egidius was not left alone in the work of enlightening the citizens of Seville. In addition to those who, like himself, had profited by the conversation of Valer, he was joined by Doctor Vargas and Constantine Ponce de la Fuente, who had been his fellow-students at the university, and were men of superior talents and learning. He imparted to them his knowledge of evangelical truth, and they in their turn contributed by their conversation to the improvement of his ministerial gifts. The three friends concerted a plan, according to which they might co-operate in advancing the common cause. Vargas read lectures 155 to the more learned, in which he expounded the Epistle to the Romans, and subsequently the book of Psalms; and Constantine, of whom we shall have occasion to speak more particularly afterwards, assisted Egidius occasionally in the pulpit. Their zeal, while it awakened the suspicions, provoked the diligence of the clergy who were devoted to the ancient superstition; and the city was divided in its attachments between the two classes of preachers. Those of the one class urged the necessity and importance of the repetition of prayers at certain stated hours, the frequent hearing of mass, the visiting of consecrated places, and the regular observance of fasting and of auricular confession; while they exhorted those who aimed at higher degrees of sanctity to dedicate their substance to pious uses, or, renouncing the world, to take on them the triple vow. Those of the other class either passed over these things entirely,

---

51. Ibid., p. 231.

or inculcated their inefficacy; exhorted their hearers to rely on the merits of Christ instead of their own works, and to prove the genuineness of their faith by obedience to the commands of God; and, in place of recommending rosaries and scales of devotion, spoke in the warmest style of the advantages to be derived from a serious and daily perusal of the sacred writings. The first class carried along with them the great body of the people, whose religion is the creature of authority and habit. But the eloquence of Egidius and his two associates, their prudence, unaffected piety, and irreproachable morals, and the harmony with

156 which they continued to act, gradually subdued the prejudices of the multitude, and thinned the ranks even of their clerical opponents. Assiduously employed in the duties of their public functions through the day, they met in the evening with the friends of the reformed doctrine, sometimes in one private house and sometimes in another; the small society in Seville grew insensibly, and became the parent stock, from which branches were taken and planted in the adjacent country.

The Inquisition had for some time fixed its jealous eyes on the three preachers; nor were there wanting persons ready to accuse them, and especially Egidius, who was most obnoxious on account of his greater openness of disposition, and his appearing more frequently in the pulpit. Surmises unfavorable to his orthodoxy were circulated, spies were set on his conduct, and consultations held in secret as to the surest method of ruining one who had become popular among all ranks. While these things were going on he was deprived of his two trusty associates; Vargas being removed by death, and Constantine called to the Low Countries. But even after he was thus left alone his enemies were afraid to proceed against him.[52]

So great was the reputation of Egidius, that in 1550 the emperor nominated him to the vacant bishopric of Torto-sa, which was one of the richest benefices in Spain, and had been held by cardinal Adrian, the preceptor of Charles V., immediately before his elevation to the popedom. This distinguished mark of royal favor inflamed the resentment of his adversaries, and determined them to proceed to extremities. Instead of confining themselves as formerly to murmurs. they now charged him openly with heresy, and predicted that his elevation to the episcopate would prove the most disastrous calamity which Spain had witnessed. He was formally denounced to the Holy Office, and, the preliminary steps having been taken, was thrown into its secret prisons. The charges against him related to the doctrine of justification, assurance of salvation, human merits, plurality of mediators, purgatory, auricular confession, and the worshipping of images. He was also accused of having favored Rodrigo de Valer on his trial, and opposed the erection of a crucifix in the room of one who had been accidentally burnt. In his defence he drew up an ample statement of his sentiments on the head of justification, with the reasons on which they were founded; a display of frankness which proved hurtful to his cause, as it furnished the procurator fiscal at once with evidence in support of his charges and materials for increasing their number. The friends of Egidius now became alarmed for his safety. The emperor, hearing of the danger to which he was exposed,

157

---

52. Montanus, p. 266.

wrote in his favor to the inquisitor general. The chapter of Seville followed his example. And, what is more strange, 158 the licentiate Correa, one of the most inexorable judges of the Holy office, became an advocate for him, influenced, it is said, by indignation at the conduct of Pedro Diaz, another inquisitor, who had formerly been a disciple of Valer along with Egidius, whom he now prosecuted with base and unrelenting hostility. In consequence of this powerful intercession the inquisitors found it necessary to adopt a moderate course, and agree, instead of remitting the articles of charge to the ordinary qualificators, to submit them to two arbiters chosen by the parties.

Egidius, after nominating Bartolomé Carranza and several other individuals, who were either absent from the country or objected to by the inquisitors, at last fixed, with the approbation of his judges, on Domingo de Soto, a Dominican and professor at Salamanca, as his arbiter. Soto came to Seville, and having obtained access to Egidius, with whom he had been acquainted at the university, professed, after mutual explanations, to coincide with him in his views on justification,[53] which was the main article in the indictment, and to think that there would be no difficulty in procuring an amicable adjustment in the affair. It was arranged between them, that each should draw up a paper containing his sentiments on the disputed point

---

53. Soto was a disciple of St. Thomas, and addicted to the sentiments of Augustine, as appears from his treatise *de Natura et Gratia*, addressed to the fathers of Trent, in opposition to Catharinus, and appended to his *Commentary on the Romans*, printed at Antwerp in 1550.

expressed in his own words, and that these papers should 159
be read in the presence of the inquisitors. As the cause had
excited great interest from its relation to a bishop elect
and a preacher so popular in Seville, it was thought proper
that it should be discussed at a public meeting held in the
cathedral. On the day appointed for the trial, pulpits were
allotted for Egidius and his arbiter Soto; but, either from
design or accident, they were placed at a great distance
from one another. After sermon was ended, Soto read the
declaration of his sentiments. Egidius, owing partly to the
distance at which he sat, and partly to the bustle prevailing
in a crowded and anxious assembly, was unable to follow
the speaker; but taking it for granted that what was read
agreed with what had passed between them in conversation, he nodded assent to it, as Soto raised his voice and
looked toward him at the end of every proposition. He
then proceeded to read his own declaration, which in the
judgment of all who were present, whether friends or foes,
contradicted the former on all the leading points. The
inquisitors availed themselves of the variance between
his gestures and language to raise an outcry against him.
These two declarations were instantly joined in process,
and sentence was given forth, declaring him violently suspected of the Lutheran heresy, and condemning him to
abjure the propositions imputed to him, to be imprisoned
for three years, to abstain from writing or teaching for ten
years, and not to leave the kingdom during that period,
under the pain of being punished as a formal and relapsed 160
heretic, or, in other words, of being burnt alive. Confounded at the unexpected issue of the process, abashed
by the exultation of his enemies, and half-convinced, by

the mortification which he read in the countenances of his friends, that he must have said something far wrong, Egidius lost courage, and silently acquiesced in the sentence pronounced against him. It was not until some time after he had returned to his prison that he learned from one of his companions the base treachery of the friend in whom he had confided.[54]

Such is the account of the process given by De Montes. The late historian of the Inquisition is disposed to call in question the truth of his statement so far as concerns the artifice imputed to the professor of Salamanca; upon this ground, that Carranza, archbishop of Toledo, during his trial, retaliated upon Soto by accusing him of "having been too indulgent in regard to Doctor Egidius of Seville."[55] But this objection is by no means conclusive. For, in the first place, Llorente bears witness to the general accuracy of De Montes, who expressly asserts that he received his information from Egidius in prison. In the second place, the charge of Carranza is not irreconcilable with the narrative which has been given; for De Montes states that Soto claimed the merit of having procured a lenient sentence for Egidius.[56] In fine, Llorente has shown, in reference to another case, that Soto was perfectly capable of the disgraceful conduct imputed to him on this occasion.[57]

161

---

54. Montanus, p. 266-272.

55 Llorente, ii. 144-147.

56. Montanus, p. 271.

57. Speaking of his letters produced on the trial of Carranza, Llorente says: "All these documents prove that F. Domingo Soto was guilty

No sooner was it known that Egidius was condemned, than a flight of hungry applicants gathered round the fat benefit of Tortosa like crows round carrion. The holy fathers assembled at Trent were not so intently occupied in watching over the interests of the catholic church as not to have one eye turned to Spain, and ready to discern what might happen there to their advantage. While the trial of the bishop elect was in dependence, cardinal Granville, then bishop of Arras and prime minister of Spain, had his table covered with applications, in which the incense of adulation was thickly sprinkled on rancid avarice. In a letter, dated from Trent on the 19th of November 1551, the titular bishop Jubin, in partibus Infidelium, writes: "We have received intelligence here, that the bishop elect of Tortosa has been condemned to perpetual imprisonment. I shall be infinitely obliged to you to think of me—the least of your servants—provided his lordship of Elna shall be translated to the bishopric of Tortosa, now vacant by this means."[58] On the preceding day, the bishop of Elna had addressed a letter to the same quarter, in which, without giving the least hint of the object he had in view, he begs the premier to command him "as the meanest domestic of his household," calls himself "his slave,"[59] and assures him that the rare qualities of his eminence, his native

162

---

of collusion in regard to two parties, which he cheated, first the one after the other, and afterwards both of them at the same time." (ii. 146.)

58. *Lettres et Mémoires de François de Vargas*, traduits par Mich. le Vassor, p. 194, 195.

59. "Esclavo."

goodness, and the favors he had conferred, were so deeply seated in the heart of his servant that he remembered him without ceasing, especially "in his poor sacrifices,[60] the fittest time to make mention of one's masters." Two days after, the modest bishop has acquired as much courage as to name his request: he acknowledges that the bishopric of Tortosa was "too weighty a burden for his weak shoulders, but urges that he could discharge his episcopal functions better in such a tranquil spot than in the frontier province of Roussillon, where his pious exercises were interrupted by the noise of warlike instruments, and that he "felt a strong desire to end his days in tending his infirm sheep in the peace of God."[61] The bishop of Algeri was equally disinterested as his brethren in seeking promotion. "It was not avarice that induced him to ask the favor" to be translated from the island of Sardinia; he only wished to "have his residence on terra firma," that his spirit being relieved from the continual agitation in which it was kept by the restless waves which surrounded him, he might be "at more liberty to serve God, and pray for the life of the king and his minister."[62] The bishop of Elna having been unsuccessful in his application, renewed it in the course of the following year, when he had recourse to a new line of argument in its support. After telling the premier "that his hands had made him," he requests him to remember, "if he pleased," that his majesty had certain rights in Valencia called les bayles de Morella, of which large sums

163

---

60. *"Mis pobres sacrificios."*

61. *Lettres et Mémoires de Vargas*, p. 193, 195, 196.

62. Ibid., p. 303.

were due to the treasury, as would appear from the lists which he had procured and took the liberty to transmit to his eminence; that most luckily the diocese of Tortosa included that district, though the episcopal seat was in his native country of Catalonia; and that, if it should please his majesty to gratify him with that bishopric, he could see to the payment of these dues without leaving his diocese, and "thus would have it in his power to serve God and the king at the same time."[63]

O the duplicity, the selfishness, the servility of the clergy! What good cause but one would they not have ruined? And how deeply has that been marred by them! Boccaccio 164 relates, (it is a tale, but deserves to be repeated for the sake of the moral it teaches,) that two persons, a Christian layman and a Jew, lived together in a retired spot on the northern boundary of Italy. The Christian had long piously labored to convert his neighbor, and had succeeded so far as to be in daily expectation of his submitting to baptism, when all at once the idea struck the latter that he would previously visit the capital of Christendom. Dreading the effects of his journey, the Christian endeavored to divert him from it; but in vain. After an absence of some weeks the Jew returned, and repairing to the house of the Christian, who had given up his convert for lost, surprised him with the intimation that he was now ready to be baptized; "for (added he) I have been at Rome, and have seen the pope and his clergy, and I am convinced that if Christianity had not been divine, it would have been ruined long ago under the care of such guardians."

---

63. Ibid. p. 514, 515, 522.

All the applicants for the bishopric of Tortosa took care to urge the services which they had done to the emperor at the council of Trent. Several authors have spoken in high terms of the liberal views and independent spirit displayed by the Spanish divines who sat in the council; and Father Simon, in particular, asserts that they were ready, upon the refusal of the ecclesiastical reforms which they sought, to join with the French church in throwing off the authority of the court of Rome, if Charles V. had not, from political motives, discouraged them by withdrawing his support.[64]

165   A perusal of their correspondence and that of the imperial embassy serves to abate, in no small degree, the high opinion which these commendations are calculated to produce. If the Italian bishops were passive tools in the hands of the papal legates, their brethren of Spain were not less under the influence of the imperial ambassadors; and it is quite as clear that their zeal for the reformation of abuses was at first excited, as that it was afterwards restrained, by the policy of the emperor. Several of the reforms which they demanded were in favor of their own order, and would have added to their power and wealth in proportion as they diminished those of the papal see; a circumstance which did not escape the observation of the court of Spain.[65] At

---

64. Simon, *Lettres Choisies*, tom. i. p. 252-254.

65. See their *Postulata to the Council in Schelhorn, Amœnit. Eccles.* tom. ii. p. 584-590. Conf. Vargas, *Lettres et Mémoires*, p. 210. The Royal Council of Castile addressed a memorial to the Council of Trent, urging a variety of ecclesiastical reforms, but desirable as many of these certainly were, we cannot help feeling pleased at the rejection of the whole, when we find the following article

the same time they satisfied themselves with murmuring in private at the shameful arts by which the council was managed, and had not the courage to resent the attacks made on its freedom, or the insults openly offered to their colleagues. The bishop of Verdun happening to apply the term pretended reformation to some of the plans proposed in the council, the papal legate, cardinal Crescentio, assailed him publicly with invective, calling him a thoughtless young man and a fool, and ordering him to be silent. "Is this a free council?" said the elector of Cologne to the Spanish bishop of Orense, who sat next to him. "It ought to be free," replied the bishop, with a caution which would not have disgraced an Italian. "But tell me your opinion candidly. Is the synod free?" "Do not press me at present, my lord," rejoined the prudent bishop; "that's a difficult question; I will answer it at home."[66] It hwas been alleged that the papal influence over the council was confined to matters of discipline and ecclesiastical polity, and did not extend to points of faith, in the decision of which all the

166

---

among them: "That the pope shall support the Inquisition, and attempt nothing to the prejudice of an institution so necessary to the welfare of these kingdoms—*porque el officio de la santa Inquisicion es muy necessario en estoys reynos, conviene ser muy favorecido.*" (*Vargas,* ut supra, p. 162, 167.)

66. Vargas, p. 235, 254. The name of this bishop was Francisco Blanco. In 1558 he gave a recommendation to the catechism of Carranza, but retracted it during the prosecution of the author for heresy, and was rewarded with the archbishopric of Santiago. (Llorente, iii. 301, 302.)

members were of one accord.[67] But this is contradicted by unquestionable documents. Some of the most learned divines who were at Trent were dissatisfied with certain parts of the doctrine of the council, and with the confused and hurried manner in which this important part of the business was transacted.[68]

After the article concerning the sacraments of penance and extreme unction had received the formal sanction of the holy and universal council, the divines of Louvain succeeded in convincing the leaders that it was erroneous. What was to be done? They agreed in a private conclave to alter it, after taking precautions to have the whole affair buried in silence, lest they should incur the ridicule of the Lutherans. "A great misfortune!" says the archbishop of Cologne; "but the least of two evils." The reflections of the counsellor of the imperial embassy are more unceremonious. "I believe (says he) that God has permitted this occurrence to cover them with shame and confusion. Surely, after this, they will open their eyes, according to the saying of the psalmist, Fill their faces with shame, that they may seek thy name. God grant they may comprehend this; but I dare not hope for so much, and have always said that nothing short of a miracle will work a change."[69] It is impossible to conceive any thing more deplorable than the picture of the council drawn in the confidential correspondence of Vargas, who was attached, as a legal adviser, to the embassy sent by Charles V. to Trent. "The legate is

67. Simon, *Lettres Choisies*, tom. i. p. 254.

68. Vargas, p. 43, 57, 224, 233.

69. Vargas, p. 66, 246-248.

always the same," says he in a letter to the cardinal-bishop of Arras; "he is a man lost to all shame. Believe me, Sir, I have not words to express the pride and effrontery which he displays in the affairs of the council. Perceiving that we are timid, and that his majesty is unwilling to hurt or offend the pope, he endeavors to terrify us by assuming stately airs and a haughty tone. He treats the bishops as slaves; threatens and swears that he will depart. It is useless 168 for his majesty to continue longer to urge the pope and his ministers. It is speaking to the deaf, and trying to soften the stones. It serves only to make us a laughing-stock to the world, and to furnish the heretics with subjects for pasquinades. We must delay till the time when God will purify the sons of Levi. That time must come soon, and, in my opinion, this purification will not be accomplished without some extraordinary chastisement. Things cannot remain long in their present state: the evils are too great. All the nerves of ecclesiastical discipline are broken, the traffic in things sacred is shameful.... The prediction of St. Paul is about to be accomplished in the church of Rome, That day cannot come, unless there come a falling away first. As to the manner of treating doctrines, I have already written you, that they precipitate every thing, examine few questions, and do not submit them to the judgment of the learned divines who are here in attendance. Many of the bishops give their vote, and say placet, on points which they do not understand and are incapable of understanding. There is no one here who appears on the side of God, or dares to speak. We are all dumb dogs that cannot bark." Notwithstanding all this, and much more to the same purpose, Vargas adds, like a true son of the church:

"As for myself, I obey implicitly, and will submit without resistance to whatever shall be determined in matters of faith. God grant that all may do this."[70]

169   These facts are not irrelative to the subject. The secrets of the council of Trent soon transpired; and several individuals, who were afterwards brought to the stake in Spain, acknowledged that their eyes were first opened to the radical corruptions of the church of Rome by the accounts they received from some of the members of that synod as to the scandalous manner in which its decisions were influenced.[71]

Egidius appeared among the criminals condemned to penance, in an auto-da-fe celebrated at Seville in 1552.[72] The term of his imprisonment having expired in 1555, he, in the course of the following year, paid a visit to Valladolid, where he found a number of converts to the reformed doctrine. His wounded spirit was refreshed by what he saw of the grace of God in that city, and after spending a short time in the company of his brethren, and exhorting them to constancy in the faith, he returned to Seville. But the fatigue of traveling, to which he had been unaccustomed for some years, brought on a fever, which cut him off in a few days. He left behind him a number of writings in his native tongue, none of which appears to have been printed.[73] His bones were afterwards taken from their grave,

---

70. Ibid., p. 207-8, 211, 225-6, 233.

71. Llorente, ii. 223; iii. 230, 231.

72. Ibid. ii. 138.

73. Montanus, p. 273. *Histoire des Martyrs*, p. 500, 501. De Montes praises his commentaries on Genesis, on some of the Psalms, the

and committed to the flames, his property confiscated, 170
and his memory declared infamous, by a sentence of the
inquisitors, finding he had died in the Lutheran faith.[74]

The first introduction of the reformed doctrine into
Valladolid was attended with circumstances nearly as extraordinary as those which had led to its reception in Seville. Francisco San-Roman, a native of Burgos, and son of
the alcayde mayor of Bribiesca, having engaged in mercan-
tile pursuits, went to the Low Countries. In the year 1540
his employers sent him from Antwerp to Bremen, to settle
some accounts due to them in that city. The reformed religion had been introduced into Bremen; and the young
Spaniard, curious to become acquainted with that doctrine
which was so much condemned in his native country, went
to one of the churches, where he heard James Sprent, formerly prior of the Augustinian monastery at Antwerp, and
one of the first persons of note who embraced the opinions
of Luther in the Netherlands.[75] The sermon made so deep
an impression on the mind of San-Roman, that he could
not refrain from calling on the preacher, who, pleased with
his candor and thirst for knowledge, introduced him to
the acquaintance of some of his pious and learned friends.
Among them was our countryman Doctor Maccabeus,[76]

Song of Solomon, and the Epistle to the Colossians; but especially a treatise on bearing the cross, which he composed in prison.

74. Montanus, p. 274. Llorente, ii. 139, 144, 273.

75. *Erasmi Epistolæ*, ep. 427. Luther's *Sämtliche Schriften*, tom. xv.
Anhang, p. 192; tom. xxi. p. 790, 806. *Gerdesii Hist. Reform.*
tom. ii. p. 131; tom. iii. p. 25.

76. *Life of John Knox*, vol. i. note. I.

then at Bremen, by whose conversation he profited greatly.
171 Like some young converts he greatly flattered himself that
he could easily persuade others to embrace those truths
which appeared to his own mind as clear as the light of
day; and he burned with the desire of returning home and
imparting the knowledge which he had received to his
relations and countrymen. In vain did Sprent endeavor
to restrain an enthusiasm from which he had himself suffered at an earlier period in his life. In the letters which
he wrote to his employers at Antwerp, San-Roman could
not help alluding to the change which his religious sentiments had undergone, and lamenting the blindness of
his countrymen. The consequence was, that on his return
to that city he was immediately seized by certain friars, to
whom the contents of his letters had been communicated; and a number of Lutheran books and satirical prints
against the church of Rome being found in his possession,
he was thrown into prison. After a rigorous confinement
of eight months, he was released at the solicitation of his
friends, who represented that his zeal was now cooled, and
that he would be duly watched in his native country. Going to Louvain, he met with Francisco Enzinas, one of his
fellow-citizens, of whom we shall afterwards speak, who
urged him not to rush upon certain danger by an indiscreet
or unnecessary avowal of his sentiments, and to confine
himself to the sphere of his proper calling, within which
he might do much good, instead of assuming the office
of a public teacher, or talking on religious subjects with
172 every person who fell in his way. San-Roman promised to
regulate his conduct by this prudential advice; but having
gone to Ratisbon, where a diet of the emperor was then

sitting, and being elated at hearing of the favor which the emperor showed to the protestants,[77] with the view of securing their assistance against the Turks, he forgot his prudent resolutions. Obtaining an introduction to Charles, he deplored the state of religion in his native country, and begged him to use his royal power in restraining the inquisitors and priests, who sought, by every species of violence and cruelty, to prevent the entrance of the only true and saving doctrine of Jesus Christ into Spain. By the mild answer which he received from the emperor, he was emboldened to renew his application, at which some of the Spanish attendants were so incensed that they would have thrown him instantly into the Danube, had not their master interposed, by ordering him to be reserved for trial before the proper judges. He was accordingly cast into chains, and conveyed, in the retinue of the emperor, from Germany into Italy, and from Italy to Africa. After the failure of the expedition against Algiers, he was landed in Spain, and delivered to the Inquisition at Valladolid. His process was short. When brought before the inquisitors, he frankly professed his belief in the cardinal doctrine of the Reformation, that salvation comes to no man by his own works, merit or strength, but solely from the mercy 173 of God through the sacrifice of the one Mediator; and he pronounced the mass, auricular confession, purgatory, the invocation of the saints, and the worshipping of images, to be blasphemy against the living God. If his zeal was impetuous, it supported him to the last. He endured the horrors of a protracted imprisonment with the utmost fortitude and patience. He resisted all the importunities used

77. *Sleidani Comment.* tom. ii. p. 222-236. edit. Am Ende.

by the friars to induce him to recant. He refused, at the place of execution, to purchase a mitigation of punishment by making confession to a priest, or bowing to a crucifix which was placed before him. When the flames first reached him on his being fastened to the stake, he made an involuntary motion with his head, upon which the friars in attendance exclaimed that he was becoming penitent, and ordered him to be brought from the fire. On recovering his breath, he looked them calmly in the face, and said, "Did you envy my happiness?" at which words he was thrust back into the flames, and almost instantly suffocated. Among a great number of prisoners brought out in this public spectacle, he was the only individual who suffered death. The novelty of the crimes with which he was charged, joined to the resolution which he displayed on the scaffold and at the stake, produced a sensible impression on the spectators. A proclamation was issued by the Inquisitors, forbidding any to pray for his soul, or to express a favorable opinion of such an obstinate heretic. Notwithstanding this, some of the emperor's body-guards collected his ashes as those of a martyr; and the English ambassador, who happened to be at Valladolid at that time, used means to procure a part of his bones as a relic. The guards were thrown into prison, and the ambassador was prohibited from appearing at court for some time. It is not unworthy of observation, that the sermon at this *auto-da-fe* was preached by the well-known Carranza, who was afterwards tried by the Inquisition, and died in prison after a confinement of seventeen years.[78]

174

78. Pellicer, *Ensayo de una Biblioteca de Traductores Espanoles*, p. 78. *Act. et Monim. Martyrum*, f. 122, 125, 4to. Histoire des Martyrs,

This event took place in the year 1544.[79] The reformed doctrine had previously been introduced into Valladolid, but its disciples contented themselves with retaining it in their own breasts, or talking of it in the most cautious way to their confidential friends. The speculation excited by the martyrdom of San-Roman took off this restraint. Expressions of sympathy for his fate, or of astonishment at his opinions, led to conversations, in the course of which the favorers of the new faith, as it was called, were easily able to recognize one another. The zeal, and even magnanimity, which he evinced in encountering public odium, and braving so horrible a death, for the sake of the truth, provoked to emulation the most timid among them; and within a few years after his martyrdom, they formed themselves into a church, which met regularly in private for the purposes of religious instruction and worship.[80]

175

---

f. 146-148, folio.

79. Pellicer, following the *Latin Martyrology*, represents San-Roman's conversion to the protestant faith as having taken place in 1545; but the large French history of Martyrs places it in 1540, which is ascertained to be the true date from collateral facts mentioned in the text. Llorente gives no account of San-Roman's martyrdom, but, in a transient allusion to it, (tom. iii. p. 188.) seems to say that it happened in 1540. The *Histoire des Martyrs*, whose authority I am inclined to prefer, fixes on 1544 as the year of his death.

80. Montanus, p. 273. Llorente, ii. 144.

V

Causes of the Progress of the Reformed Doctrine in Spain

BEFORE PROCEEDING farther with the narrative of the religious movement in Spain, it may be proper to give an account of some facts which happened without the kingdom. This will furnish the reader with interesting information respecting Spaniards who embraced the Reformation abroad, and whose pious and enlightened exertions, in publishing the scriptures and other books in their native tongue, had great influence in disseminating the knowledge of the truth among their countrymen at home.

About the year 1540, three brothers, Jayme, Francisco, and Juan, sons of a respectable citizen of Burgos in Old Castile, were sent to study at Louvain, a celebrated seat of education, to which the Spanish youth had long been accustomed to resort. The family name of the young men was Enzinas, though they were better known among

177 the learned in Germany by their assumed name of Dryander.[1] Polite letters had been form some time cultivated
in the university of Louvain, and the students indulged
in a freedom of opinion, which was not tolerated at Paris
and other places where the old scholastic ideas and modes
of teaching were rigidly preserved. Along with a taste
for elegant literature, the young Spaniards acquired the
knowledge of the reformed doctrines. They lived in terms
of great intimacy with the celebrated George Cassander,[2]
who corresponded with the leading protestant divines,
and afterwards distinguished himself by a fruitless attempt
to reconcile the popish and reformed churches. Dissatisfied with the temporizing principles of this learned man,
and the partial reforms in which he was disposed to rest,
the three brothers entered with the most cordial zeal into
the views of those who had formally separated from the

---

1. Encina in Spanish, like δρυς in Greek, signifies an oak. Pellicer
    thinks that Francisco Enzinas adopted the name of Dryander
    for the purpose of concealment, after his escape from prison at
    Brussels in 1545. (*Ensayo*, p. 80.) But we find him subscribing
    Franciscus Dryander to a letter written in 1541. (*Gerdesii Hist.
    Reform.* tom. iii. append. 0. 86.) It was customary at that pe-
    riod for learned men to change their names into Greek ones of
    the same signification; as Reuchlin (smoke) into Capnio, Gerard
    (amiable) into Erasmus, and Schwartzerd (black earth) into Mel-
    anchthon.

2. *Illustrium et clarorum Virorum Epistolæ Selectiores, scriptæ a Belgis
    vel ad Begas*, p. 55, 58. Lugd. Bat. 1617. The letter from Jacobus
    Dryander, inserted in that work, throws much light on his
    character and family.

church of Rome.

Juan Enzinas, or Dryander, the younger brother, chose   178
the medical profession, and having settled in Germany,
became a professor in the university of Marburg. He was
the author of several works on medicine and astronomy,
and acquired a reputation by the ingenuity which he displayed in the invention and improvement of instruments
for advancing these sciences.[3]

Jayme Enzinas, the elder brother, removed in 1541,
by the direction of his father, to Paris. During his residence in that city he became confirmed in his attachment
to the Reformation, and was successful in communicating his impressions to some of his countrymen who were
prosecuting their studies along with him. The expectations
which he had formed from the far-famed university of
the French metropolis were miserably disappointed. He
found the professors to be generally pedants and bigots,
and the students equally destitute of good manners and a
love for liberal pursuits. It was with the deepest emotion
that he beheld the Christian heroism shown by protestant
martyrs under the cruel treatment to which they were exposed. There was something solemn, though appalling, in
the composure with which a Spanish assembly witnessed
the barbarous spectacle of an auto-da-fe; but the wanton
ferocity with which a Parisian mob shouted, when the executioner, with his pincers, tore the tongue from the mouth   179

---

3.   Teissier, *Eloges*, tom. i. p. 199. *Melanchthonis Epistolæ*, col. 817.
     In another letter, written in the course of the same year, 1543,
     Melanchthon bestows great praise on an orrery which Juan
     Dryander had constructed. (Ibid. col. 818.)

of his victim, and struck him with it repeatedly in the face, before binding his body to the stake, was disgustingly horrible and fiendish.[4] Unable to remain in a place where he could find neither learning nor humanity, Jayme Enzinas left Paris and returned to Louvain. Thence he went to Antwerp to superintend the printing of a catechism which he had drawn up in his native language for the benefit of his countrymen.[5] Soon after this he received orders from his father, who entertained sanguine hopes of his advancement in the church, to visit Italy and spend some time in the capital of Christendom. Nothing could be more contrary to his inclinations; but yielding to the dictates of filial duty he set out, leaving his heart with his brothers and other friends in the Netherlands. To a delicate taste and generous independence of spirit, Jayme Enzinas added a tenderness of conscience and candor of disposition which exposed him to peculiar danger in Italy, at a time when the jealousy of the priests was roused by the recent discovery that the reformed tenets had spread extensively in that country. After spending several years in great uneasiness of

---

4. *Jacobus Dryander Georgio Cassandro: Epistolæ Selectiores*, ut supra, p. 55-65. Eustathius a Knobelsdorf Georgio Cassandro: ibid. p. 38-45. Had not the facts been attested by two such credible eyewitnesses we might have suspected the author of the *Martyrology* of exaggeration in his narrative of the shocking scene. Dryander's letter is dated "20 Februarii;" and that it was written in 1541, appears from comparing it with the *Histoire des Martyrs*, f. 119, b.

5. *Epistolæ Selectiores*, p. 66. I have not seen this catechism mentioned elsewhere.

mind, without being able to procure liberty from his father to return, he resolved at least, in compliance with the urgent request of his brothers, to repair to Germany, and 180 was preparing to quit Rome, when he was betrayed by one of his countrymen, who denounced him as a heretic to the Inquisition. The circumstance of a Spaniard being accused of Lutheranism, together with the character which he bore for learning, attracted much interest in Rome; and his examination was attended by the principal bishops and cardinals. Undaunted by the solemnity of the court, he avowed his sentiments, and defended them with such spirit that his judges, irritated at his boldness, condemned him instantly to the flames; a sentence which was loudly called for by such of his countrymen as were present. Attempts were afterwards made to induce him to recant, by the offer of reconciliation to the church upon his appearing publicly with the san-benito, according to the custom of his native country. But he refused to purchase his life on such conditions, and died at the stake with the utmost constancy and courage. His martyrdom happened in the year 1546.[6]

About the same time that Enzinas suffered, one of his 181

---

6. Pellicer, *Ensayo*, p. 78, 79. *Hist. des Martyrs*, f. 159. Beza places his martyrdom in 1545, by mistake. (Icones, sig. Kk ij.) Gerdes (*Hist. Reform.* iii. 165.) calls him Nicolas Ensinas; probably misled by the letter N. put before his name in the *Actiones et Monim. Martyrum*, (f. 151, a.) which merely intimates that the writer of the article was ignorant of the martyr's Christian name. Pellicer calls him "*el doctor Juan de Ensinas*," confounding him with one of his brothers already mentioned.

countrymen and intimate friends met with a still more tragical fate in Germany. Juan Diaz, a native of Cuenca, after he had studied for several years at Paris, was converted to the protestant religion by the private instructions of Jayme Enzinas. Being liberally educated, he had, previously to that event, conceived a disgust at the scholastic theology, and made himself master of the Hebrew language, that he might study the Bible in the original. With the view of enjoying the freedom of professing the faith which he had embraced, he left Paris in company with Matthew Budé and John Crespin, and went to Geneva, where he resided for some time in the house of his countryman Pedro Gales.[7] Having removed to Strasburg in the beginning of the year 1546, his talents and suavity of manners recommended him so strongly to the celebrated Bucer, that he prevailed on the senate to join the Spanish stranger with himself in a deputation which they were about to send to a conference on the disputed points of religion to be held at Ratisbon. On going thither Diaz met with his countryman Pedro Malvenda, whom he had known at Paris, and was now to confront as an antagonist at the conference. To the pride and religious prejudices of his countrymen, Malvenda added the rudeness of a doctor of the Sorbonne, and the insolence of a minion of the court.[8] When informed by Diaz of the change which had taken place in his sentiments, he expressed the utmost surprise and horror; saying, that the heretics would boast more of making a convert of a single Spaniard than of ten thousand Ger-

182

7.   *Calvini Epist.* p. 39; *Opera*, tom. ix.

8.   Seckendorf, *Hist. Lutheranismi*, lib. iii. p. 623.

mans. Having labored in vain, at different interviews, to reclaim him to the catholic faith, he laid the matter before the emperor's confessor. It is not known what consultations they had; but a Spaniard, named Marquina, who had transactions with them, repaired soon after to Rome, and communicated the facts to a brother of Diaz, Doctor Alfonso,[9] who had long held the office of advocate in the sacred Rota. The pride and bigotry of Alfonso was inflamed to the highest degree by the intelligence of his brother's defection; and taking along with him a suspicions attendant, he set out instantly for Germany, determined, in one way or other, to wipe off the infamy which had fallen on the hitherto spotless honor of his family. In the mean time, alarmed at some expressions of Malvenda, and knowing the inveteracy with which the Spaniards hated such of their countrymen as had become protestants, Bucer and the other friends of Juan Diaz had prevailed upon him to retire for a season to Neuburg, a small town in Bavaria situated on the Danube. On arriving at Ratisbon, Alfonso 183 succeeded in discovering the place of his brother's retreat, and after consulting with Malvenda, repaired to Neuburg. By every art of persuasion he sought during several days to bring his brother back to the church of Rome. Disappointed in this, he altered his method,—professed that the arguments which he had heard had shaken his confidence, and listened with apparent eagerness and satisfaction to

---

9.   He had another brother named Esteban, who entered his noviciate, along with Father Ribadeneyra, among the Jesuits, but left the order, and is said to have been killed in a duel (Ribadeneyra, *Dialogo sobre los que se salen de Religion*, MS.: Pellicer, *Ensayo*, p. 74.)

his brother while he explained to him the protestant doctrines, and the passages of scripture on which they rested.
Finding Juan delighted with this unexpected change, he
proposed that he should accompany him to Italy, where
there was a greater field of usefulness in disseminating the
doctrines of the gospel than in Germany, which was already provided with an abundance of laborers. The guile-
less Juan promised to think seriously on this proposal,
which he submitted to the judgment of his protestant
friends. They were unanimously of opinion that he should
reject it; and in particular Ochino, who had largely fled
from Italy and was then at Augsburg, pointed out the danger and hopeless nature of the project. Alfonso did not yet
desist. He insisted that his brother should accompany him
at least as far as Augsburg, promising to acquiesce in the
decision which Ochino should pronounce after they had
conversed with him on the subject. His request appeared
so reasonable that Juan agreed to it; but he was prevented
from going by the arrival of Bucer and two other friends,
184 who, having finished their business at Ratisbon, and fearing that Juan Diaz might be induced to act contrary to
their late advice, had agreed to pay him a visit. Concealing the chagrin which he felt at this unexpected obstacle,
Alfonso took an affectionate leave of his brother, after he
had, in a private interview, forced a sum of money on him,
expressed warm gratitude for the spiritual benefit he had
received from his conversation, and warned him to be on
his guard against Malvenda. He proceeded to Augsburg on
the road to Italy; but next day, after using various precautions to conceal his route, he returned, along with the man
whom he had brought from Rome, and spent the night

in a village at a small distance from Neuburg. Early next morning, being the 27th of March 1546, they came to the house where his brother lodged. Alfonso stood at the gate, while his attendant, knocking at the door and announcing that he was the bearer of a letter to Juan Diaz from his brother, was shown up stairs to an apartment. On hearing of a letter from his brother, Juan sprang from his bed, hastened to the apartment in an undress, took the letter from the hand of the bearer, and as it was still dark, went to the window to read it, when the ruffian, stepping softly behind him, despatched his unsuspecting victim with one stroke of an axe which he had concealed under his cloak. He then joined the more guilty murderer, who now stood at the stair-foot to prevent interruption, and ready, if necessary, to give assistance to the assassin whom he had hired to execute his purpose.[10]

Alarmed by the noise which the assassin's spurs made on the steps as he descended, the person who slept with Juan Diaz rose hastily, and going into the adjoining apartment beheld, with unutterable feelings, his friend stretched on the floor and weltering in his blood, with his hands clasped, and the instrument of death fixed in his head. The murderers were fled, and had provided a relay of horses to convey them quickly out of Germany; but the pursuit

185

---

10. *Y si es asi, la daré*
   Senor á mi mismo hermano
   Y en nada reparare.
So let him die, for sentence Ortiz pleads;
   Were he my brother, by this hand he bleeds.
Lope de Vega, *Estrella de Sevilla.*

after them, which commenced as soon as the alarm could be given, was so hot, that they were overtaken at Inspruck, and secured in prison. Otho Henry, count palatine of the Rhine and duke of Bavaria, within whose territories the crime was perpetrated, lost no time in taking the necessary measures for having it judicially tried. Lawyers were sent from Neuburg with the night-cap of the deceased, the bloody axe, the letter of Alfonso, and other documents; but though the prisoners were arraigned before the criminal court at Inspruck, the trial was suspended through the influence of the cardinals of Trent and Augsburg, to whom the fratricide obtained liberty to write at the beginning of his imprisonment. When his plea for the benefit of clergy was set aside as contrary to the laws of Germany, various legal quirks were resorted to; and, at last, the judges produced an order from the emperor, prohibiting them from proceeding with the trial, and reserving the cause for the judgment of his brother Ferdinand, king of the Romans. When the protestant princes, at the subsequent diet of Ratisbon, demanded, first of the emperor and afterwards of his brother, that the murderers should be punished, their requests were evaded;[11] and, in the issue, the murderers were allowed to escape untried and with impunity, to the outraging of humanity and justice, and the disgrace of the church of Rome, whose authorities were bound to see that the most rigorous scrutiny was made into the horrid deed, under the pain of being held responsible for it to heaven and to posterity. The liberated fratricide appeared openly at Trent, along with his bloody accomplice, without exciting a shudder in the breasts of the holy fathers

186

11. *Sleidani Comment.* tom. ii. p. 458.

met in council; he was welcomed back to Rome; and finally returned to his native country, where he was admitted to the society of men of rank and education, who listened to him while he coolly related the circumstances of his sanctified crime.[12] Different persons published accounts,[13] agreeing in every material point, of a murder which, all circumstances considered, has scarcely a parallel in the annals of blood since the time of the first fratricide, and affords a striking proof of the degree in which fanatical zeal will stifle the tenderest affections of the human breast, and stimulate to the perpetration of crimes the most atrocious and unnatural. The narrative which I have followed was drawn up and published at the time by Claud Senarcle,[14] a noble young Savoyard, who was strongly attached to Juan Diaz, had accompanied him from the time he left Paris,

187

---

12. *Supulvedæ Opera*, tom. ii. p. 132.

13. One of these narratives was written by Malanchthon, under the title of *Historie von Alfonso Diacio*. (Sleidan, ii. 440, not. i.) An ample account is given in *Act. et Monim. Martyrum*, f. 126, b.-129, a. conf. *Sleidan*, ii. 435-441. *Seckendorf,* lib. iii. p. 653-658. *Calvini Epist.* p. 39: *Opera*, tom. ix.

14. Calvin mentions that Diaz had left Geneva, "*cum duobus Senarclenis.*" (*Epistolæ*, p. 39; *Opera*, tom. ix.) Maimbourg imputes the departure of Diaz from Geneva to his dislike of the harsh temper and opinions of the Genovese reformer; one of the fictions of that disingenuous historian, which is refuted by the statement of Senarcle, (*Hist. Diazii*, ut infra, p. 33, 34.) and by the fact that Diaz maintained a confidential correspondence with Calvin after the period referred to. (*Lettres de Calvin a Jaque de Burgogne, Seigneur de Falais et de Bredam*, p. 48, 56. Amst. 1744.)

and slept in the same bed with him on the night before his murder. Its accuracy is confirmed by the attestation of Bucer, who was personally acquainted with many of 188 the facts, as well as with the character of the author.[15] But indeed so far were the Roman catholics from denying the facts, that many of them, and especially the countrymen of Diaz, justified and even applauded the deed.[16] Juan Ginez de Sepulveda, who professes to have received the facts from the mouth of the terrible hero of the tragedy, has given an account of them so completely in accordance with Senarcle's, that we might suppose he had abridged

---

15. *Historia vera de orte sancti uiri Joannis Diazii Hispani, quem eius frater germanus Alphonsus Diazius, exemplum sequutus primi prricidæ Cain, uelut alterum Abelem, nefariè interfecit:* per Claudium Senarclæum, 1546, 8vo. Prefixed to the work is an epistle from Martin Bucer to count Otho Henry, and another from the author to Bucer. Appended to it is a short treatise by the martyr, under the following title: *Christianæ Religionis Summa: ad illustrissimum principem Dominuum D. Ottonem Heinricum. Palatinum Rheni, et utriusque Barvariæ Ducem. Joanne Diazio Hispano autore.*

16. Senarclaeus, *Hist. de Morte Diazii*, p. 169; et *Buceri Epist.* præfix. sig. α 5, b. Bezae Icones, sig. Kk. iij. *Act. et Monim. Martyrum*, f. 138, b, 139, a. Sepulveda expressly says, "the news of the slaughter were disagreeable to none of our countrymen—*de patrata nece nuntius nulli nostrorum ingratus*;" and he adds that the emperor evidently showed, by protecting Alfonso, that he approved of his spirit and deed. (*Sepulvedæ Opera*, tom. ii. p. 132.) Maimbourg, who wrote at the close of the 17th century, condemns the murder, but his narrative shows that he felt little abhorrence at it. (*Hist. du Lutheranisme*, sect. 37.)

that work, in the way of substituting the atrocious moral of fanaticism for the touching sentiments of friendship, charity, and piety, which pervade the whole narrative of the protestant historian.[17] It is humbling to think that Sepulveda was one of the most elegant prose writers who flourished at that time in Spain.

Francisco Enzinas continued, after his brother's departure to Italy, to reside at Louvain. But though he lived on good terms with the professors of the university, he found his situation becoming daily more irksome and painful. Among the learned protestants in the neighborhood with whom he carried on a confidential correspondence were 189 Albert Hardenberg, preacher to the Cistercian monastery of Adwert, which, since the days of John Wessel, the Dutch Wicliffe, had resembled an academy more than a convent; and the celebrated Polish nobleman, John a Lasco, who had left his native country from attachment to the reformed faith, and was eminently successful in diffusing the knowledge of the truth in East Friesland. It would appear that the parents of Enzinas had intended him for the army, to which he was now decidedly averse. In a letter to A Lasco, accompanying the present of an ancient and richly-mounted sword, which he had received from a nobleman, he says: "All the world will, I know, be in arms against me on account of the resolution which, in opposition to the advice of some worthy men, I have now formed to devote myself to literary pursuits. But I will not suffer myself, from respect to the favor of men, to hold

---

17. *Joannis Genesii Sepulvedæ Opera*, tom. ii. p. 127-132. *Matriti*, 1780, 4to.

the truth in unrighteousness, or to treat unbecomingly those gifts which God in his free mercy has been pleased to confer on me, unworthy as I am. On the contrary, it shall be my endeavor, according to my ability, to propagate divine truth. That I may do this by the grace of God, I find that it will be necessary for me, in the first place, to fly from the Babylonian captivity, and to retire to a place in which I shall be at liberty to cultivate undefiled religion and true Christianity, along with liberal studies. It is therefore my purpose to repair to Wittenberg, because that city contains an abundance of learned professors in all the sciences, and I entertain so high an esteem for the learning, judgment, and dexterity in teaching possessed by Philip Melanchthon in particular, that I would go to the end of the world to enjoy the company and instructions of such men. I therefore earnestly beg that, as your name has great weight, you will have the goodness to favor me with letters of introduction to Luther, Philip, and other learned men in that city.[18] He accordingly paid a visit to Wittenberg, where he was warmly received by all, and especially by the individual for whom he had expressed so high a veneration. But he returned to the Low Countries, probably by the advice of Melanchthon, to labor in a work which promised to be of the greatest benefit to his native country. This was the translation of the New Testament into the Spanish language.

Though Spain was the only nation which at that time

190

---

18. Franciscus Dryander Joanni a Lasco Baroni, Lovanii x. die Maii 1541: *Gerdesii Hist. Reform.* tom. iii. append. no. vii. *Conf. Epist. Selectiores*, p. 58.

did not possess the scriptures in the vulgar language, it had not always labored under that deficiency. In the year 1233, Juan I. of Aragon, by a public edict, prohibited the use of any part of the Old or New Testament in the vernacular tongue, and commanded all, whether laity or clergy, who possessed such books, to deliver them to their ordinaries to be burnt, on the pain of being held suspected of here- 191 sy.[19] On the other hand, Alfonso X. of Castile caused the sacred scriptures to be translated into Castilian, with the view of improving the native language of his people; and a copy of that translation, executed in the year 1260, is still preserved in manuscript.[20] Other ancient versions of the scriptures into the Limosin, or Catanolian, and Castilian dialects, are still to be seen, in whole or in part, among the manuscripts in the public libraries of Spain and France.[21] Bonifacio Ferrer, brother of St. Vincente Ferrer, and prior of the Carthusian monastery of Portaceli in Valencia, who died in the year 1417, translated the whole scriptures into the Valencian or Catalonian dialect of Spain. His translation was printed at Valencia in the year 1478, at the expense of Philip Vizlant, a merchant of Isny in Ger-

---

19. Du Cange, *Glossarium, v. Romancium. Constitutiones Jacobi regis Aragonum adversus Hæreticos: Martene et Durand, Veter. Script. et Monum. Hist. Collect.* tom. vii. p. 123, 124.

20. Rodriguez de Castro, *Bibl. Espanola,* tom. i, p. 411-426, where extracts of the translation are given from the MS. in the Library of the Escurial.

21. *Le Long, Bibl. Sacr.* tom. i. p. 361. Paris, 1723, 2. tom fol. Rodriguez de Castro, i. 431-440. *Ocios de Espanoles Emigrados,* tom. i. p. 39.

many, by Alfonso Fernandez, a Spaniard of Cordova, and Lambert Philomar, a German. But, although it was the production of a catholic author, and underwent the examination and correction of the inquisitor James Borrell, it had scarcely made its appearance when it was suppressed by the Inquisition, who ordered the whole impression to be devoured by the flames.[22] So strictly was this order carried into execution, that scarcely a single copy appears to have escaped. Long after the era of the Reformation, it was taken for granted by all true Spaniards, that their language had never been made the unhallowed instrument of exposing the Bible to vulgar eyes; and with the exception of two incidental allusions, the translation of Ferrer remained unnoticed for nearly two hundred years after its publication.[23] At length, in 1645, the last four leaves of a copy of this edition were discovered in the library belonging to the monastery of Portaceli. The number was reduced within a short time to one leaf; but happily this contained the imprint, or final epigraph, indicating the names of the translators and printers, together with the

192

22. Ferdinand and Isabella prohibited all, under the severest pains, from translating the sacred scriptures into the vulgar tongue, or from using it when translated by others. (*Alphonsus de Castro contra Hæreses*, lib. i. cap. 13; apud *Schelhorn, Amænit. Liter.* tom. viii. p. 485.)

23. It is mentioned by Frederico Furio, in a treatise entitled *Bonomia*, printed in 1556; (Rodriguez de Castro, *Bibl. Espan.* i. 448.) and by Cypriano de Valera, in his *Exhortacion al Christiano Lector*, prefixed to his Spanish Bible printed in 1602.

place and year of the impression.[24] According to some authors, the version of Ferrar underwent, about the year 1515, a second impression, which shared the same fate as its predecessor; but of this statement the evidence is less complete and satisfactory.[25]

193

Apparently ignorant that his native country had once possessed such a treasure, and anxious that they should be supplied with it, Francisco de Enzinas undertook a translation of the New Testament into the Castilian tongue. Having finished his task, he submitted the work to the judgment of the divines of Louvain. They allowed that there was no law of the state prohibiting the printing of translations of the scriptures, but expressed their fears that such works would lead to the spread of heresy and disturbance of the peace of the church, and excused themselves

---

24. The imprint has been copied in Bayer's edition of *Antonii Bibl. Hisp. Vet.* tom. ii. p. 214, note (2.); in Mendez, *Typogr. Espan.* p. 62; and in *Ocios de Espanoles Emigrados*, tom. i. p. 36. Along with the imprint, the translation, from Rev. xx. 8. to the close of the book, is given by Rodriguez de Castro, *Biblioteca Espanola*, tom. i. p. 444-448.

25. Frederici Furii Bononia, apud *Le Long, Bibl. Sacra*, tom. i. p. 362. Before meeting with this authority, I was inclined to think that Dr. Alexander Geddes had alluded to the original impression of Ferrer's version, of which he mistook the date, when he says, "A Spanish translation of the Bible was printed in 1516. It has been so totally destroyed that hardly a copy of it is to be found." (*Prospectus of a New Translation of the Bible*, p. 109.) Quere: Was a single copy to be found? According to Furio, the date of printing was 1515.

from either sanctioning or censuring the undertaking, on the ground of their ignorance of the Spanish tongue. The private friends of the translator, who were acquainted with both languages, gave it as their opinion, after examining the work that it would be a great honor as well as benefit to Spain.[26] It was accordingly printed at Antwerp in the year 1543, under the title of "The New Testament, that is, the New Covenant of our only Redeemer and Saviour Jesus Christ, translated from Greek into the Castilian language." The purblind monks, to whom it was submitted before publication, could not proceed farther than the title-page. One of them, whose pretensions to learning were not the least among those of his order, smelled Lutheranism in "the new covenant." The leaf was cancelled, and the suspicious phrase struck out. He next pointed out the palpable heresy in the expression "our only Redeemer." Recourse was again had to the operation of cancelling, and the obnoxious particle expelled. But his success in discovery only served to quicken the censorial organ of the monk; so that the author, despairing to see an end of the process, gave directions for putting the work into the hands of the booksellers.[27]

194

---

26. *Gerdesii Hist. Reform.* tom. iii. p. 166.

27. The work appeared under the following title: "*El Nuevo Testamento de nuestro Redemptor y Salvador Jesu-Christo, traduzido de Griego en lengua Castellana, por Françisco de Enzinas, dedicado a la Cesarea Megestad. Habla Dios. Josue, i. No se aparte el libro de esta ley, &c. M.D.XLIII.*" On the reverse is a quotation from Deut. xvii. Then follows the dedication to Charles V., to which are added four Spanish coplas. The imprint at the end of the work is, "*Aca-*

The emperor having soon after arrived at Brussels, the author presented a copy of the work to him, and requested his permission to circulate it among his countrymen. Charles received it graciously, and promising his patronage, if it were found to contain nothing contrary to the faith, gave it to his confessor Pedro de Soto[28] to examine. After various delays, Enzinas, having waited on the confessor, was upbraided by him as an enemy to religion, who had tarnished the honor of his native country; and refusing to acknowledge a fault, was seized by the officers of justice and thrown into prison. Besides the crime of translating the scriptures, he was charged with having made a translation of a work of Luther, and visiting Melanchthon.[29] To add to his distress, his father and uncles, hearing of his imprisonment, paid him a visit, and participating in the common prejudices of their countrymen, reproached

195

---

bose de imprimir este libro en la insigne çibdad de Enveres, en casa de Estevan Mierdmanno, impressor de libros, a 25. de Octubre, en el anno del Senor de M.D.XLIII." The work is divided into chapters, but not into verses, and is beautifully printed in small 8vo.

28. Soto afterwards accompanied Philip II. into England, and was incorporated at Oxford, 14 Nov. 1555. (*Wood's Fasti Oxon*, edit. Bliss, p. 148.) After taking an active part in the prosecution of the English protestants, he was himself prosecuted, on his return to Spain, before the inquisition of Valladolid, as suspected of heresy. (Llorente, iii. 88.)

29. One fault found with the translation was, that Rom. iii. 28, was put in large characters, which had been done by the printer without any directions from the author. Enzinas was at Wittenberg in February 1543. (*Melanchthonis Epist.* col. 570.)

him for bringing calamity on himself, and dishonor on his kindred. He continued however to possess his soul in patience,[30] employed his time in translating the Psalms, and received many marks of sympathy from the citizens of Brussels, of whom he knew far more than four hundred warmly attached to the protestant faith. After a confinement of fifteen months, he one day found his prison doors open, and walking out without the slightest opposition, escaped from Brussels and arrived safely at Wittenberg; an escape the more remarkable that a hot persecution raged at that time throughout the Netherlands, and the portraits of the protestant preachers, accompanied with the offer of a reward for their apprehension, were to be seen affixed to the gates of all the principal cities.[31] The following extract shows the steps taken against him after his flight. "The inquisitors in Belgium have summoned my guest, the wise, upright and pious Spaniard, in his absence; and from the

196

30. "I am persuaded," says Melanchthon, in a letter to Camerarius, 25 Dec. 1545, "you will feel great pleasure in reading the letter of Francis my Spanish guest, written from his prison in Belgium. His magnanimity will delight you." (*Epistolæ*, COL. 842.)

31. *Melanchthonis Epist.* col. 848. *Gerdesii hist. Reform.* iii. 173. In a letter to his friend Camerarius, 16 cal. Aprilis 1545, Melanchthon says, "Our Spanish friend Franciscus has returned, being set free by a divine interposition, without the help of any man, so far as he knows at least. I have enjoined him to draw up a narrative of the affair, which shall be sent you." (*Epist.* col. 848.) This narrative was printed at Antwerp in 1545. It is inserted at length by Rabus, in his German *Martyrology*, vol. vii. p. 1707-2319, and abridged by Gerdes, in his *Hist. Reform.* tom. iii. p. 166-172.

day fixed for his appearance, we conclude that sentence has already been pronounced against him. He sets out for your town to ascertain the fact, and to learn if there are any letters for him from that quarter. I have given him a letter to you, both that I may acquaint you with the cause of his journey, and because I know you feel for the calamities of all good men. He evinces great fortitude, though he evidently sees that his return to his parents and native country is now cut off. The thought of the anguish which this will give to his parents distresses him. These inquisitors are as cruel to us as the thirty tyrants were of old to their fellow-citizens at Athens; but God will preserve the remnant of his church, and provide an asylum for the truth somewhere."[32] In another letter, written in the year 1546, the same individual says, "Franciscus the Spaniard has resolved to go to Italy, that he may assuage the grief of his mother."[33] Whether he accomplished that journey or not, is uncertain; but in 1548 he went to England, on which occasion he was warmly recommended by Melanchthon to Edward VI, and archbishop Cranmer, as a person of excellent endowments and learning, averse to all fanatical and seditious tenets, and distinguished by his piety and grave manners. He obtained a situation at Oxford; but returning soon after to the continent, he resided sometimes at Strasburg and sometimes at Basle, where he spent his time in literary pursuits, and in the society of the wise and good.[34]

197

---

32. Melanchthon Camerario, 20 Aug. 1545: *Epistolæ*, col. 858.

33. Ibid. col. 874.

34. *Malanchthonis Epist.* col. 494, 522, 911. *Strype's mem. of Cran-*

198   In the same year in which the New Testament of Enzinas came from the press, a Spanish translation of the seven
penitential Psalms, the Song of Solomon, and the Lamen-
tations of Jeremiah, was printed at Antwerp by Ferdinand
Jarava, who, three years before, had printed the Book of
Job, and the Psalms for the office of the dead, in the same
language and at the same place. There exists also a copy of
a Spanish psalter in Gothic letter, without date, but apparently ancient.[35]

The Jews appear to have early had translations of the
Old Testament, or parts of it, in Spanish. In 1497, only
five years after their expulsion from the peninsula, they
printed the Pentateuch in that language at Venice. In 1547
this work was printed at Constantinople in Hebrew characters, and in 1552 it was reprinted at the same place in
Roman characters.[36] In 1553 they printed at Ferrara two
editions of the Old Testament in Spanish; the one edited

---

mer, p. 404. Gerdesii Scrin. Antiquar. tom. iii. p. 644; iv. 666.
Letters from him are to be found in Gabbema, Collect. epist.
Clar. Viror. p. 40; Olympiæ Moratæ Opera, p. 333; Fox's Acts and
Monuments, p. 1628, edit. 1596; and in the Library of Corpus
Christi; Nasmyth's Catalogue, no. cxix. 94. Enzinas was the author
of a Spanish translation of Plutarch's Lives, (Antonii Bibl. Hisp.
Nova, tom. i. p. 422.) and of "Breve Description del Pais Baxo, y
Razon de la Religion en Espana;" which last work, according to
Gerdes, contains the narrative of his imprisonment and escape,
and was printed both in Latin and French. (Gerdesii Florilegium
Librorum Rariorum, p. 111.) Pellicer, Ensayo, p. 80.

35. Rodriguez de Castro, Bibl. Espan. tom. i. p. 449.

36. Rodriguez de Castro, Bibl. Espan. tom. i. p. 448.

by Abraham Usque, and the other by Duarte Pinel. Bibliographers have generally held that the first of these was intended for the use of Jews, and the last for the use of Christians;[37] an opinion which does not seem to rest on good grounds.[38]

At the time that Egidius was thrown into prison, several of his religious friends became alarmed for their safety, and took refuge in Germany and Switzerland. Among these were Juan Perez, Cassiodoro de Reyna, and Cypriano de Valera, who were industriously employed during their exile, in providing the means of religious instruction for their countrymen. Juan Perez was born at Montilla, a town of Andalusia. He was sent to Rome in 1527, as charge d'affaires of Charles V., and procured from the pope a suspension of the decree by which the Spanish divines had condemned the writings of Erasmus.[39] Subsequently

199

---

37. Such is the opinion of Wolfius, (*Bibl. Hebr.* tom. ii. p. 451.) who has been followed by Clement, Brunet, and Dibdin, in his *Ædes Althorpianæ*, tom. i. p. 86.

38. Cassiodoro de Reyna, *Amonestacion*, prefixed to his Spanish translation of the Bible. Rodriguez de Castro, i. 401-408; where the opinion of the writers referred to in the preceding note is examined. Usque dedicated his edition to Dona Gracia Naci; and Pinel to the duke of Ferrara. The latter adopts the Christian era, and in the translation of Isa. vii. 14. makes use of the word *virgen*, whereas the former uses *moza*. But they agree exactly in their translation of all the other passages which have been the subject of dispute between Jews and Christians; and the versions are almost entirely the same.

39. Llorente (ii. 280.) calls him "Jean Perez de Pineda." Beza desig-

he was placed at the head of the College of Doctrine, an endowed school at Seville, where he contracted an intimacy with Egidius and other favorers of the reformed opinions. He received the degree of doctor of divinity in his native country; and his talents and probity secured him a high place in the esteem of the foreigners among whom he resided, first at Geneva and afterwards in France.[40] The works which he composed in his native tongue were of the most valuable kind. His version of the New Testament came from the press in 1556;[41] his version of the Book of Psalms followed in the course of the subsequent year;[42]

200

---

nates him "Joannes Pierius."

40. Pellicer, *Ensayo de Traductores Espan.* p. 120. *Bezae Icones*, sig. Ii. iij.

41. "*El Testamento Nuevo de nuestro Senor y Salvador Jesu Christo. Nueva y fielmente traduzido del original Griego en Romance Castellano. En Venecia, en casa de Juan Philadelpho.* M.D.LVI." It is dedicated, "*Al todo poderoso Rey de cielos y tierra Jesu Christo,*" &c. (Pellider, *Ensayo*, p. 120, 121. Riederer, *Nachrichten*, tom. ii. p. 145-152.) The author's name does not appear in the book; but Le Long says that Juan Perez states, in the prologue to his version of the Psalms, that he had published a version of the New Testament in the preceding year. This prologue was not in the copy examined by Pellicer. Cypriano de Valera says, "*El doctor Juan Perez, de pia memoria, ano de 1556, imprimio el Testamento Nuevo.*" (Exhortacion prefixed to his Spanish Bible. *Conf. Abbate D. Giov. Andres dell' Origine d'ogni Letteratura*, tom. xix. p. 238.)

42. *Los Psalmos de David, con sus sumarios, en que se declara con brevedad lo contenido en cada Psalmo, agora nueva y fielmente traduzidos en romance Castellano, por el doctor Juan Perez, conforme a la*

and his Catechism, and Summary of Christian doctrine, appeared about the same time.[43] They were all printed at Venice. Besides these, he published in Spanish several of the works of his countryman Juan Valdez.[44] Being called from Geneva, and having officiated as a preacher at Blois, and as chaplain to Renée, duchess of Ferrara, in the castle of Montargis, he died of the stone at Paris, after he had bequeathed all his fortune to the printing of the Bible in his native tongue.[45] The task which he left unfinished was continued by Cassiodoro de Reyna, who, after ten years' labor, produced a translation of the whole Bible, which was printed in 1569 at Basle.[46] It was revised and corrected by Cypriano de Valera, who published the New Testament in 1596 at London, and both Testaments in 1602 at Amsterdam.[47] It is no slight proof of the zeal with which the

201

---

verdad de la Lengua Sancta. En Venecia, en casa de Pedro Daniel. M.D.LVII." The work is dedicated, "A Dona Maria de Austria, Reyna de Hungaria y de Bohemia." A Spanish translation of the Psalter, the Proverbs of Solomon, and the Book of Job, had been printed at Lyons in 1550. (Riederer, Nachrichten, tom. ii. p. 146.)

43. Antonii Bibl. Hisp. Nova, i. 757. Llorente, ii. 280. The last-named author, by mistake, ascribes to Perez a translation of the Bible.

44. See above, p. 145; and Pellicer, Ensayo, p. 120.

45. Bezæ Icones, sig. Ii. iij.

46. Miscellanea Groningana, tom. iii. p. 98-100. Rodriguez de Castro, tom. i. p. 464-468.

47. Rodriguez de Castro, i. 468-470. Antonii Bibl. Hisp. Nova, tom. i. p. 234, 235. In 1602, the same year in which De Valera's Bible was printed at Amsterdam, another edition of De Reyna's was

Spanish protestants sought to disseminate the scriptures among their countrymen, that Juan Lizzarago published, in 1571, a translation of the New Testament in Basque, or the language of Biscay, which differs widely from the other dialects spoken in the Peninsula.[48] The versions of
202 the three writers last mentioned did not appear until the Reformation was suppressed in Spain; but they were of great utility to many individuals, and the reprinting of De Valera's translation at a recent period was the means of provoking the Spanish clergy to make the dangerous experiment of translating the scriptures into their native tongue.[49]

---

printed at Frankfort, in 4to. (Riederer, *Nachrichten*, tom. iv. p. 265-270.)

48. The Basque New Testament was printed at Rochelle, and dedicated to Joan d'Albret, queen of Navarre. (Larramendi, *Diccionario Trilingue del Castellano, Bascuence y Latin*, prologo, sect. 20. *Andres dell' Origine d'ogni Letteratura*, tom. xix. p. 239.) It would be improper to pass over another version, as it bears the name of Enzinas, so honorably connected with the translation of the scriptures. In 1708, there was printed at Amsterdam, a Spanish version of the New Testament, "*corregido y revisto por D. Sebastian de la Enzina, ministro de la Yglesia Anglicana y Predicador de la illustre congregacion de los honorables senores tratantes en Espana.*" This translation is the same with that of Valera, except that the contents of chapters are not inserted, and the marginal notes are either omitted or put at the foot of the page. (Pellicer, *Ensayo*, p. 156. Rodriguez de Castro, i. 499-501.)

49. Dr. Alexander Geddes's *Prospectus*, p. 109. Preface by Don Felix Torres Amat, bishop elect of Barcelona, to his Spanish translation

All these versions were accompanied with vindications of the practice of translating the scriptures into vernacular languages, and the right of the people to read them. This formed one of the points most warmly contested between the Romanists and reformers. The Spanish divines distinguished themselves by their intemperate support of the illiberal side of the question; and the determination of Alfonso de Castro, "that the translation of the scriptures into the vernacular tongue, with the reading of them by the vulgar, is the true fountain of all heresies," continued long to be the standard of orthodoxy in Spain.[50] There was, however, one honorable exception. Frederico Furio,[51]   203 a learned native of Valencia, defended the cause of biblical translation intrepidly and ably, first, in an academical dispute with John de Bononima, rector of the university of Louvain and afterwards from the press.[52] This raised

of the New Testament, in 1823. Scio's Bible consisted of no fewer than 19 volumes 8vo. *Of Amat's New Testament*, in 2 vols. 4to, 2000 copies were printed in Latin and Castilian, and only 500 in Castilian alone.

50. *Gerdesii Hist. Reform.* tom. iii. p. 169, 170. So late as 1747, D. Francisco Perez del Prado, the inquisitor general, lamented, "that some men carried their audacity to the execrable extreme of asking permission to read the sacred scriptures in the vulgar tongue, not afraid of finding in them the most deadly poison." (Llorente, i. 481.)

51. He is commonly called Fredericus Furius Caeriolanus, that is, of Seriol, the vulgar name of Valencia.

52. The title of his work is *Bononia; sive de Libris Sacris in vernacu-lam linguam con vertendis Libri duo.*" Basileæ, a. 1556. He has

against him a host of enemies, and his book was strictly prohibited;[53] but he was protected by Charles V., and what is singular, continued during life about the person of Philip II., that most determined patron of ignorance and the Inquisition.[54]

The versions of the scriptures by which the Reformation was promoted in Spain, were those of Enzinas and Perez. In spite of the suppression of the former in the Low Countries, copies of it were conveyed to the Peninsula. Accordingly pope Julius III. states in a bill addressed to the inquisitors in 1550, that he was informed that there were in the possession of booksellers and private persons a great number of heretical books, including Spanish Bibles, marked in the catalogue of prohibited books which the university of Louvain, at the desire of the emperor, had drawn up in the preceding year. And at a period somewhat later, Philip, who governed Spain during the absence of his father, ordered an examination of certain Bibles introduced into the kingdom but not mentioned in the late index; and the council of the Supreme, having pronounced them dangerous, gave instructions to the provincial inquisitors to seize all the copies, and proceed with the utmost rigor against those who should retain them, with out excepting

204

---

commemorated the opposition which he met with, in some elegant Latin verses addressed to cardinal Mendoza. (Schelhorn, *Amœnit. Literariæ*, tom. vii. p. 485, 486.) Furio also wrote encomiastic verses on Castalio's version of the Bible. (*Colomesii Italia et Hispania Orientalis*, p. 102.)

53. *Index Libr. Prohib.* a. 1559. lit. F.

54. *Thuani Hist.* lib. civ. cap. 7.

members of universities, colleges, or monasteries.[55]

At the same time the strictest precautions were adopted to prevent the importation of such books by placing officers at all the sea-ports and land-passes, with authority to search every package that should enter the kingdom. It might be supposed that those measures would have reared an insuperable barrier to the progress of illumination in Spain. But the thirst for knowledge, when once excited, is irresistible; and tyranny, when it goes beyond a certain point, inspires its victims at once with daring and ingenuity. The books provided by the Spanish refugees remained for some time locked up in Geneva, none choosing to engage in the hazardous and almost desperate attempt to convey them across the Pyrenees. But at last a humble individual had the courage to undertake, and the address to execute the task. This was Julian Hernandez, a native of Villaverda in the district of Campos, who on account of his small stature was commonly called Julian the Little. Having imbibed the reformed doctrine in Germany, he had come to Geneva and entered into the service of Juan Perez as amanuensis and corrector of the press.[56] Two large casks, filled with translations of the scriptures, and other protestant books in Spanish, were in 1557 committed to his trust, which he undertook to convey by land; and having eluded the vigilant eyes of the inquisitorial familiars, 205

---

55. Llorente, i. 464, 465.

56. Montanus, p. 217. *Bezæ Icones*, sig. Ii. iij. b. *Histoire des Martyrs*, p. 497. Llorente represents Hernandez as having undertaken a journey from Spain to Geneva with the view of bringing home the contraband books. (ii. 282.)

he lodged his precious charge safely in the house of one of the chief protestants of Seville, by whom the contents were quickly dispersed among his friends in different parts of the country.[57]

57. Montanus, *et Histoire des Martyrs*, ut supra.

VI

Progress of the Reformation in Spain

THE CIRCUMSTANCES attending the condemnation of 206
Egidius inflicted a severe shock on the infant church of
Seville. While the enemies of truth triumphed in his fall,
its friends felt "as when a standard-bearer fainteth." His
release from imprisonment, and the proofs which he gave
of unabated attachment to the doctrine which he had formerly taught, were consolatory to them; but the obstinan-
cy with which he continued to the last to upbraid himself
for his imbecility, together with the restraints under which
he was laid, threw a melancholy air over his instructions,
which had a tendency to discourage those who needed to
be animated by the countenance and advice of a person of
unbroken courage and high reputation. Providence furnished them with such a head, a little before the death of
Egidius, by the return of the individual who had been his
associate in his early labors, and who was unquestionably 207
the greatest ornament of the reformed cause in Spain.

Constantine Ponce de la Fuente was a native of San
Clemente de la Mancha, in the diocese of Cuença.[1] Pos-

---

1. *Antonii Bibl. Hisp. Nov.* tom. i. p. 256.

sessing a good taste and a love of genuine knowledge, he evinced an early disgust for the barbarous pedantry of the schools, and attachment to such of his countrymen as sought to revive the study of polite letters. Being intended for the church, he made himself a master of Greek and Hebrew, to quality him for interpreting the scriptures. At the same time he spoke and wrote his native language with uncommon purity and elegance. Like Erasmus, with whose writings he was first captivated, he was distinguished for his lively wit, which he took pleasure in indulging at the expense of foolish preachers and hypocritical monks. But he was endowed with greater firmness and decision of character than the philosopher of Rotterdam. During his attendance at the university, his youthful spirit had betrayed him into irregularities, of which his enemies afterwards took ungenerous advantage; but these were succeeded by the utmost decorum and correctness of manners, though he always retained his gay temper, and could never deny himself a jest. One of his contemporaries remarked, "that he never knew any man who loved or hated Constantine moderately;" a treatment which is experienced by every person who possesses superior talents and poignancy of wit combined with generosity and benevolence. His knowledge of mankind made him scrupulous in forming intimate friendships, but he treated all his acquaintance with a cordial and easy familiarity.

Notwithstanding the opportunities he had of enriching himself, he was so exempt from avarice that his library, which he valued above all his property, was never large. His eloquence caused his services in the pulpit to be much sought after; but he was free from vanity, the besetting sin of orators, and scorned to prostitute his talents at the shrine of popularity. He declined the situation of preacher in the cathedral of Cuença, which was offered him by the unanimous vote of the chapter. When the more honorable and lucrative office of preacher to the metropolitan church of Toledo was afterwards put in his offer, and thanking the chapter for their good opinion of him he declined it, alleging as a reason, "that he would not disturb the bones of their ancestors;" alluding to a dispute between them and the archbishop Siliceo, who had insisted that his clergy should prove the purity of their descent. Whether it was a predilection for the reformed opinions that induced him at first to fix his residence in Seville, is uncertain; but we have seen that he co-operated with Egidius in his plans for disseminating scriptural knowledge. The emperor having heard him preach during a visit to that city, was so much pleased with the sermon, that he immediately named him one of his chaplains, to which he added the office of 209 almoner; and he soon after appointed him to accompany his son Philip to Flanders, "to let Flemings see that Spain was not destitute of polite scholars and orators."[2] Constantine made it a point of duty to obey the orders of his sovereign, and reluctantly quitted his residence in Seville, for which he had hitherto rejected the most tempting offers. His journey gave him the opportunity of becoming personally acquainted with some of the reformers. Among these was James Schopper, a learned man of Biberach in Suabia, by whose conversation his views of evangelical

---

2. *Geddes's Miscell. Tracts*, vol. i. p. 556. Montanus, p. 269, 282.

doctrine were greatly enlarged and confirmed.[3] In 1555 he returned to Seville, and his presence imparted a new impulse to the protestant cause in that city. A benevolent and enlightened individual having founded a professorship of divinity in the College of Doctrine, Constantine was appointed to the chair; and by means of the lectures which he read on the scriptures, together with the instructions of Fernando de St. Juan, provost of the institution, the minds of many of the young men were opened to the truth.[4] On the first Lent after his return to Seville, he was chosen by the chapter to preach every alternate day in the cathedral

210 church. So great was his popularity, that though the public service did not begin till eight o'clock in the morning, yet when he preached, the church was filled by four and even by three o'clock. Being newly recovered from a fever when he commenced his labors, he felt so weak that it was necessary for him repeatedly to pause during the sermon, on which occasions he was allowed to recruit his strength by taking a draught of wine in the pulpit; a permission which has never been granted to any other preacher.[5]

While Constantine was pursuing this career of honor and usefulness, he involved himself in difficulties by coming forward as a candidate for the place of canon magistral in the cathedral of Seville. There are three canonries in every episcopal church in Spain, which must be obtained by comparative trials. These are chiefly filled by fellows

---

3. *Jacobi Schopperi Oratio de vita et obitu Parentis*, p. 26-28: *Gerdesii Scrin. Antiq.* tom. iv. p. 648.

4. Montanus, p. 283; conf. p. 214.

5. Ibid., p. 279, 283.

belonging to the six Colegios Mayores, who form a kind of learned aristocracy, which has long possessed great influence in that country. No place of honor or emolument in the church or the departments of law is left unoccupied by these collegians. Fellows in orders, who possess abilities, are kept in reserve for the literary competitions; such as cannot appear to advantage in these trials, are provided through court-favour to stalls in the wealthier cathedrals; while the absolutely dull and ignorant are placed in the tribunals of the Inquisition, where, passing judgment in their secret halls, they may not by their blunders disgrace the college to which they belonged.[6] The place of canon 211 magistral in Seville having become vacant by the death of Egidius, the chapter, in accordance with the general wish of the city, fixed their eyes upon Constantine, as the person most fitted by his talents for filling that important office. Egidius had been introduced into it without engaging in the literary competition; but, in consequence of his unpopularity when he first ascended the pulpit, the canons had entered on their records a resolution that the usual trials should take place in all future elections. Constantine had uniformly ridiculed these literary jousts, as resembling the exercises of schoolboys and the tricks of jugglers. Finding him obstinate in refusing to enter the lists, the chapter were inclined to dispense with their resolution, when Fernando Valdes, the archbishop of Seville and inquisitor general, who had conceived a strong dislike to Constantine on account of a supposed injury which he had received from him when he was preacher to the emperor, interposed his authority to prevent the suspension

6. *Doblada's Letters from Spain*, p. 106, 107.

of the law. A day was accordingly fixed for the trial, and edicts were published in all the principal cities, requiring candidates to make their appearance. The friends of Constantine now pressed him to lay aside his scruples; and an individual, who had great influence over his mind, represented so strongly the services which he would be able to render to the cause of truth in so influential a situation, and the hurtful effects which would result from its being occupied by some noisy and ignorant declaimer, that he consented at last to offer himself as a candidate. The knowledge of this fact prevented others from appearing, with the exception of two individuals who came from a distant part of the country. One of them declined the contest as soon as he became acquainted with the circumstances; but the other, a canon of Malaga, instigated by the archbishop, who wished to mortify his competitor, descended into the arena. Despairing, however, of being able to succeed by polemical skill, or by interest with the chapter, he had recourse to personal charges and insinuations, in which he was supported by all those who envied the fame of Constantine, had felt the sting of his satire, or hated him for his friendship with Egidius. He was accused of having contracted a marriage before he entered into holy orders; it was alleged that there were irregularities in his ordination and the manner in which he obtained his degree of doctor of divinity; and an attempt was made to fasten on him the charge of heresy. In spite of these accusations he carried his election, was installed in his new office, and commenced his duty as preacher in the cathedral with high acceptance. But this contest arrayed a party against him, which sought in every way to thwart his measures,

and afterwards found an opportunity to make him feel the   213
weight of its vengeance.[7]

Constantine, while he instructed the people of Seville
from the pulpit, was exerting himself to diffuse religious
knowledge through the nation at large by means of the
press. In the character of his writings, we have one of the
clearest indications of the excellence of his heart. They
were of that kind which was adapted to the spiritual wants
of his countrymen, and not calculated to display his own
talents, or to acquire for himself a name in the learned
world. They were composed in his native tongue, and in
a style level to the lowest capacity. Abstruse speculations
and rhetorical ornaments, in which he was qualified both
by nature and education to excel, were rigidly sacrificed
to the one object of being understood by all, and useful
to all. Among his works were a Catechism, whose highest
recommendation is its artless and infantine simplicity; a
small treatise on the doctrine of Christianity, drawn up in
the familiar form of a Dialogue between a master and his
pupil; an Exposition of the first Psalm in four sermons,
which show that his pulpit eloquence, exempt from the
common extremes, was neither degraded by vulgarity, nor
rendered disgusting by affectation and effort at display;
and the Confession of a sinner, in which the doctrines of
the gospel, poured from a contrite and humbled spirit,
assume the form of the most edifying and devotional pi-   214
ety.[8] His Summary of Christian Doctrine, without being

---

7.   Montanus, p. 284-287.

8.   Montanus, p. 294-297. *Histoire des Martyrs*, f. 502, b. -506, a.
     Antonii Bibl. Hisp. Nova, tom. i. p. 256.

deficient in simplicity, is more calculated to interest persons of learning and advanced knowledge. In this work he proposed to treat first of the articles of faith; and secondly, of good works and the sacrament. The first part only came from the press;[9] the second being kept back until such time as it could be printed with greater safety, a period which never arrived. It was not the author's object to lay down or defend the protestant doctrines, but to exhibit from the scriptures, and without intermeddling with modern disputes, the great truths of the gospel. The work was translated into Italian, and has been highly praised by some Roman catholic writers.[10] But it was viewed with great suspicion by the ruling clergy, who took occasion from it to circulate reports unfavorable to the author's orthodoxy, and held secret consultations on the propriety of denouncing him to the Inquisition. They complained that he had not condemned the Lutheran errors, nor vindicated the supremacy of the bishop of Rome; and that, if at any time he mentioned indulgences, purgatory and human merit, instead of extolling, he derogated from these authorized doctrines of the church, by warning his readers not to risk their salvation on them. When these charges came to the ears of Constantine, he contented himself with saying, that these topics did not properly belong to

215

---

9. It was printed at Antwerp, without date, under the title of "*Summa de Doctrina Christiana*;" and appended to it was "*El Sermon de Christo nuestro Redemptor en el monte, traducido por el mismo autor, con declaraciones.*"

10. Ulloa, *Vita di Carlo V.* p. 237. Joan. Pineda, *Comment. in Fab. Justiniani Indic. Univ.* præf. cap. xiii. sect. 6.

the first part of his treatise, but that he would explain his views respecting them in his second volume, which he was preparing for the press. This reply, backed by the popularity of which he was in possession, silenced his adversaries for that time.[11]

Previously to the period of which we have been speaking, an occurrence took place which had nearly proved fatal to the disciples of the reformed faith in Seville. Francisco Zafra, a doctor of laws, and vicar of the parish church of San Vicente, had long cherished a secret predilection for the Lutheran sentiments. Being a many of learning, he was frequently called, in the character of *qualificator*, to pronounce judgment on the articles laid to the charge of persons denounced to the Holy Office, and had been instrumental in saving the lives of many individuals, who otherwise would have been condemned as heretics.[12] He had received into his house Maria Gomez, a widow, who was a zealous and constant attendant on the private meetings of the protestants, and consequently well acquainted with all the persons of that persuasion in the city. In 216 the year 1555 she became deranged in her intellect, and having conceived, as is not unusual with persons in that unhappy state of mind, a violent antipathy to her former friends, she talked of nothing but vengeance on heretics. It was found necessary to lay her under an easy restraint; but, escaping from her domestic confinement, she went

---

11. Montanus, p. 294, 295.

12. Llorente (ii. 256-7.) refers to De Montes in support of this fact. I do not find it stated by that writer, whom he probably confounded with some other authority.

straight to the castle of Triana, in which the inquisitors held their sittings, and, having obtained an audience, told them that the city was full of Lutherans, while they, whose duty it was to guard against the entrance and spread of this plague, were slumbering at their post. She ran over the names of those whom she accused, amounting to the number of more than three hundred. The inquisitors had no apprehension of the extent to which the reformed doctrines had been embrace in Seville, and could not but perceive marks of derangement in the appearance and incoherent talk of the informer; but, acting according to the maxim of their tribunal, that no accusation is to be disregarded, they resolved to make inquiry, and ordered the instant attendance of Zafra. Had he yielded to the sudden impressions of fear, and attempted to make his escape, the consequences would have been fatal to himself and his religious connections. Instead of this, he, with great presence of mind, repaired on the first notice to the Holy Office, treated the accusation with indifference, stated the symptoms of the woman's distemper, with the reason which induced him to confine her, and referred to the members of his family and neighbours for the truth of the facts. His statement, together with the character which he bore, succeeded in removing the suspicions of the inquisitors, who were persuaded that Maria labored under a confirmed lunacy, and that her representations had no other foundation than the visionary workings of a disordered brain. Accordingly they requested Zafra to take the unfortunate woman along with him, and to keep her under a stricter confinement than that from which she had escaped. Thus did this dark cloud pass away, by the kindness of Providence, which watched over a tender flock, yet not sufficiently prepared for encountering the storm of persecution.[13]

In the meantime the protestant church in Seville was regularly organized, and placed under the pastoral inspection of Christobal Losada, a doctor of medicine. He had paid his addresses to the daughter of a respectable member of that society, and was rejected on a religious ground; but having afterwards become acquainted with Egidius, he embraced the reformed opinions, and recommended himself so strongly to those of the same faith by his knowledge of the scriptures, and other gifts, that they unanimously chose him as their pastor. His future conduct did not disgrace their choice.[14] He was assisted by a friar named Cassiodoro, whose ministry was uncommonly success- 218 ful.[15] The church met ordinarily in the house of Isabella de Baena, a lady not less distinguished for her piety than for her rank and opulence.[16] Among the nobility who at-

---

13. Montanus, p. 50-53. Llorente (ii. 267.) is of opinion that the inquisitors did not entirely discredit the information of Maria Gomez, and that it led to the subsequent discovery and apprehension of the protestants in Seville. When afterwards aroused by new informations, the names mentioned by her might assist their inquiries; but it is not very probable that they would have remained inactive during two years, if they had credited her testimony.

14. Cypriano de Valera, Dos Tratados, p. 249, 251. Montanus, p. 231, 232.

15. Llorente, ii. 264, 270.

16. Cypriano de Valera, ut supra, p. 241. Montanus, p. 210, 211.

tached themselves to it, the two most distinguished were Don Juan Ponce de Leon, and Domingo de Guzman. The former was a younger son of Don Rodrigo, count de Baylen, cousin german of the duke D'Arcos, and allied to the principal grandees of Spain. So unbounded was this nobleman in charity to the poor, that, by distributing to their necessities, he encumbered his patrimonial estate, and reduced himself to those straits in which others of his rank involve themselves by prodigality and dissipation. He was equally unsparing in his personal exertions to promote the reformed cause.[17] Domingo de Guzman was a son of the duke de Medina Sidonia, and being destined for the church, had entered the order of St. Dominic. His extensive library contained the principal Lutheran publications, which he lent and recommended with uncommon industry.[18]

219   Most of the religious institutions in Seville and the neighborhood were leavened with the new doctrines. The preacher of the Dominican monastery of St. Paul's was zealous in propagating them.[19] They had disciples in the convent of St. Elizabeth, a nunnery established according

---

17. Montanus, p. 200. 201.

18. Sepulveda says he was "of the illustrious house of the Guzmans." (*De Rebus gestis Caroli V.* p. 541.) Skinner, in his additions to Montanus, says, "He was bastarde brother to the duke de Medina Sidonia." (*A Discovery and playne Declaration of sundry subtill Practises of the Holy Inquisition of Spayne*, sig. D d. iiij. b. 2d edit. Lond. 1569, 4to.)

19. Ibid.

to the rule of St. Francis d'Assisa.[20] But they made the greatest progress in the Hieronymite convent of San Isidro del Campo, situated within two miles of Seville. This was owing in a great degree to a person whose singular character merits examination.

Garcia de Arias, commonly called Doctor Blanco, on account of the extreme whiteness of his hair, possessed an acute mind and extensive information; but he was undecided and vacillating in his conduct, partly from timidity and partly from caution and an excess of refinement. He belonged to that class of subtle politicians, who, without being destitute of conscience, are wary in committing themselves, forfeit the good opinion of both parties by failing to yield a consistent support to either, and trusting to their address and dexterity to extricate themselves from difficulties, are sometimes caught in the toils of their own intricate management. There is no reason to question the sincerity of his attachment to the reformed tenets, but his adoption of them was known only to the leaders of the Sevillian church, with whom he was secretly in corre- 220 spondence. By the ruling clergy, he was regarded not only as strictly orthodox, but as the ablest champion of their cause, and accordingly was consulted by them on every important question relative to the established faith. An anecdote which has been preserved is strikingly illustrative of his character and mode of acting. Gregorio Ruiz, in a sermon preached by him in the cathedral of Seville, employed expressions favorable to the protestant doctrine concerning justification and the merits of Christ's death, in conse-

20. Montanus, p. 229.

quence of which he was denounced to the Inquisition, and had a day fixed for answering the charges brought against him. In the prospect of this, he took the advice of Arias, with whose real sentiments he was perfectly acquainted, and to whom he confidentially communicated the line of defence which he meant to adopt. But on the day of his appearance, and after he had pleaded for himself, what was his surprise to find the man whom he had trusted rise, at the request of the inquisitors, and in an elaborate speech refute all the arguments which he had produced! When his friends remonstrated with Arias on the impropriety of his conduct, he vindicated himself by alleging that he had adopted the course which was safest for Ruiz and for them; but, galled by the censures which they pronounced on the duplicity and baseness with which he had acted, he began to threaten that he would inform against them to the Holy Office. "And if we shall be forced to descend into the arena," said Constantine to him, "do you expect to be permitted to sit among the spectators?"

221

Yet this was the man who was made the instrument of conveying the light of divine truth into the convent of San Isidro, when it was immersed in the most profound ignorance and superstition. Without laying aside his characteristic caution, he taught his brethren, that true religion was something very different from what it was vulgarly supposed to be; that it did not consist in chanting matins and vespers, or performing any of those acts of bodily service, in which their time was consumed; and that if they expected to obtain the approbation of God, it behoved them to have recourse to the scriptures to know his mind. By inculcating these things in his sermons and in private conversation, he produced in the breasts of the monks a feeling of dissatisfaction with the circular and monotonous devotions of the cloister, and a spirit of inquiry after a purer and more edifying piety. But from versatility, or with the view of providing for his future safety, he all at once altered his plans, and began to recommend, by doctrine and example, austerities and bodily mortifications more rigid than those which were enjoined by the monastic rules of his order. During Lent he urged his brethren to remove every article of furniture from their cells, to lie on the bare earth, or sleep standing, and to wear shirts of haircloth, with iron girdles, next to their bodies. The monastery was for a time thrown into confusion, and some individuals were reduced to a state of mind bordering on distraction. But this attempt to revive superstition produced a reaction 222 which led to the happiest consequences. Suspecting the judgment or the honesty of the individual to whom they had hitherto looked up as an oracle, some of the more intelligent resolved to take the advice of Egidius and his friends in Seville; and having received instructions from them, began to teach the doctrines of the gospel to their brethren in a plain and undisguised manner; so that, within a few years, the whole convent was leavened with the new opinions.[21] The person who had the greatest influence in effecting this change was Cassiodoro de Reyna, afterwards celebrated as the translator of the Bible into the language of his country.[22]

---

21. Montanus, p. 237-247.

22. Llorente (ii. 262.) merely calls him "Fr. Cassiodore," but I have no doubt that he was the individual mentioned in the text.

A more decided change on the internal state of this monastery took place in the course of the year 1557. An ample supply of copies of the scriptures and protestant books, in the Spanish language, having been received, they were read with avidity by the monks, and contributed at once to confirm those who had been enlightened, and to extricate others from the prejudices by which they were in-thralled. In consequence of this, the prior and other official persons, in concurrence with the fraternity, agreed to re-form their religious institute. Their hours of prayer, as they 223 were called, which had been spent in solemn mummeries, were appointed for hearing prelections on the scriptures; prayers for the dead were omitted, or converted into les-sons for the living; papal indulgences and pardons, which had formed a lucrative and engrossing traffic, were entirely abolished; images were allowed to remain, without receiv-ing homage; habitual temperance was substituted in the room of superstitious fasting; and novices were instructed in the principles of true piety, instead of being initiated into the idle and debasing habits of monachism. Nothing remained of the old system but the monastic garb and the external ceremony of the mass, which they could not lay aside, without exposing themselves to imminent and inev-itable danger.[23]

The good effects of this change were felt without the monastery of San Isidro del Campo. By their conversa-tion, and by the circulation of books, these zealous monks diffused the knowledge of the truth through the adjacent country, and imparted it to many individuals who resided

---

23. Montanus, p. 247, 248.

in towns at a considerable distance from Seville.[24] In particular, their exertions were successful in religious houses of the Hieronymite order; and the prior and many of the brotherhood of the Valle de Ecija, situated on the banks of the Xenil, were among the converts to the reformed faith.[25] Individuals of the highest reputation belonging to that order incurred the suspicion of heresy. Juan de Regla, prior of Santa Fe, and provincial of the Hieronymites in Spain, was a divine greatly celebrated for his talents and learning, and had assisted at the council of Trent during its second convocation. Being denounced to the inquisition of Saragossa, he was condemned to penance, and the abjuration of eighteen propositions savoring of Lutheranism. After his recantation, he verified the maxim respecting apostates, by his bitter persecution of those who were suspected of holding the new opinions, and was advanced to the office of confessor, first to Charles V. and afterwards to Philip II.[26] Francisco de Villalba, a Hieronymite monk of Montamarta, sat in the council of Trent along with Regla, and was preacher to Charles and Philip. He waited on the former in his last moments, and pronounced his funeral oration with such appalling eloquence, that several of his hearers declared that he made their hair stand erect. After the emperor's death, a process was commenced against Villalba before the inquisition of Toledo, in which he was accused of having taught certain Lutheran errors. At the same time an attempt was made, in a chapter of the monks

224

---

24. Ibid. p. 249.

25. Cypriano de Valera, *Dos Tratados*, p. 248.

26. Llorente, ii. 160, 161; iii. 84, 85.

of St. Jerome, to attaint his blood, by showing that he was of Jewish extraction. This charge was refuted. But it was not so easy to put a stop to his trial before the inquisitors; all that he could obtain, through the intervention of the court, was, that his incarceration should be delayed until
225 additional witnesses should be found; and while matters remained in this state, he was released from persecution, by the hand of death.[27]

While the reformed doctrine was advancing in Seville and its vicinity, it was not stationary at Valladolid. The protestants in this city had for their first pastor Domingo de Roxas, a young man of good talents, and allied to some of the principal grandees of Spain. His father was Don Juan, first marquis de Poza; his mother was a daughter of the conde de Salinas, and descended from the family of the marquis de la Mota. Being destined for the church, Domingo de Roxas had entered into the order of Dominicans. He was educated under Bartolomé de Carranza, from whom he imbibed opinions more liberal than those which were common either in the colleges or convents of Spain. But the disciple did not confine himself to the timid course pursued by the master. The latter made use of the same language with the reformers respecting justification, and some other articles of faith; but he cautiously accompanied it with explications intended to secure him against the charge of heterodoxy. The former was bolder in his speculations, and less reserved in avowing them. Notwithstanding the warnings which he received from Carranza to be diffident of his own judgment, and submissive to

---

27. Llorente, iii. 85, 86.

the decisions of the church, De Roxas repudiated as un-
scriptural the doctrine of purgatory, the mass, and other 226
articles of the established faith. Besides the books of the
German reformers, with which he was familiar, he circulated certain writings of his own, and particularly a treatise
entitled, Explication of the Articles of Faith; containing a
brief statement and defence of the new opinions. By his
zealous exertions, many were induced to join themselves
to the reformed church in Valladolid, among whom were
several individuals belonging to his own family, as well as
that of the marquis of Alcagnizes, and other noble houses
of Castille.[28]

The protestants at Valladolid obtained an instructor of
greater talents and reputation, though of inferior courage,
in Doctor Augustin Cazalla. This learned man was the son
of Pedro Cazalla, chief officer of the royal finances, and of
Leonor de Vibero, both of them descended from Jewish
ancestors. In 1526 a process was commenced before the
Inquisition against Constanza Ortiz, the mother of Leanor de Vibero, as having died in a state of relapse to Judaism; but her son-in-law, by his influence with the inquisitor Moriz, prevented her bones from being disturbed, and
averted the infamy which otherwise would have been entailed on his family.[29] His son, Augustin Cazalla, was born 227

---

28. Llorente, ii. 228-230; iii. 202-217, 220-1. The leading facts concerning Dr. Roxas, stated by Llorente in the passages referred to,
are confirmed by the Register appended to the English translation of Montanus's work on the Inquisition, by V. Skinner, sig. E.
ij.

29. Llorente, ii. 25-27.

in 1510, and at seventeen years of age had Bartolomé Carranza for his confessor. After attending the college of San Gergorio at Valladolid, he finished his studies at Alcala de Henares, and was admitted a canon of Salamanca.[30] The interest possessed by his father, together with his own talents, opened up to him the most flattering prospect of advancement in the church. Being esteemed one of the first pulpit orators in Spain,[31] he was in 1545 chosen preacher and almoner to the emperor, whom he accompanied in the course of the following year to Germany. During his residence in that country, he was engaged in opposing the Lutherans, by preaching and private disputation.[32]

Spanish writers impute the extensive spread of the protestant opinions in the Peninsula, in a great degree, to the circumstance that their learned countrymen, being sent into foreign parts to confute the Lutherans, returned with their minds infected with heresy; an acknowledgement not very honorable to the cause which they maintain, as it implies that their national creed owes its support chiefly to ignorance, and that, when brought to the light of scripture and argument, its ablest defenders were convinced of its weakness and falsehood. "Formerly," says the author of the Pontifical History, "such Lutheran heretics as were now and then apprehended and committed 228 to the flames, were almost all either strangers,—Germans, Flemings, and English, or, if Spaniards, they were mean people and of a bad race; but in these later years, we have

---

30. Llorente, ii. 222.

31. Illescas, *Historia Pontifical*, tom. ii. f. 337, b.

32. Llorente, ii. 223.

seen the prisons, scaffolds, and stakes, crowded with persons of noble birth, and, what is still more to be deplored, with persons illustrious, in the opinion of the world, for letters and piety. The cause of this, and many other evils, was the affection which our catholic princes cherished for Germany, England, and other countries without the pale of the church, which induced them to send learned men and preachers from Spain to these places, in the hopes that, by their sermons, they would be brought back to the truth. But unhappily, this measure was productive of little good fruit; for of those who went abroad to give light to others, some returned home blind themselves, and being deceived, or puffed up with ambition, or a desire to be thought vastly learned, and improved by their residence in foreign countries, they followed the example of the heretics with whom they had disputed."[33] This important fact is confirmed by the testimony of contemporary protestant writers, with a particular reference to those divines whom Philip II. brought along with him into England on his marriage with queen Mary. "It is much more notable," says the venerable Pilkington, "that we have seen come to pass in our days, that the Spaniards sent for into the realm 229 on purpose to suppress the gospel, as soon as they were returned home, replenished many parts of their country with the same truth of religion to the which before they were utter enemies."[34] It is probable that these authors in-

---

33. Illescas, ut supra.

34. Sermon by James Pilkington, master of St. John's College, Cambridge, (afterwards bishop of Durham at the interring of the bones of Martin Bucer and Paul Fagius; apud *Strype's Memorials*

clude in their statement those divines who were accused
to the Inquisition, and thrown into prison, on suspicion
of heresy, though they were averse to Lutheranism, or, at
most, favorably inclined to it in some points connected
with the doctrine of justification. But there are at least
two striking instances of the truth of their remark. It was
during his attendance on the emperor in Germany, as we
have already seen, that Constantine Ponce de la Fuente decidedly embraced the reformed faith; and Augustin de Cazalla became a convert to it in the same circumstances.[35]

On returning to Spain in 1552, Cazalla took up his
residence at Salamanca, where he remained for three years.
But he kept up an epistolary correspondence with the
protestants of Sevilla; and his office of royal chaplain leading him occasionally to visit Valladolid, he was induced
by Domingo de Roxas to fix his abode in this city. He still
continued, however, to be regarded as a patron of the established faith, and was consulted on the most important
230   questions of an ecclesiastical kind. Soon after his return
to Spain he was nominated by the emperor as a member of a junta of divines and lawyers, who were called to
give their opinion on the conduct of Julius III. in transfer-
ring the general council from Trent to Bologna; on which
occasion he joined with his colleagues in declaring that
the pope was actuated in that measure more by personal
considerations than regard to the good of the church.[36]
He also preached at different times before Charles V. after

---

of Cranmer, p. 246.

35. *Sepulveda de Rebus gestis Philippi II.* p. 55. Opera, tom. iii.

36. Llorente, ii. 222, 223.

his retirement into the convent of St. Juste, when he had for hearers the princess Joanna, who governed Spain in the absence of her brother Philip II., together with other members of the royal family. In spite of the caution which he used on these occasions, his real sentiments were discovered by the more intelligent of those who frequented the court; but they were unwilling to fix the stigma of heresy on a person of so great reputation, and could not permit themselves to believe that he would rush upon certain danger by transgressing the line of prudence which he appeared to have prescribed to himself.[37] In this opinion, however, they were deceived. After his settlement at Valladolid his mother's house became the ordinary place in which the protestant church was assembled for worship. The greater part of his relations were among its members. 231 He could not resist the pressing requests which were made to him to take charge of its spiritual interests; and favored with his talents and the authority of his name, it increased daily in numbers and respectability.[38]

At Valladolid, as at Seville, the reformed doctrine penetrated into the monasteries. It was embraced by a great portion of the nuns of Santa Clara, and of the Cistercian order of San Belen;[39] and had its converts among the class

---

37. Sepulveda, after mentioning that he had heard Cazalla preach at St. Juste, says, *"Animadverti, id quod ex ipso etiam audivi, eum magna solicitudine cavere, nequod verbum excideret concionanti, quod ab æmulis et invidis, quos vehementer extimescebat, ad calumniam trahi posset."* (*De Rebus gestis Philippi II.* p. 55.)

38. Cypriano de Valera, *Dos Tratados*, p. 251. Llorente, ii. 221, 222.

39. Llorente, ii. 229, 240-243.

of devout women, called in Spain beatas, who are bound by no particular rule, but addict themselves to works of charity.[40]

The protestant opinions spread in every direction round Valladolid. They had converts in almost all the towns, and in many of the villages, of the ancient kingdom of Leon. In the town of Toro they were embraced by the licenciate Antonio Herezuelo, an advocate of great spirit, and by individuals belonging to the houses of the marquises de la Mota and d'Alcagnizes.[41] In the city of Zamora the protestants were headed by Don Christobal de Padilla, a cavalier, who had undertaken the task of tutor to a noble family of that place, that he might have the better opportunity of propagating the knowledge of the truth.[42] The reformed opinions were also introduced into Aldea del Palo and Pedroso, in the diocese of Zamora. In the last of these villages they had numerous converts, who enjoyed the instructions of Pedro de Cazalla, their parish priest.[43] Their spread was equally extensive in the diocese of Palencia. In the episcopal city they were taught by Doctor Alfonso Perez, a priest, and patronized by Don Pedro Sarmiento, a cavalier of the order of Santiago, commander of Quintana, and a son of the marquis de Roxas. The parish priest of the neighboring villages of Hormigos belonged to the family of Cazalla, which was wholly prot-

232

40. Ibid. ii. 231, 242.

41. Ibid, ii. 227, 229. Register appended to Skinner's translation of Montanus, sig. E. I. b.

42. Llorente, ii. 227, 241. Register, ut supra.

43. Illescas, *Hist. Pontif.* tom. ii. f. 337, b. Llorente, ii. 228, 233, 237.

estant.[44] From Valladolid, the new opinions were diffused through Old Castile to Soria in the diocese of Osma, and to Logrono on the borders of Navarre. In the last-named town they were embraced by numbers, including the individual who was at the head of the custom-house, and the parish priest of Villamediana in the neighbourhood of Logrono.[45]

The propagation of the reformed doctrine in all these places was owing in a great degree to Don Carlos de Seso. This distinguished nobleman was born at Verona in Italy. 233 Having performed important services for Charles V., he was held in great honor by that monarch, through whose interest he obtained in marriage Donna Isabella de Castilla, a descendant of the royal family of Castile and Leon. De Seso was not less elevated by dignity of character, mental accomplishments and decorum of manners, than by his birth and connexions. While he resided at Valladolid he connected himself with the protestants in that city. At Toro, of which he was corregidor, or mayor, at Zamora, and at Palencia, he zealously promoted the cause of reformation, by the circulation of books and by personal instructions. After his marriage, he settled at Villamediana, and was most successful in diffusing religious knowledge in the city of Logrono, and in all the surrounding country.[46]

The reformed cause did not make so great progress in

---

44. *Sepulveda de Rebus gestis Philippi II.* p. 57. Llorente, ii. 224, 226, 228.

45. Register, ut supra, sig. E. i. a. E. ij. b. Llorente, ii. 227, 238, 407.

46. Illescas, *Hist. Pontif.* tom. i. f. 337, b. Llorente, ii. 235-6, 407.

New Castile, but it was embraced by many in different parts of that country, and particularly in the city of Toledo.[47] It had also adherents in the provinces of Granada,[48] of Murcia,[49] and of Valencia.[50] But, with the exception of the places around Seville and Valladolid, nowhere were they more numerous than in Aragon. They had formed settlements in Saragossa, Huesca, Balbastro, and many other towns.[51] This being the case, it may appear singular that we have no particular account of the protestants in the eastern parts of Spain. But one reason serves to account for both facts. The inhabitants of Bearn were generally protestants; and many of them, crossing the Pyrenees, spread themselves over Aragon, and, at the same time that they carried on trade, found the opportunity of circulating their religious books and tenets among the natives. When violent measures were adopted for crushing the Reformation in Spain, the greater part of them made good their retreat, without difficulty and without noise, to their native country, where the proselytes they had made found an asylum along with them; whereas their brethren who were situated in the interior of the kingdom either fell into the hands of their persecutors, or, escaping with great difficulty, were dispersed over all parts of Europe; and thus the tragical fate of the one class, and the narrow and next to miraculous escape of the other, by exciting deep interest in

234

---

47. Illescas, ut supra. Llorente, ii. 384, 386.

48. Llorente, ii. 401.

49. Ibid. p. 340-343.

50. Ibid. p. 411.

51. Ibid. p. 386, 389.

the public mind, caused their names and their history to be inquired after and recorded.

By the facts which have been brought forward, the reader will be enabled to form an estimate of the extent to which the reformed doctrine was propagated in Spain, and of the respectability, as well as number, of its disciples. Perhaps there never was in any other country so large a proportion of persons, illustrious either from their rank or their learning, among the converts to a new and pro-scribed religion. This circumstance helps to account for 235 the singular fact, that a body of dissidents, who could not amount to fewer than two thousand persons, scattered over an extensive country, and loosely connected with one another, should have been able to communicate their sen-timents and hold their private meetings, for a number of years, without being detected by a court so jealous and vigilant as that of the Inquisition. In forming a judgment of the tendency which existed at this time in the minds of Spaniards toward the reformed doctrine, we must take into account, not only the numbers who embraced it, but also the peculiar and almost unprecedented difficulties which resisted its progress. At the beginning of Christi-anity, the apostles had for some time the external liber-ty of preaching the gospel; and when persecution forced them to flee from one city, they found an "effectual door" opened to them in another. Luther, and his co-adjutors in Germany, were enabled to proclaim their doctrine from the pulpit and the press, under the protection of princes and free cities, possessing an authority within their own territories which was independent of the emperor. The reformers of Scotland enjoyed a similar advantage under their feudal chiefs. The breach of Henry VIII. with the pope, on a domestic ground, gave the people of England the Bible in their own language, which they were at least permitted to hear read from the pulpits, to which it was chained. In France, a Hugonot could not be seized without the concurrence and orders of the magistrates, who sometimes proved reluctant and dilatory. And the same

236 check was imposed on the violence of a persecuting priesthood, in many of the Italian states. But not one of these advantages was enjoyed by the friends of the Reformation in Spain, where the slightest expression of public opinion in favor of the truth was prevented or instantly put down by a terrific tribunal, armed with both swords, and present at once in every part of the kingdom. That flame must have been intense, and supplied with ample materials of combustion, which could continue to burn and to spread in all directions, though it was closely pent up, and the greatest care was taken to search out and secure every aperture and crevice by which it might find a vent, or come into communication with the external atmosphere. Had these obstructions to the progress of the reformed doctrine in Spain been removed, though only in part and for a short time, it would have burst into a flame, which resistance would only have increased, and which, spreading over the Peninsula, would have consumed the Inquisition, the hierarchy, the papacy, and the despotism by which they had been reared and were upheld. These were not the sanguine anticipations of enthusiastic friends to the Reformation, but the deliberately-expressed sentiments of its decided enemies.[52] "Had not the Inquisition taken care

---

52. Authorities for this assertion, besides those which are subjoined,

in time," says one of them, "to put a stop to these preachers, the protestant religion would have run through Spain
like wildfire; people of all ranks, and of both sexes, having
been wonderfully disposed to receive it."[53] The testimony 237
of another popish writer is equally strong. "All the prisoners in the inquisitions of Valladolid, Seville, and Toledo,
were persons abundantly well-qualified. I shall here pass
over their names in silence, that I may not, by their bad
fame, stain the honor of their ancestors, and the nobility of the several illustrious families which were infected
with this poison. And as these prisoners were persons thus
qualified, so their number was so great, that had the stop
put to that evil been delayed two or three months longer,
I am persuaded all Spain would have been set in a flame
by them."[54] I subjoin the reflection of a protestant author,
who resided for a considerable time in Spain, and, feeling
a deep interest in this portion of its history, drew up a
short account of its protestant martyrs. "So powerful (says
he) were the doctrines of the Reformation in those days,
that no prejudices nor interests were any where strong
enough to hinder piously-disposed minds, after they came
thoroughly to understand them, from embracing them.
And that the same doctrines have not still the same divine

---

may be seen in La Croze, *Histoire de Christianisme des Indes*, p.
256, 257.

53. Paramo, *Hist. Inquisitionis: Preface to Spanish Martyrology*, in
Geddes's Miscell. Tracts, vol. i. p. 555.

54. Illescas, *Hist. Pontifical*, tom. ii. f. 451, a. Burgos, 1578. The edition of Illescas quoted in the former parts of this work was printed at Barcelona, in 1606.

238   force, is neither owing to their being grown older, nor to popery's not being so gross, nor to any change in people's natural dispositions, but is owning purely to the want of the same zeal for those doctrines in their professors, and especially for the three great doctrines of the Reformation, which the following martyrs sealed with their blood: which were, that the pope is antichrist; that the worship of the church of Rome is idolatrous; and that a sinner is justified in the sight of God by faith, and through Christ's and not through his own merits.[55]

---

55. *Geddes, Miscell. Tracts,* vol. i. p. 556.

VII

Suppression of the Reformation in Spain

WE CANNOT CONDEMN, either upon the principles of na- 239
ture or revelation, those individuals who, finding themselves in the utmost peril of their lives, chose to forsake
their native country, and to seek abroad for a place in
which they were at liberty to worship God according to
their consciences. Yet it was this step on the part of some of
the Spanish protestants which led to the discovery of their
brethren who remained behind. Their sudden disappear-
ance led to inquiries as to the cause, and the knowledge of
this excited suspicions that they were not the only persons
who were disaffected to the religion of their country. The
divines attached to the court of Philip II. at Brussels kept a
strict watch upon the refugees from Spain who had settled
in Geneva and different places of Germany; and, having
got possession of their secrets by means of spies, conveyed 240
information to the inquisitors, that a large quantity of heretical books had been sent to Spain, and that the protestant doctrine was spreading rapidly in the kingdom. This

intelligence was received in the close of the year 1557.[1]

Roused from their security, the inquisitors instantly put their extensive police in motion, and were not long in discovering the individual who had been active in introducing the heretical books. Juan Hernandez, in consequence of information received from a smith, to whom he had shown a copy of the New Testament, was apprehended and thrown into prison.[2] He did not seek to conceal his sentiments, and gloried in the fact that he had contributed to the illumination of his countrymen by furnishing them with the scriptures in their native tongue. But the inquisitors were disappointed in their expectations that they had formed from his apprehension. His life indeed was in their hands, and they could dispose of it according to their pleasure; but the blood of an obscure individual appeared, in their eyes, altogether inadequate to wash away the disgrace which they had incurred by their failure in point of vigilance, or to expiate the enormous crime which had defiled the land. What they aimed at was, to obtain from the prisoner such information respecting his associates as would enable them "at once to crush the viper's nest," (to use their own words) and set them at ease for the future. But they found themselves mortifyingly baffled in all their attempts to accomplish this object. In vain they had recourse to those arts of deceit in which they were so deeply practiced, in order to draw from Hernandez his secret. In vain they employed promises and threats,

241

---

1. Llorente, iii. 191, 258.

2. Register appended to Skinner's translation of *Montanus*, sig. Dd. iiij. a.

examinations and cross-examinations, sometimes in the hall of audience, and at other times in his cell, into which they sent alternately their avowed agents, and persons who "feigned themselves just men," and friendly to the reformed doctrine. When questioned concerning his own faith, he answered frankly; and though destitute of the advantages of a liberal education, he defended himself with boldness, silencing, by his knowledge of the scriptures alone, his judges, together with the learned men whom they brought to confute him. But when asked to declare who were his religious instructors and companions, he refused to utter a word. Nor were they more successful when they had recourse to that horrid engine which had often wrung secrets from the stoutest hearts, and made them betray their nearest and best-beloved friends. Hernandez displayed a firmness and heroism altogether above his physical strength and his station in life. During the three years complete that he was kept in prison, he was frequently put to the torture, in every form and with all the aggravations of cruelty which his persecutors, incensed at his obstinacy, could inflict or devise; but, on every fresh occasion, he appeared before them with unsubdued forti- 242 tude; and when led, or rather dragged, from the place of torment to his cell, he returned with an air of triumph, chanting this refrain, in his native tongue:

> *Vencidos van los frayles, vencidos van:*
> *Corridos van los lobos, corridos van.*[3]

> Conquered return the friars, conquered return:
> Scattered return the wolves, scattered return.

---

3. *Histoire des Martyres*, f. 497, b. Llorente, ii. 282.

At length the inquisitors got possession of the secret which they were so eager to know. This was obtained at Seville, by means of the superstitious fears of one member of the protestant church, and the treachery of another, who had for some time acted as a concealed emissary of the Inquisition.[4] At Valladolid, it was obtained by one of those infernal arts, which that tribunal, whenever it served its purposes, has never scrupled to employ. Juan Garcia, a goldsmith, who had been in the habit of summoning the protestants to sermon; and aware of the influence which superstition exerted over the mind of his wife, he concealed from her the place and times of assembling. Being gained by her confessor, this demon in woman's shape dogged her husband one night, and having ascertained the place of meeting, communicated the fact to the Inquisition. The traitress received her earthly reward in an annuity for life, paid from the public funds.[5]

243

Having made these important discoveries, the council of the Supreme dispatched messengers to the several tribunals of inquisition through the kingdom, directing them to make inquiries with all secrecy within their respective jurisdictions, and to be prepared, on receiving further instructions, to act in concert. The familiars were employed in tracing out the remoter ramifications of heresy; and guards were planted at convenient places, to intercept and seize such persons as might attempt to escape. These precautions having been taken, orders were issued to the

---

4. *Montanus*, p. 218.

5. Register appended to Skinner's translation of *Montanus*, sig. E. i. a. Llorente, ii. 227.

proper agents; and by a simultaneous movement, the protestants were seized at the same time in Seville, in Valladolid, and in all the surrounding country. In Seville and
its neighborhood two hundred persons were apprehended
in one day; and, in consequence of information resulting
from their examinations, the number soon increased to
eight hundred. The castle of Triana, the common prisons,
the convents, and even private houses, were crowded with
the victims. Eighty persons were committed to prison in
Valladolid, and the number of individuals seized by the
other tribunals was in proportion.[6] When the alarm was
first given, many were so thunderstruck and appalled as   244
to be unable to take the least step for securing their safety.
Some ran to the house of the Inquisition, and informed
against themselves, without knowing what they were doing; like persons who, rushing out of a house which has
taken fire in the night-time, precipitate themselves into
a devouring flood. Others, in attempting to make their
escape, were pursued and overtaken; and some, who had
reached a protestant country, becoming secure, fell into the
snares laid for them by the spies of the Holy Office, were
forcibly carried off, and brought back to Spain. Among
those who made good their retreat, was the licentiate Zafra, formerly mentioned, who was peculiarly obnoxious to
the inquisitors. He was apprehended among the first, but,
during the confusion caused by want of room to contain
the prisoners, contrived to make his escape, and to conceal
himself, until he found a favorable opportunity of retiring

6.   *Montanus*, p. 218, 219. *Puigblanch's Inquisition Unmasked*, vol. ii.
     p. 183. Llorente, ii. 250, 258.

into Germany.[7]

The reader will recollect the reform which the monks of San Isidro had introduced into their convent.[8] Desirable as this change was in itself, and commendable as was their conduct in adopting it, it brought them into a situation both delicate and painful. They could not throw off the monastic forms entirely, without exposing themselves to the fury of their enemies; nor yet could they retain them, without being conscious of acting to a certain degree hypocritically, and giving countenance to 245 a pernicious system of superstition, by which their country was at once deluded and oppressed. In this dilemma, they held a consultation on the propriety of deserting the convent, and retiring to some foreign land, in which, at the expense of sacrificing their worldly emoluments and spending their lives in poverty, they might enjoy peace of mind and the freedom of religious worship. The attempt was of the most hazardous kind, and difficulties presented themselves to any plan which could be suggested for carrying it into execution. How could so many persons, well known in Seville and all around it, after having left one of the most celebrated monasteries in Spain deserted, expect to accomplish so long a journey, without being discovered? If, on the other hand, a few of them should make the attempt and succeed, would not this step bring the lives of the remainder into the greatest jeopardy; especially as the suspicions of the inquisitors, which had for a considerable time been laid asleep, had been lately aroused? This last

---

7. *Montanus*, p. 52.

8. See before, p. 222.

consideration appeared so strong that they unanimously resolved to remain where they were, and commit themselves to the disposal of an all-powerful and gracious providence. But the aspect of matters becoming hourly darker and more alarming, another chapter was held, at which it was agreed that it would be tempting instead of trusting providence to adhere to their former resolution, and that therefore every one should be left at liberty to adopt that course which in the emergency appeared to his own mind best and most advisable. Accordingly, twelve of their 246 number left the monastery, and taking different routes, got safely out of Spain, and at the end of twelve months met in Geneva, which they had previously agreed upon as the place of their rendezvous. They were gone only a few days when the storm of persecution burst on the heads not only of their brethren who remained in San Isidro, but of all their religious connexions in Spain.[9]

It was in the beginning of the year 1558 that this calamitous event befell Spain. Previously to that period Charles V., having relinquished his schemes of worldly ambition, and resigned the empire in favor of his brother Ferdinand, and his hereditary dominions to his son Philip, had retired into the convent of St. Juste, situated in the province of Estremadura, where he spent the remainder of his days in the society and devotional exercises of monks. Several historians of no inconsiderable reputation have asserted, that Charles, during his retreat, became favorable to the sentiments of the protestants of Germany, that he died in their faith, that Philip charged the Holy Office to investi-

---

9.   Cypriano de Valera, *Dos Tratados*, p. 178. *Montanus*, p. 249, 250.

gate the truth of this report, and that he had at one time serious thoughts of disinterring the bones of his father as those of a heretic.[10] Various causes may be assigned for the currency of these rumors. Charles had three years before been involved in a dispute with Paul IV., who had threatened him with excommunication; Constantine Ponce and Augustin Cazalla, two of his chaplains, had embraced the protestant opinions; his confessor De Regla had been forced to abjure them; and Carranza and Villalba, who exhorted him on his death-bed, were soon after denounced to the Inquisition. To these presumptions it may be added, that the manner in which Philip treated his son Don Carlos, and the known fact that he never scrupled to employ the Inquisition as an engine for accomplishing purposes purely political, if not domestic also, have induced historians, from supposing him capable of any crime, to impute to him those of which he was never guilty.[11]

There is the best reason for believing that Charles, instead of being more favorably disposed, became more averse to the protestants in his latter days, and that, so far from repenting of the conduct which he had pursued towards them, his only regret was that he had not treated them with greater severity. When informed that Lutheranism was spreading in Spain, and that a number of persons had been apprehended under suspicion of being infected with it, he wrote letters, from the monastery of St. Juste, to his daughter Joanna, governess of Spain, to Juan

---

10. See the authorities quoted by Burnet, in his *History of the Reformation*, vol. iii. p. 253.

11. Llorente, tom. ii. chap. xviii. art. 2.

de Vega, president of the council of Castile, and to the inquisitor general, charging them to exert their respective powers with all possible vigor "in seizing the whole party, and causing them all to be burnt, after using every means 248 to make them Christians before their punishment; for he was persuaded that none of them would become sincere catholics, so irresistible was their propensity to dogmatize." He afterwards sent Luis Quixada, his major-domo, to urge the execution of these measures.[12] In conversation with the prior and monks of the convent, he took great credit to himself for having resisted the pressing solicitations of the protestant princes to read their books and admit their divines to an audience; although they promised on that condition to march with all their forces, at one time against the king of France, and at another against the Turk.[13] The only thing for which he blamed himself was his leniency to them, and particularly keeping faith with the heresiarch. Speaking of the charge he had given to the inquisitors respecting the heretics in Spain, "if they do not condemn them to the fire," said he, "they will commit a great fault, as I did in permitting Luther to live. Though I spared him solely on the ground of the safe-conduct I had sent him, and the promise I had made at a time when I expected to suppress the heretics by other means, I confess nevertheless that I did wrong in this, because I was not bound to keep my promise to that heretic, as he had of-

---

12. Sandoval, *Historia de la Vida y Hechos del Emperador Carlos V.* tom. ii. p. 829, 881.

13. Sandoval, ut supra, . p. 388. *Sepulvedæ Opera*, tom. ii. p. 542-544.

fended a master greater than I, even God himself. I was at liberty then, yea I ought, to have forgotten my word, and avenged the injury he had done to God. If he had injured me only, I should have kept my promise faithful; but, in consequence of my not having taken away his life, heresy continued to make progress, whereas his death, I am persuaded, would have stifled it in its birth."[14] Nor does this rest merely on the evidence of reported conversations. In his testament, made in the Low countries, he charged his son "to be obedient to the commandments of holy mother church, and especially to favor and countenance the holy office of the Inquisition against heretical pravity and apostasy." And in a codicil to it, executed in the convent of St. Juste a few weeks before his death, after mentioning the instructions he had formerly given on this subject, and the confidence which he placed in his son for carrying them into execution, he adds: "Therefore I entreat him and recommend to him with all possible and due earnestness, and moreover command him as a father, and by the obedience which he owes me, carefully to attend to this, as an object which is essential and nearly concerns him, that heretics be pursued and punished as their crime deserves, without excepting any who are guilty, and without showing any regard to entreaties, or to rank or quality. And that my intentions may be carried into full effect, I charge him to favour and cause to be favoured the holy Inquisition, which is the means of preventing and correcting so many evils, as I have enjoined in my testament; that so he may fulfil his duty as a prince, and that our Lord may prosper him in his reign, and protect him against his enemies, to

14. Sandoval, ut supra, p. 829.

my great peace and contentment."[15]

But though it appears from these facts that the imprisoned protestants had nothing to hope from Charles V., yet their calamities were aggravated by his retirement and the succession of Philip II. That bigotry which in the father was paralysed by the incipient dotage which had inflamed it, was combined in the son with all the vigor of youth, and with a temper naturally gloomy and unrelenting. Other circumstances conspired to seal the doom of the reformers in Spain. The wars which had so long raged between that country and France were terminated by the treaty of Chateau Cambresis, and the peace between the rival kingdoms was ratified by the marriage of Philip to the eldest daughter of the French king. Previously to that event the dissension between the Spanish monarch and the court of Rome had been amicably adjusted. The papal throne was filled at this time by Paul IV., a furious persecutor, and determined supporter of the Inquisition. And the office of inquisitor general in Spain was held by Francisco Valdes, a prelate who had already distinguished himself from his two immediate predecessors by the severity of his administration, and whose worldly passions 251 were unmitigated by the advanced age to which he had arrived. The supreme pontiff, the inquisitor general, and the monarch, were alike disposed to adopt the most illegal and sanguinary measures for extinguishing heresy in the Peninsula.

When only sixteen years of age, Philip gave a proof of his extreme devotion to the Inquisition, and of the prin-

---

15. Ibid., ut supra, p. 863, 881, 882.

ciples on which his future reign was to be conducted. In the year 1543 the marquis de Terranova, viceroy of Sicily, ordered two familiars of the Holy Office to be brought before the ordinary tribunals, for certain crimes of which they were guilty. Though this was in perfect accordance with a law which, at the request of the inhabitants, Charles V. had promulgated, suspending for ten years the powers of the inquisitors to judge in such causes within the island, yet a complaint was made, on the part of the familiars, to Philip, then acting as regent of the Spanish dominions, who addressed a letter to the viceroy, exhorting him, as an obedient son of the church, to give satisfaction to the holy fathers whom he had offended. The consequence was, that the marquis, who was grand constable and admiral of Naples, one of the first peers of Spain, and sprung from the royal stock of Aragon, felt himself obliged to do penance in the church of the Dominical monastery, and to pay a hundred ducats to the catchpolls of the Inquisition, whose vices he had presumed to correct.[16] During the regency of the prince, the Spanish inquisitors in more than one instance obtained the revival of those powers which had been suspended, as at once injurious to the civil judicatures and to the liberties of the subject.[17]

During the negotiation in 1557 between the court of Spain and the Roman see, which ended so disgracefully to the former, Philip wrote to his general, the duke of Alva, "that Rome was a prey to great calamities at the time of his birth, and it would be wrong in him to subject it to sim-

16. Llorente, ii. 84-88.

17. Puigblanch, ii. 272.

ilar evils at the commencement of his reign; it was therefore his will that peace should be speedily concluded on
terms no way dishonorable to his Holiness; for he would
rather part with the rights of his crown than touch in the
slightest degree those of the holy see."[18] In pursuance of
these instructions, Alva, as viceroy of Naples, was obliged
to fall on his knees, and, in his own name, as well as that
of his master and his emperor, to beg pardon of the pope
for all the offenses specified in the treaty of peace; upon
which they were absolved from the censures which they
had respectively incurred. After this ceremony was over, 253
the haughty and gratified pontiff, turning to the cardinals,
told them "that he had now rendered to the holy see the
most important service it would ever receive; and that the
example which the Spanish monarch had just given would
teach popes henceforth how to abase the pride of kings,
who knew not the extent of that obeisance which they le-
gitimately owed to the heads of the church."[19] With good

---

18. Philip was not without a precedent in using such language. When
the deputies of Aragon petitioned for a reform on the Inquisition,
Charles V. answered, "that on no account would he forget his
soul, and that he would lose part of his dominions rather than
permit any thing to be done therein contrary to the honor of
God, or the authority of the Holy Office." (Dormer, *Anales de
Aragon*, lib. i. cap. 26: Puigblanch, ii. 266, 267.

19. The duke of Alva, who had retired before this address, when informed of it, is reported to have said, that if he had been Philip
II., cardinal Caraffa (Paul IV.) should have come to Brussels, and
done that obeisance at the feet of the king of Spain, which he, as
viceroy, had done before the pope. (Llorente, ii. 181-183.)

reason might Charles V. say in his testament, when leaving his dying charge to extirpate heresy, "that he was persuaded the king his son would use every possible effort to crush so great an evil with all the severity and promptitude which it required."[20]

Paul IV. acceded with the utmost readiness to the applications which were now addressed to him by Philip, in concurrence with Valdes, the inquisitor general, for such enlargements of the authority of the Holy Office as would enable it to compass the condemnation of the heretics who were in prison, and to seize and convict others. On the 15th of February 1558 he issued a summary brief, renewing all the decisions of councils and sovereign pontiffs against heretics and schismatics; declaring that this measure was rendered necessary by the information he had received of the daily and increasing progress of heresy; and charging Valdes to prosecute the guilty, and inflict upon them the punishments decreed by the constitutions, particularly that which deprived them of all their dignities and functions, "whether they were bishops, archbishops, patriarchs, cardinals or legates,—barons, counts, marquises, dukes, princes, kings or emperors."[21] This sweeping brief, from whose operation none was exempted but his Holiness, was made public in Spain with the approbation of the monarch, soon after he himself and his father had been threatened with excommunication and dethronement. Valdes, in concurrence with the council of the Su-

254

---

20. Sandoval, *Historia de la Vida y Hechos del Emperador Carlos V.* tom. ii. p. 881.

21. Llorente, ii. 183, 184.

preme, prepared instructions to all the tribunals of the Inquisition, directing them, among other things, to search for heretical books, and to make a public auto-de-fe of such as they should discover, including many works not mentioned in any former prohibitory index.[22] This was also the epoch of that terrible law of Philip which ordained the punishment of death, with confiscation of goods, against all who sold, bought, read, or possessed any book that was forbidden by the Holy Office.[23] To ferret the poor heretics from their lurking-places, and to drive them into the toils of the bloody statute, Paul IV., on the 6th of January 1559, issued a bull, enjoining all confessors strictly to examine their penitents of whatever rank, from the lowest to that of cardinal or king, and to charge them to denounce all whom they know to be guilty of this offence, under the pain of the greater excommunication, from which none but the pope or the inquisitor general could release them; and subjecting such confessors as neglected this duty to the same punishment that was threatened against their penitents.[24] On the following day the pope declared, in full consistory, that the heresy of Luther and other innovators being propagated in Spain, he had reasons to suspect that it had been embraced by some bishops; on which account he authorized the grand inquisitor, during two years from that day, to hold an inquest on all bishops, archbishops, patriarchs, and primates of that kingdom, to commence their processes, and, in case he had grounds to suspect that

255

---

22. Ibid. i. 468.

23. Ibid. p. 470.

24. Llorente, ii. 471.

they intended to make their escape, to seize and detain them, on condition of his giving notice of this immediately to the sovereign pontiff, and conveying the prisoners, as soon as possible, to Rome.[25]

256 As if these measures had not been calculated sufficiently to multiply denunciations, Philip seconded them by an edict renewing a royal ordinance, which had fallen into desuetude or been suspended, and which entitled informers to the fourth part of the property of those found guilty of heresy.[26] But the existing code of laws, even after those which had been long disabled or forgotten were revived, was too mild for the rulers of this period. Statutes still more barbarous and unjust were enacted. At the request of Philip and Valdes, the pope, on the 4th of February 1559, gave forth a brief, authorizing the council of the Supreme, in derogation of the standing laws of the Inquisition, to deliver over to the secular arm those who were convicted of having taught the Lutheran opinions, even though they had not relapsed, and were willing to recant. It has been justly observed, that though history had had nothing else with which to reproach Philip II. and the inquisitor general Valdes, than their having solicited this bull, it would have been sufficient to consign their names to infamy. Neither Ferdinand V. and Torquemada, nor Charles V. and Manriquez, had pushed matters to this length. They never thought of burning alive, or subjecting to capital punishment, persons who were convicted of falling into heresy for the first time, and who confessed their errors;

---

25. Ibid. iii. 228.

26. ibid. ii. 216-7.

nor did they think themselves warranted to proceed to this extremity by the suspicion that such confessions were dictated by the fear of death. This was the last invention of tyranny, inflamed into madness by hatred and dread of the truth. Were it necessary to point out aggravations of this iniquity, we might state that the punishment was to be inflicted for actions done before the law was enacted; and that it was unblushingly applied to those who had long 257 been immured in the cells of the Inquisition.

The next object was to find fit agents for carrying these sanguinary statutes into execution. It is one of the wise arrangements of a merciful providence for thwarting designs hurtful to human society, and for inspiring their authors with the dread of ultimate discomfiture, that wicked men and tyrants are disposed to suspect the most slavish and devoted instruments of their will. The individuals at the head of the inquisitorial tribunals of Seville and Valladolid had incurred the suspicions of Valdes, as guilty of culpable negligence, if not of connivance at the protestants, who had held their conventicles in the two principal cities of the kingdom, almost with open doors. To guard against any thing of this kind for the future, and to provide for the multiplicity of business which the late disclosures had created, he delegated his powers of inquisitor general to two individuals, in whom he could place entire confidence, Gonzales Munebrega, archbishop of Tarragona, and Pedro de la Gasca, archbishop of Palencia, who fixed their residence, the former at Seville, and the latter at Valladolid, in the character of vice-inquisitors general.[27] Both substitutes

---

27. *Montanus*, p. 90, 91. Llorente, ii. 217.

proved themselves worthy of the trust reposed on them; but the conduct of Munebrega gratified the highest ex-
258 pectations of Valdes and Philip. When engaged in super-intending the examinations of the prisoners, and giving directions as to the torture to which they should be put, he was accustomed to indulge in the most profane and cruel raillery, saying that these heretics had the commandment, "Thou shalt love thy neighbor as thyself," so deeply seated in their hearts, that it was necessary to tear the flesh from their bones, to make them inform against their brethren. During the intervals of business, he was to be seen sailing in his barge on the river, or walking in the gardens of the Triana, dressed in purple and silk, accompanied with a train of servants, surrounded by wretched poetasters, and followed by hired crowds, who at one time saluted him with their huzzas, and at another insulted the prot-estants, whom they descried through the grated windows of the castle.[28] An anecdote which is told of him, though trifling compared with the horrors of that time, deserves to be repeated as a proof of the insolence of office, and one among many instances of the shameless manner in which the inquisitors converted their authority into an in-strument of gratifying their meanest passions. A servant of the vice-inquisitor general snatched a stick one day from the gardener's son, who was amusing himself in one of the avenues. The father, attracted by the cries of his child, came to the spot, and having in vain desired the servant
259 to restore the stick, wrested it from his hand, which was slightly injured in the struggle. A complaint was instant-ly made to Munebrega; and the conduct of the gardener

---

28. *Montanus*, p. 92, 93.

being found sufficient to fasten on him a suspicion of heresy de levi, he was thrown into prison, where he lay nine months heavily ironed.[29]

The reader will mistake very much, if he suppose that the holy fathers undertook all these extraordinary services from pure zeal for the truth, or under the idea that their superabundant and supererogatory labors would secure to them an unseen and future recompense. If heretics were visited in this life with exemplary punishment for the sins of which they had been guilty, why should not the defenders of the faith have "their good things" in this life? To meet the expenses of this domestic crusade, the pope, at the request of the inquisitors, authorized them to appropriate to their use certain ecclesiastical revenues, and granted them, in addition, an extraordinary subsidy of a hundred thousand ducats of gold, to be raised by the clergy. The bull issued for that purpose stated, that the heresy of Luther had made an alarming progress in Spain, where it was embraced by many rich and powerful individuals; that, with the view of putting a stop to it, the inquisitor general had been obliged to commit to prison a multitude of suspected persons, to increase the number of judges in the provincial tribunals, to employ supernumerary familiars, and to purchase and keep in readiness a supply of horses in the different parts of the kingdom for the pursuit 260 of fugitives; and that the ordinary revenue of the Holy Office was quite insufficient to defray the expenses of so enlarged an establishment, and at the same time to maintain such of the prisoners as were destitute of means to support

---

29. Ibid., p. 190-192.

themselves. Zealous as the clergy in general were against heresy, they fretted exceedingly against this tax on their income; and after the Inquisition had succeeded in exterminating the Lutherans, it needed to direct its thunders, and even to call in the assistance of the secular arm, against certain refractory canons, who resisted the payment of the sums in which they had been assessed.[30]

While these preparations were going on, it is not easy to conceive, but easier to conceive than describe, the situation and feelings of the captive protestants. To have had the prospect of an open trial, though accompanied with the certainty of being convicted and doomed to an ignominious death, would have been relief to their minds. But, instead of this, they were condemned to a protracted confinement, during which their melancholy solitude was only broken in upon by attempts to bereave them of their best consolation; distracted, on the one hand, by the entreaties of their disconsolate friends, who besought them to purchase their lives by an early recantation, and harassed, on the other, by the endless examinations to which they were subjected by their persecutors; assured to-day that they would escape provided they made an ingenuous confession of all they knew, and told to-morrow that the confessions which they had made in confidence had only served to confirm the suspicions entertained of their sincerity; hearing, at one time, of some unhappy individual who was added to their number, and receiving, at another time, the still more distressing intelligence that a fellow-prisoner, entangled by sophistry, or overcome by

261

---

30. Llorente, ii. 218.

torments, had consented to abjure the truth. A milder tribunal would have been satisfied with making an example of the ringleaders, or would have brought out the guilty for execution as soon as their trials could be overtaken. The policy of Philip II. and his inquisitors was different. They wished to strike terror into the minds of the whole nation, and exhibit to Europe a grand spectacle of zeal for the catholic faith, and vengeance against heresy. Filled with those fears which ever haunt the minds of tyrants, they imagined that heresy had spread more extensively than was really the case, and therefore sought to extort from their prisoners such confessions as would lead to the discovery of those who still remained concealed, or who might be in the slightest degree infected with the new opinions. While they had not the most distant intention of extending mercy to those who professed themselves penitent, and had already procured a law which warranted them to withhold it, they were nevertheless anxious to secure a triumph to the catholic faith, by having it in their power to read, in the public auto-de-fe, the forced retractions of those who 262 had embraced the truth. With this view, the greater part of the protestants were detained in prison for two, and some of them for three years, during which their bodily health was broken, or their spirit subdued, by the rigor of confinement and the severity of torture. The consequence of this treatment was, that the constancy of some of them was shaken, while others ended their days by a lingering and secret martyrdom.

Among those of the last class was Constantine Ponce de la Fuente. Exposed as he was to the hatred of those who envied his popularity, and the jealousy of those who looked upon him as the ablest supporter of the new opinions,[31] it is not to be supposed that this learned man could escape the storm that overwhelmed the reformed church in Spain. He was among the first who were apprehended, when the familiars were let loose on the protestants of Seville.[32] When information was conveyed to Charles V. in the monastery of St. Juste, that his favorite chaplain was thrown into prison, he exclaimed, "If Constantine be a heretic, he is a great one!" and when assured, at a subsequent period, by one of his inquisitors, that he had been found guilty, he replied with a sigh, "You cannot condemn a greater!"[33]

263   The joy which the inquisitors felt at obtaining possession of the person of a man whom they had long eyed with jealousy, was in no small degree abated by the difficulties which they found in the way of procuring his conviction. Knowing the perilous circumstances in which he was placed, he had for some time back exercised the utmost circumspection over his words and actions. His confidential friends, as we have already stated, were always few and select. His penetration enabled him with a single glance to detect the traitor under his mask; and his knowledge of human nature kept him from committing himself to the weak though honest partisans of the reformed faith. The veneration and esteem in which he

---

31. See before, p. 210-215.

32. *Montanus*, p. 287.

33. Sandoval, *Historia del Emperador Carlos V.* tom. ii. p. 829. When told of the imprisonment of Domingo de Guzman, the emperor said, "They should have confined him as a fool!" (Ibid.)

was held by his friends was so great, that they would have died sooner than compromise his safety by their confessions. When brought before his judges, he maintained his innocence, challenged the public prosecutor to show that he had done any thing criminal, and repelled the charges brought against him with such ability and success as threw his adversaries into the greatest perplexity. There was every probability that he would finally baffle their efforts to convict him of heresy, when an unforeseen occurrence obliged him to abandon the line of defence which he had hitherto pursued. Dona Isabella Martinia, a widow lady of respectability and opulence, had been thrown into prison as a suspected heretic, and her property confiscated. The inquisitors being informed, by the treachery of a servant in the family, that her son, Francisco Bertran, had con- 264 trived, before the inventory was taken, to secrete certain coffers containing valuable effects, sent their alguazil, Luis Sotelo, to demand them. As soon as the alguazil entered the house, Bertran, in great trepidation, told him he knew his errand, and would deliver up what he wanted, on condition that he screened him from the vengeance of the Inquisition. Conducting the alguazil to a retired part of the building, and breaking down a thin partition-wall, he disclosed a quantity of books which Constantine Ponce had deposited with his mother for the purpose of security, some time before his imprisonment. Sotelo signified that these were not exactly what he was in search of, but that he would take charge of them, along with the coffers which he was instructed to carry to the Holy Office. Dazzling as were the jewels of Isabella Martinia, the eyes of the inquisitors glistened still more at the sight of the books of Constantine. On examining them, they found, beside various heretical works, a volume of his own handwriting, in which the points of controversy between the church of Rome and the protestants were discussed at considerable length. In it the author treated of the true church according to the principles of Luther and Calvin, and, by an application of the different marks which the scriptures gave for discriminating it, showed that the papal church had no claim to the title. In a similar way he decided the questions respecting justification, the merit of good works, the sacraments, indulgences, and purgatory; calling this last the wolf's head, and an invention of the monks to feed idle bellies. When the volume was shown to Constantine, he acknowledged at once that it was in his handwriting, and contained his sentiments. "It is unnecessary for you (added he) to produce further evidence: you have there a candid and full confession of my belief. I am in your hands; do with me as seemeth to you good."[34]

No arts or threatenings could prevail on him to give any information respecting his associates. With the view of inducing the other prisoners to plead guilty, the agents of the Holy Office circulated the report that the had informed against them when put to the question; and they even suborned witnesses to depone that they had heard his cries on the rack, though he never endured that inhuman mode of examination. By what motives the judges were restrained from subjecting him to it, is uncertain. I can only conjecture that it proceeded from respect to the feelings of the emperor; for, soon after his death, Constantine

---

34. *Histoire des Martyrs*, f. 502, a. *Montanus*, p. 239, 290.

was removed from the apartment which he had hitherto occupied, and thrust into a low, damp, and noisome vault, where he endured more than his brethren did from the application of the engines of torture. Oppressed and worn out with a mode of living so different from what he had been used to, he was heard to exclaim, "O my God, were 266 there no Scythians, or cannibals, or pagans still more savage, that thou hast permitted me to fall into the hands of these baptized fiends?" He could not remain long in such a situation. Putrid air and unwholesome diet, together with grief for the ruin of the reformed cause in his native country, brought on a dysentery, which put an end to his days, after he had been nearly two years in confinement.[35]

Not satisfied with wreaking their vengeance on him when alive, his adversaries circulated the report that he had put an end to his own life by opening a vein with a piece of broken glass; and ballads grounded on this fabricated story, and containing other slanders, were indecently hawked through the streets of Seville. Had there been the least foundation for this report, we may be sure the inquisitors would have taken care to verify it, by ordering an inquest to be held on the dead body. But the calumny was refuted by the testimony of a young monk of San Isidro, named Fernando, who being providentially confined in the same cell with Constantine, ministered to him during his sickness, and closed his eyes in peace.[36]

---

35. *Montanus*, p. 287-292. Llorente, ii. 275-277.

36. Cypriano de Valera, *Dos Tratados*, p. 251, 252. *Montanus*, p. 291, 292. Paramo mentions the calumny hesitatingly. (*Hist. Inquis.* lib. ii. tit. iii. cap. 5; apud Puigblanch, vol. ii. p. 210.) Illescas

The slanders which were at this time so industriously propagated against him, only serve to show the anxiety of the inquisitors to blast his fame, and the dread which they 267 felt lest the reformed opinions should gain credit from the circumstance of their having been embraced by a person of so great eminence and popularity.[37] In this object, however, they did not succeed altogether to their wish. This appeared when his effigy and bones were brought out in the public auto-de-fe celebrated at Seville on the 22d of December 1560. The effigies of such heretics as had escaped from justice, by flight or by death, usually consisted of a shapeless piece of patch-work surmounted by a head; that of Constantine Ponce consisted of a regular human figure, complete in all its parts, dressed after the manner in which he appeared in public, and representing him in his most common attitude of preaching, with one arm resting on the pulpit and the other elevated. The production of this figure in the spectacle, when his sentence was about to be read, excited a lively recollection of a preacher so popular, and drew from the spectators an expression of feeling by no means pleasing to the inquisitors. In consequence of this they caused it to be withdrawn from the

---

states it as a mere report. (*Hist. Pontif.* tom. ii. f. 451, a.)

37. The slanders referred to are contained int he work of Illescas. (*Historia Pontifical*, ut supra.) But this is no proof that they were believed by that author; for, as we shall afterwards see, his original history was suppressed, and he was obliged to write another, agreeably to the instructions of the inquisitors, and to insert in it statements the very opposite of those which he had formerly published.

prominent situation which it occupied, and to be brought near to their own platform, where they commenced the reading of the articles of the libel on which Constantine had been condemned. The people, displeased at this step, 268 and not hearing what was read, began to murmur; upon which Calderon, who, as mayor of the city, presided on the occasion, desired the acting secretary to go to the pulpit provided for that part of the ceremony. This intimation being disregarded, the murmurs were renewed, and the mayor, raising his voice, ordered the service to be suspended. The inquisitors were obliged to restore the effigy to its former place, and to recommence the reading of the sentence in the audience of the people; but the secretary was instructed, after naming a few of the errors into which the deceased had fallen, to conclude by saying, that he had vented others so horrible and impious that they could not be heard without pollution by vulgar ears. After this the effigy was sent to the house of the Inquisition, and another of ordinary construction was conveyed to the stake to be burnt along with the bones of Constantine. The inquisitors were not a little puzzled how to act respecting his works, which had already been printed by their approbation; but they at last agreed to prohibit them, "not because they had found any thing in them worthy of condemnation," as their sentence runs, "but because it was not fit that any honorable memorial of a man doomed to infamy should be transmitted to posterity."[38] But they had a still more delicate task to perform. The history of a voy- 269 age to Flanders by Philip II. when prince of Asturias, had been printed at Madrid by royal authority, in which his

---

38. *Montanus*, p. 293, 294, 297. Llorente, ii. 278, 279.

chaplain Constantine was described as "the greatest philosopher, the pro-foundest divine, and the most eloquent
preacher, who has been in Spain for many ages." Whether
Philip himself gave information of this work, we know
not; but there can be no doubt that he would have run the
risk of excommunication by retaining it in his library, after
it was stigmatized by the inquisitorial censors of the press.
They ordered all the copies of the book to be delivered
to them, that they might delete the obnoxious panegyric;
"and on this passage," says one who afterwards procured a
copy of the History in Spain, "the expurgator of the book,
which is in my hands, was so liberal of his ink, that I had
much ado to read it."[39]

Constantine Ponce was not the only protestant who
fell a sacrifice to the noxious vapors and ordure of the
inquisitorial prisons. This was also the fate of Olmedo,
a man distinguished for his learning and piety, who fell
into the hands of the inquisitors of Seville, and was often heard to exclaim, that there was no species of torture
which he would not endure in preference to the horrors of
his present situation.[40] Considering the treatment which
270 the prisoners received, it is wonderful that many of them
were not driven to distraction. One individual only, a female, had recourse to the desperate remedy of shortening
her days. Juana Sanchez, a beata, after having long kept in
prison at Valladolid, was found guilty of heresy. Coming
to the knowledge of her sentence before it was formally
intimated to her, she cut her throat with a pair of scissors,

---

39. *Geddes, Miscell. Tracts*, vol. i. p. 567.

40. *Montanus*, p. 104, 105. Cypriano de Valera, *Dos Tratados*, p. 250.

and died of the wound in the course of a few days. During the interval every effort was employed by the friars to induce her, not to repent of her suicide, but to recant the errors which she had cherished. She repulsed them with indignation, as monsters equally devoid of humanity and religion.[41]

I must again refer my readers to the common histories of the Inquisition, for information as to the modes of torture and other cruel devices used for procuring evidence to convict those who were imprisoned on a charge of heresy. One or two instances, however, are of such a character that it would be unpardonable to omit them in this place. Among the protestants seized at Seville was the widow of Fernando Nugnez, a native of the town of Lepe, with three of her daughters and a married sister. A there was no evidence against them, they were put to the torture, but refused to inform against one another. Upon this the presiding inquisitor called one of the young women into the audience-chamber, and after conversing with her for some time, professed an attachment to her person. Having repeated this at another interview, he told her, that he could be of no service to her unless she imparted to him the whole facts of her case; but if she intrusted him with these, he would manage the affair in such a way as that she and all her friends should be set at liberty. Falling into the snare, the unsuspecting girl confessed to him that she had at different times conversed with her mother, sisters, and aunt, on the Lutheran doctrines. The wretch immediately brought her into court, and obliged her to declare judi-

271

---

41. Llorente, ii. 240.

cially what she had owned to him in private. Nor was this all: under the pretence that her confession was not sufficiently ample and ingenuous, she was put to the torture by the most excruciating engines, the pulley and the wooden horse; by which means evidence was extorted from her, which led, not only to the condemnation of herself and her relations, but also to the seizure and conviction of others who afterwards perished in the flames.[42] Another instance relates to a young countryman of our own. An English vessel, which had entered the port of St. Lucar, was visited by the familiars of the Inquisition, and several of her crew, who, with the frankness of British seamen, avowed them-

272 selves protestants, were seized before they came on shore. Along with them the familiars conveyed to prison a boy of twelve years of age, the son of a respectable merchant to whom the principal part of the cargo belonged. The pretext for his apprehension was, that an English psalm-book was found in his portmanteau; but there is reason to believe that the real ground was the hope of extorting from the father a rich ransom for his son's liberation. Having been piously educated, the youth was observed to be regular in his devotions, and to relieve the irksomeness of his confinement by occasionally singing one of the psalms which he had committed to memory. Both of these were high offenses; for every piece of devotion not conducted under the direction of its ghostly agents, and even every

---

42. *Montanus*, p. 82-85. Llorente has corrected a mistake of Monta-
    nus as to the degrees of consanguinity among these female pris-
    oners, and by doing this confirms the general statement of the
    protestant historian, while he passes over some of the aggravating
    circumstances of the case. (Tom. ii. p. 286.)

mark of cheerfulness on the part of the prisoners, is strictly prohibited within the gloomy walls of the Holy Office.[43] On the report of the jailer, the boy's confinement was rendered more severe; in consequence of which he lost the use of both his limbs, and it was found necessary, for the preservation of his life, to remove him to the public hospital.[44]

So shameful were the measures taken for procuring the conviction of the prisoners at this time, that a legal investigation of the procedure in the inquisitorial tribunals was afterwards demanded by persons of great respectability in the church. In 1560, Senor Enriquez, an ecclesiastic of rank in the collegiate church of Valladolid, presented to 273 Philip a remonstrance against the inquisition of that city, in which he charged it with tyranny and avarice. Among other things he asserted, that in the cause of Cazalla the officers had allowed the nuns, who like him were imprisoned for Lutheranism, to converse together, that, by confirming one another in their errors, the judged might have it in their power to condemn them, and thus to confiscate their property. Having accomplished the object which they had in view, they changed their measures, kept the prisoners apart, and, by examinations and visits, promises and threatenings, tried every method to induce them to recant and die in the bosom of the church.[45]

Nearly two years having been spent in the previous

---

43. *Montanus*, p. 116-7.

44. Ibid. p. 119-121.

45. Original Proceedings against Cazalla, taken from the archives of the tribunal of Valladolid: Puigblanch, ii. 273. Llorente, iii. 202-217.

290 | THE SPANISH REFORMATION IN SPAIN

steps, the time was considered as come, according to Spanish ideas of unity of action, for the exhibition of the last scene of the horrible tragedy. Orders were accordingly issued by the council of the Supreme for the celebration of public autos-de-fe, under the direction of the several tribunals of inquisition through the kingdom. Those which took place in Seville and Valladolid were the most noted for the pomp with which they were solemnized, and for the number and rank of their victims. Before describing these, it may be proper to give the reader a general idea of the nature of these exhibitions, and the order in which they were usually conducted.

An auto-de-fe, or act of faith, was either particular or general. In the particular auto, or autillo, as it is called, the offender appeared before the inquisitors in their hall, either alone or in the presence of a select number of witnesses, and had his sentence intimated to him. A general auto, in which a number of heretics were brought out, was performed with the most imposing solemnity, and formed an imitation of an ancient Roman triumph, combined with the last judgment.[46] It was always celebrated on a

---

46. The last-mentioned resemblance is noticed in a letter written by a Moor in Spain to a friend in Africa, giving him an account of the sufferings of his countrymen from the Inquisition: "After this they meet in the square of Hatabin, and there having erected a large stage, they make all resemble the day of judgment; and he that reconciles himself to them is clothed in a yellow mantle, and the rest are carried to the flames with effigies and horrible figures." (Marmol, *Historia del Rebelion del Reyno de Granada*, lib. iii. cap. 3.)

Sunday or holyday, in the largest church, but more frequently in the most spacious square, of the town in which it happened to be held. Intimation of it was publicly made beforehand in all the churches and religious houses in the neighbourhood. The attendance of the civil authorities as well as of the clergy, secular and regular, was required; and, with the view of attracting the multitude, an indulgence of forty days was proclaimed to all who should witness the ceremonies of the act.

On the evening preceding the auto, such of the prisoners as were penitent, and were to suffer a punishment milder than death, were assembled, the males in one apartment of the prison, and the females in another, when they had their respective sentences intimated to the. At midnight a confessor entered the cell of the prisoners who were sentenced to the stake, and intimated to them for the first time the fate which awaited them, accompanying the intimation with earnest exhortations to recant their errors, and die reconciled to the church; in which case they obtained the favor of being strangled before their bodies were committed to the flames. On such occasions the most heart-rending scenes sometimes took place.

Early on the following morning the bells of all the churches began to toll, when the officials of the Inquisition repaired to the prison, and having assembled the prisoners, clothed them in the several dresses in which they were to make their appearance at the spectacle. Those who were found suspected of having erred in a slight degree were simply clothed in black. The other prisoners wore a sanbenito, or species of loose vest of yellow cloth, called zamarra in Spanish. On the sanbenito of those who were

275

to be strangled were painted flames burning downwards, which the Spaniards call fuego revolto to intimate that they had escaped the fire. The sanbenito of those who were doomed to be burnt alive was covered with figures of flames burning upwards, around which were painted dev-
276 ils carrying fagots, or fanning the fire. Similar marks of infamy appeared on the pasteboard cap, called coroza, which was put on their heads. After this ceremony was over, they were desired to partake of a sumptuous breakfast, which, on their refusal, was devoured by the menials of the office.

The persons who were to take part in the ceremony being all assembled in the court of the prison, the procession moved on, generally in the following order. Preceded by a band of soldiers to clear the way, came a certain number of priests in their surplices, attended by a company of young persons, such as the boys of the college of Doctrine in Seville, who chanted the liturgy in alternate choruses. They were followed by the prisoners, arranged in different classes according to the degrees of their supposed delinquencies, the most guilty being placed last, having either extinguished torches or else crosses in their hands, and halters suspended from their necks. Every prisoner was guarded by two familiars, and, in addition to this, those who were condemned to die were attended each by two friars. After the prisoners came the local magistrates, the judges, and officers of state, accompanied by a train of nobility on horseback. They were succeeded by the secular and monastic clergy. At some distance from these were to be seen moving forward, in slow and solemn pomp, the members of the Holy Office, the persons who principally shared the triumph of the day, preceded by their fiscal,

bearing the standard of the Inquisition, composed of red 277
silk damask, on which the names and insignia of pope Sixtus IV. and Ferdinand the Catholic, the founders of the
tribunal, were conspicuous, and surmounted by a crucifix
of massive silver, overlaid with gold, which was held in the
highest veneration by the populace. They were followed by
the familiars on horseback, forming their body-guard, and
including many of the principal gentry of the country as
honorary members. The procession was closed by an immense concourse of the common people, who advanced
without any regular order.

Having arrived at the place of the auto, the inquisitors
ascended the platform erected for their reception, and the
prisoners were conducted to another which was placed opposite to it. The service commenced with a sermon, usually preached by some distinguished prelate; after which the
clerk of the tribunal read the sentences of the penitents,
who, on their knees, and with hands laid on the missal,
repeated their confessions. The presiding inquisitor then
descended from the throne on which he sat, and advancing to the altar, absolved the penitents a culpa, leaving
them under the obligation to bear the several punishments
to which he had been adjudged, whether these consisted
of penances, banishment, whipping, hard labour, or imprisonment. He then administered an oath to all who were
present at the spectacle, binding them to live and die in
the communion of the Roman church, and to uphold and
defend, against all its adversaries, the tribunal of the Holy 278
Inquisition; during which ceremony the people were to be
seen all at once on their knees in the streets. The more tragical part of the scene now followed. The sentences of those

who were doomed to die having been publicly read, such of them as were in holy orders were publicly degraded, by being stripped, piece by piece, of their priestly vestments; a ceremony which was performed with every circumstance calculated to expose them to ignominy and execration in the eyes of the superstitious beholders. After this they were formally delivered over to the secular judges, to suffer the punishment awarded to heretics by the civil law. It was on this occasion that the inquisitors performed that impious farce which has excited the indignation of all in whose breasts fanaticism, or some worse principle, has not extinguished every sentiment of common feeling. When they delivered the prisoner into the hands of the secular judges whom they had summoned to receive him, they besought them to treat him with clemency and compassion.[47] This they did to escape falling under the censure of *irregularity*, 279 which the canons of the church had denounced against ecclesiastics who should be accessory to the inflicting of any bodily injury. Yet they not only knew what would be the consequence of their act, but had taken all the precautions necessary for securing it.

---

47. The protestant historian of the inquisition, *De Montes*, states the matter thus: when the person who is relaxed has confessed, the inquisitors, on delivering him to the secular judges, "beseech them to treat him with much commiseration, and not to break a bone of his body, nor shed his blood;" but when he is obstinate, they "beseech them, if he shall show any symptoms of true repentance, to treat him with much commiseration." &c. (*Montanus*, p. 148.) I do not observe any such distinction in the accounts of the popish historians. (Llorente, ii. 250-253. Puigblanch, i. 279-281.)

Five days before the auto-de-fe, they acquainted the ordinary royal judge with the number of prisoners to be delivered over to him, in order that the proper quantity of stakes, wood, and every thing else requisite for the execution, might be in readiness. The prisoners once declared by the inquisitors to be impenitent or relapsed heretics, nothing was competent to the magistrate but to pronounce the sentence adjudging them to the flames; and had he presumed in any instance to change the sentence of death into perpetual imprisonment, though it were in one of the remotest forts of Asia, Africa, or America, he would soon have felt the vengeance of the Holy Office.[48] Besides, the statues adjudging heretics to the fire had been confirmed by numerous bulls of popes, which commanded the inquisitors to watch over their exact observance. And in accordance with this, they, at every auto-de-fe, required the magistrates to swear that they would faithfully execute the sentences against the persons of heretics, without delay, "in the way and manner prescribed by the sacred canons, and the laws which treated on the subject."[49] Were it necessary to say more on this topic, we might add that the very appearance of the prisoners, when brought out in the public spectacle, proclaimed the unblushing hypocrisy of the inquisitors.[50] They implored the secular judge to treat 280

---

48. Llorente, ii. 253, 254. Puigblanch, i. 350-353.

49. Puigblanch, i. 351, 352.

50. With the view of preventing such appearances as much as possible, the inquisitors have laid it down as a rule, that no prisoner shall be tortured within fifteen days of the auto-de-fe. The Portuguese regulation on this head is very plain in assigning the rea-

with lenity and compassion persons whom they themselves had worn to skeletons by a cruel incarceration,—
not to shed the blood of him from whose body they had
often made the blood to spring, nor to break a bone of her
whose tender limbs were already distorted and mangled by
their hellish tortures![51]

The penitents having been remanded to their several
prisons, the other prisoners were led away to execution.
Some writers have spoken as if they were executed on the
spot where their sentence was read, and in the presence of
all who had witnessed the preceding parts of the spectacle.
This however is a mistake. The stakes were erected without
the walls of the town where the auto-de-fe was celebrated; but though the last act was deemed too horrid to be
exhibited on the same stage with those which we have de-
281   scribed, yet it was performed publicly, and was witnessed,
not only by the mob, but by persons who from their rank
and station might have been expected to turn with disgust
from so revolting a spectacle.

Seville contained by far the greatest number of protestants under confinement; and the long period during
which its prisons has been crowded gave it a claim to the

---

son: "*por naõ hirem os prezos a elle mostrando os sinaes do tormento
lho daraõ no potro.*" Yet their anxiety to obtain information often
induces them to transgress this prudential regulation; in which
cases they have recourse to the rack, which does not distort the
body like the pulley. (*Puigblanch*, i. 294.)

51. The apologies made for this hypocritical deprecation, not only
by De Castro in the sixteenth, but by several writers in the nineteenth century, may be seen in *Puigblanch*, vol. i. p. 354-359.

benefit of the first jail delivery. Valladolid, however, was preferred; for no other reason, apparently, than that it afforded the Inquisition the opportunity of exhibiting the greatest proportion of criminals of whom it could boast as converts from heresy.

The first public auto-de-fe of protestants was accordingly celebrated at Valladolid on the 21st of May 1559, being Trinity Sunday, in the presence of Don Carlos the heir apparent to the crown, and his aunt Juana, queen dowager of Portugal and governess of the kingdom during the absence of her brother Philip II.; attended by a great concourse of persons of all ranks. It was performed in the grand square between the church of St. Francis and the house of the Consistory. In the front of the town-house, and by the side of the platform occupied by the inquisitors, a box was erected, which the royal family could enter without interruption from the crowd, and in which they had a full view of the prisoners. The spectacle continued from six o'clock on the morning till two in the afternoon, during which the people exhibited no symptoms of impatience, nor did the queen retire until the whole 282 was concluded.[52] The sermon was preached by the celebrated Melchior Cano, bishop of the Canaries; the bishop of Palencia, to whose diocese Valladolid at that time belonged, performed the ceremony of degrading such of the victims as were in holy orders. When the company were assembled and had taken their places, Francisco Baca, the presiding inquisitor, advancing to the bed of state on

---

52. Register appended to *Skinner's translation of Montanus*, sig. E. i. b. E. ij. a.

which the prince and his aunt were seated, administered to them the oath to support the Holy Office, and to reveal to it every thing contrary to the faith which might come to their knowledge, without respect of persons. This was the first time that such an oath had been exacted from any of the royal family; and Don Carlos, who was then only fourteen years of age, is said from that moment to have vowed an implacable hatred to the Inquisition.

The prisoners brought forth on this occasion amounted to thirty, of whom sixteen were reconciled, and fourteen were "relaxed," or delivered over to the secular arm. Of the last class, two were thrown alive into the flames, while the remainder were previously strangled.

The greater part of the first class were persons distinguished by their rank and connections. Don Pedro Sarmiento de Roxas,[53] son of the first marquis de Poza, and of a daughter of the conde de Salinas y Ribadeo, was stripped of his ornaments as chevalier of St. James, deprived of his office as commander of Quintana, and condemned to wear a perpetual sanbenito, to be imprisoned for life, and to have his memory declared infamous. His wife Dona Mercia de Figueroa, dame of honor to the queen,[54] was sentenced to wear the coat of infamy, and to be confined during the remainder of her life. His neph-

283

---

53. Don Juan de Roxas Sarmiento, a brother of the prisoner, was celebrated as a mathematician, and addressed a consolatory letter to his sister Dona Elvira de Roxas, marchioness d' Alcagnizes, which was printed at Louvain in 1544.

54. Skinner says she was "one of the maydes of honour to the queene of *Boheme*."

ew don Luis de Roxas, eldest son of the second marquis de Poza, and grandson of the marquis d'Alcagnizes, was exiled from the cities of Madrid, Valladolid, and Palencia, forbidden to leave the kingdom, and declared incapable of succeeding to the honors or estates of his father. Dona Ana Henriquez de Roxas, daughter of the marquis d'Alcagnizes, and wife of Don Juan Alonso de Fonseca Mexia, was a lady of great accomplishments, understood the Latin language perfectly, and though only twenty-four years of age, was familiar with the writings of the reformers, particularly those of Calvin. She appeared in the sanbenito, and was condemned to be separated from her husband and spend her days in a monastery. Her aunt Dona Maria de Roxas, a nun of St. Catherine in Valladolid, and forty years of age, received sentence of perpetual penance and imprisonment, from which, however, she was released by an influence which the inquisitors did not choose to resist.[55] Don 284 Juan de Ulloa Pereira, brother to the marquis de la Mota, was subjected to the same punishment as the first-mentioned nobleman. This brave chevalier had distinguished himself in many engagements against the Turks both by sea and land, and performed so great feats of valor in the expeditions to Algiers, Bugia, and other parts of Africa, that Charles the Fifth had advanced him to the rank of first captain, and afterwards of general. Having appealed

---

55. "This Donna Maria (de Roxas) was intirely beloved of king Phillip's sister the queene of Portugall, by whose meanes and procurement she was released for wearying the Sambenite, and restored immediately into her cloyster agayne, whereat the inquisitours greatly repyned." (Register appended to *Skinner's translation of Montanus*, sig. E. iu. a.)

to Rome against the sentence of the inquisitors, and rep-
resented the services which he had done to Christendom,
De Ulloa was eventually restored to his rank as commander of the order of St. John of Jerusalem. Juan de Vibero
Cazalla, his wife Dona Silva de Ribera, his sister Dona
Constanza, Dona Francisca Zunega de Baeza, Marina de
Saavedra the widow of a hidalgo named Juan Cisneros de
Soto, and Leanor de Cisneros, (whose husband Antonio
Herezuelo was doomed to a severer punishment) with four
others of inferior condition, were condemned to wear the
sanbenito, and be imprisoned for life. The imprisonment
of Anthony Wasor, an Englishman, and servant to Don
285   Luis de Roxas, was restricted to one year's confinement in
a convent. Confiscation of property was an article in the
sentence of all these persons.[56]

Among those who were delivered over to the secular
arm, one of the most celebrated was Doctor Augustin Cazalla.[57] His reputation, and the office he had held as chaplain to the late emperor, made him an object of particular
attention to the inquisitors. During his confinement he
underwent frequent examinations, with the view of establishing the charges against himself and his fellow-prisoners. Cazalla was deficient in the courage which was requisite for the situation into which he had brought himself.
On the 4th of March 1559 he was conducted into the place
of torture, when he shrunk from the trial, and promising
to submit to his judges, made a declaration, in which he

---

56. Llorente, ii. 228-223. Register appended to *Skinner's translation
of Montanus*, sig. E. ij. a.

57. See before, p. 226.

confessed that he had embraced the Lutheran doctrine, but denied that he had ever taught it, except to those who were of the same sentiments with himself. This answered all the wishes of the inquisitors, who were determined that he should expiate his offence by death, at the same time that they kept him in suspense as to his fate, with the view of procuring from him additional information. On the evening before the auto-de-fe, Antonio de Carrera, a monk of St. Jerome, being sent to acquaint him with his sentence, Cazalla begged earnestly to know, if he might 286 entertain hopes of escaping capital punishment; to which Carrera replied, that the inquisitors could not rely on his declaration, but that, if he would confess all that the witnesses had deponed against him, mercy might perhaps be extended to him. This cautious reply convinced Cazalla that his doom was fixed. "Well, then," said he, "I must prepare to die in the grace of God; for it is impossible for me to add to what I have said, without falsehood." He confessed himself to Carrera that night, and next morning. On the scaffold, seeing his sister Constanza passing among those who were sentenced to perpetual imprisonment, he pointed to her, and said to the princess Juana, "I beseech your highness, have compassion on this unfortunate woman, who has thirteen orphan children!" At the place of execution, he addressed a few words to his fellow-prisoners in the character of a penitent, in virtue of which he obtained the poor favor of being strangled before his body was committed to the fire. His confessor was so pleased with his behavior as to say, he had no doubt Cazalla was in heaven.[58] His sister Dona Beatriz de

---

58. Llorente, ii. 222-225. If we may believe Illescas, or rather his

Vibero, Doctor Alonso Perez, a priest of Palencia, Don Christobal de Ocampo, chevalier of the order of St. John of Jerusalem, and almoner to the grand prior of Castile, Don Christobal de Padilla, and seven others, shared the same fate as Cazalla. Among these were the husband of the woman who had informed against the protestant coventicle in Valladolid, and four females, one of whom, Dona Catalina de Ortega, was daughter-in-law to the fiscal of the royal council of Castile.[59] They were all protestants, except Gonzales Baez, a Portuguese, who was condemned as a relapsed Jew.[60]

The two individuals who on this occasion had the honor to endure the flames were Francisco de Vibero Cazalla,[61] parish priest of Hormigos, and Antonio Herezue-

---

interpolators, Cazalla confessed, to the great edification of those who heard him, that in embracing the new opinions he had been actuated by ambition and a desire to have his followers in Spain called Cazallites, as those of the same sentiments were called Lutherans in Germany, Zuinglians in Switzerland, and Hugonots in France. (*Hist. Pontif.* tom. ii. f. 450, b.)

59. "Donna Katalina de Ortega, in common reputation a widow, daughter to the fischal, the king's attorney in the court of Inquisition, and at that time a chief councellour to the high inquisitour, howbeit she was privily contracted and married to the same Doct. Caçalla." (Register appended to *Skinner's translation of Montanus*, sig. E. i. a.)

60. Ibid. Llorente, ii. 222-228.

61. Llorente, ii. 225-6. "Francisco de Vibero, a priest, brother to the same D. Cazalla, having his tong pinched betwixt a clefte sticke, because he remayned most constant in the open profession of the

lo, an advocate of Toro. Some writers say that the former begged, when under the torture, to be admitted to reconciliation; but it is certain that he gave no sign of weakness or a wish to recant on the day of the auto-de-fe. Seeing his brother Augustin Cazalla, not at the stake, but on the adjoining scaffold among the penitents, and being prevented from speaking by the gag, he signified his sorrow by an expressive motion of his hands; after which he bore the fire without shrinking. Herezuelo conducted himself with surpassing intrepidity. From the moment of his apprehension 288 to that of his death, he never exhibited the least symptom of a wish to save his life, or to mitigate his sufferings, by compromising his principles. His courage remained unshaken amidst the horrors of the torture, the ignominy of the public spectacle, and the terrors of the stake. The only thing that moved him, on the day of the auto-de-fe, was the sight of his wife in the garb of a penitent; and the look which he gave, (for he could not speak) as he passed her to go to the place of execution, seemed to say, "This is hard to bear!" He listened without emotion to the friars who teazed him with their importunate exhortations to repent, as they conducted him to the stake; but when, at their instigation, his former associate and instructor, Doctor Cazalla, began to address him in the same strain, he threw upon him a glance of disdain, which froze the words on his recreant lips. "The bachelor Herezuelo (says the popish author of the Pontifical History) suffered himself to be burnt alive with unparalleled hardihood. I stood so near him that I had a complete view of his person, and observed all his motions and gestures. He could not speak, for his mouth

---

fayth." (Register, ut supra.)

was gagged on account of the blasphemies which he had uttered; but his whole behaviour showed him to be a most resolute and hardened person, who, rather than yield to believe with his companions, was determined to die in the flames. Though I marked him narrowly, I could not observe the least symptom of fear, or expression of pain; only, there was a sadness in his countenance beyond any thing I had ever seen. It was frightful to look in his face, when one considered that in a moment he would be in hell with his associate and master, Luther."[62] Enraged to see such courage in a heretic, one of the guards plunged his lance into the body of Herezuelo, whose blood was licked up by the flames with which he was already enveloped.[63]

289

Herezuelo and his wife, Leanor de Cisneros, were divided in their death, but it was in the time of it only, not the kind or manner; and their memory must not be divided in our pages. Leanor was only twenty-two years of age when she was thrown into the Inquisition; and when we consider that, during her imprisonment, she was precluded from all intercourse with her husband, kept in ignorance of his resolutions, and perhaps deceived into the belief that she would find him among the class of penitents in the auto, we need not wonder that one of her tender sex and age should have fainted in the day of trial, suffered herself to be overcome by the persuasions of the monks, or, yielding to the feelings of nature, consented to renounce with the hand the truth which she continued to believe with the

---

62. Illescas, *Hist. Pontif.* tom. ii. f. 450, b.

63. Register appended to *Skinner's translation of Montanus*, sig. E. i. b. Llorente, ii. 227, 231.

heart. Such assaults have shaken, and threatened to throw to the ground pillars in the church. But Leanor was not long in recovering from the shock. The parting look of her 290 husband never departed from her eyes;[64] the reflection that she had inflicted a pang on his heart, during the arduous conflict which he had to maintain, fanned the flame of attachment to the reformed religion which secretly burned in her breast; and having resolved, in dependence on that strength which is made perfect in weakness, to emulate the example of constancy set by one in every respect so dear to her, she resolutely broke off the course of penance on which she had entered. The consequence of this was, that she was again thrown into the secret prisons. During eight years that she was kept in confinement, every effort was made in vain to induce her to renew her recantation. At last she was brought out in a public auto-de-fe celebrated at Valladolid; and we have the account of her behavior from the same pen which so graphically described that of her husband. "In the year 1568, on the 26th of September, justice was executed on Leanor de Cisneros, widow of the bachelor Herezuelo. She suffered herself to be burnt alive, notwithstanding the great and repeated exertions made to bring her to a conviction of her errors. Finally, she resisted, what was sufficient to melt a stone, an admirable sermon

---

64. Llornte has adopted the monkish slander, that Herezuelo, on descending from the scaffold, seeing his wife in the dress of a penitent, expressed his indignation at her conduct by kicking her with his foot. (Tom. ii. p. 231.) Illescas, who has given a minute account of the behavior of both parties, takes no notice of any thing of this nature, which is irreconcilable with all the circumstances of the case.

291   preached, at the auto of that day, by his excellency Don
Juan Manuel, bishop of Zamora, a man no less learned
and eloquent in the pulpit than illustrious in blood. But
nothing could move the impenetrable heart of that obstinate woman."[65]

One part of the solemnities in the first auto at Valladolid, though not so shocking to the feelings as some
others which have been related, was nevertheless a flagrant
violation both of justice and humanity. Dona Leanor de
Vibero, the mother of Doctor Cazalla and of four other children who appeared as criminals in this auto-de-fe,
had died some years before, and was buried in a sepulchral
chapel of which she was the proprietress. No suspicion of
heresy attached to her at the time of her death; but, on the
imprisonment of her children, the fiscal of the inquisition
at Valladolid commenced a process against her; and certain witnesses under the torture having deponed that her
house was used as a temple for the Lutherans, sentence
was passed, declaring her to have died in a state of heresy,
her memory to be infamous, and her property confiscated;
and ordering her bones to be dug up, and, together with
her effigy, publicly committed to the flames; her house to
be razed, the ground on which it stood to be sown with
salt, and a pillar, with an inscription stating the cause of its
demolition, to be erected on the spot. All this was done,
and the last-mentioned monument of fanaticism and fe-
292   rocity against the dead was to be seen until the year 1809,
when it was removed during the occupation of Spain by

---

65. Illescas, *Hist. Pontif.* tom. ii. i. 451, a.

the French.[66]

There were still a great number of protestant prisoners in Valladolid; but though the processes of most of them were terminated, they were kept in confinement, to afford a gratifying spectacle to the monarch on his arrival from the Low Countries. The second auto-de-fe in this city was celebrated on the 8th of October 1559. Philip II. appeared at it, attended by his son, his sister, the prince of Parma, three ambassadors from France, with a numerous assemblage of prelates, and nobility of both sexes. The inquisitor general Valdes administered the oath to the king; on which occasion Philip, rising from his seat, and drawing his sword in token of his readiness to use it in support of the Holy Office, swore and subscribed the oath, which was afterwards read aloud to the people by one of the officers of the Inquisition.

Twenty-nine prisoners appeared on the scaffold, of whom sixteen wore the garb of penitents, while the flames painted on the sanbenitos and corozas of the remainder marked them out for the stake. Among the former were Dona Isabella de Castilla, wife of Don Carlos de Seso, her niece Dona Catalina, and three nuns of St. Belen.[67] The

---

66. Cypriano de Valera, *Dos Tratados*, p. 251. Llorente, ii. 221-2.

67. Another nun of that order, Dona Catalina de Reynoza, daughter of the baron de Auzillo, and sister of the bishop of Cordova, was delivered to the secular arm. She was only twenty-one years of age, and was charged with having said to the sisters, when engaged in their monkish devotions, "Cry aloud, that Baal may hear you; break your heads, and see if he will heal them." (Register appended to the translation of *Montanus*, sig. E. ij. b. Llorente, ii. 241.)

293 first two were condemned to lose all their property, to wear the sanbenito, and be imprisoned during life. To the Lutherans subjected to penances were added two men, one of whom was convicted of having sworn falsely that a child had been circumcised, with the view of bringing the father to the stake; the other of having personated an alguazil of the Holy Office. The former was sentenced to receive two hundred lashes, to lose the half of his property, and to work in the galleys for five years; the latter to receive four hundred lashes, to lose the whole of his property, and to work in the galleys for life;—a striking specimen of the comparative estimate which the Inquisition forms of meditated murder, and an insult on its own prerogatives.

At the head of those devoted to death was Don Carlos de Seso, with whose name the reader is already acquainted.[68] Arrested at Logrono, he was thrown into the secret prisons of the inquisition of Valladolid; and, on the 28th of June 1558, answered the interrogatories of the fiscal. His conduct during the whole of his imprisonment, and in the formidable scene by which it terminated, was worthy of his character, and the active part he had taken in the cause of religious reform. In the examinations which he underwent, he never varied, nor sought to excuse himself

294 by affixing blame to those whom he knew his judges were anxious to condemn.[69] When informed of his sentence on the night before his execution, he called for pen, ink, and paper, and having written a confession of his faith,

---

68. See before, p. 232.

69. This appears from his answers on the trial of archbishop Carranza. (Llorente, iii. 204.)

gave it to the officer, saying, "This is the true faith of the gospel, as opposed to that of the church of Rome which has been corrupted for ages: in this faith I wish to die, and in the remembrance and lively belief of the passion of Jesus Christ, to offer to God my body now reduced so low." "It would be difficult (says one who read this document in the archives of the Inquisition) to convey an idea of the uncommon vigor of sentiment with which he filled two sheets of paper, though he was then in the presence of death."[70] The whole of that night and next morning was spent by the friars in ineffectual attempts to induce him to recant. He appeared in the procession with a gag in his mouth, which remained while he was in the auto-de-fe, and on the way to the place of execution. It was removed after he was bound to the stake, and the friars began again to exhort him to confess. He replied, in a loud voice, and with great firmness, "I could demonstrate to you that you ruin yourselves by not imitating my example; but there is no time. Executioners, light the pile which is to consume me." They obeyed, and De Seso expired in the flames without a struggle or a groan. He died in the forty-third year of his age.[71]

Pedro de Cazalla, parish priest of Pedrosa, when arrested on the 25th of April 1558, confessed that he had embraced the protestant doctrines. Having afterwards supplicated reconciliation, he could obtain only two votes of the court of Inquisition for a punishment milder than death, and the decision of the majority was confirmed by the

295

---

70. Llorente, ii. 236.

71. Llorente, ii. 237.

council of the Supreme. He refused to make confession to the priest sent to intimate his sentence, and appeared in the auto with a gag; but after he was bound to the stake, having asked, or the attendant monks having represented him as asking a confessor, he was strangled and then cast into the fire. He was only in the thirty-fourth year of his age.

Domingo de Roxas, son of the marquis of Poza, two of whose children appeared in the former auto, was seized, in the garb of a laic, at Calahorra, where he had stopped, in his flight to the Low Countries, in order to have an interview with his friend De Seso. Subsequently to the 13th of May 1558, when he made his first appearance before the Inquisition, he underwent frequent examinations. The inquisitors having ordered the torture to be administered with a view of extorting from him certain facts which they were anxious to possess, he promised to tell all he knew, provided they would spare him the horrors of the 296 question, which he dreaded more than death. Deluded by the prospect of a merciful sentence which was held out to him, he was induced to make certain professions of sorrow, and to throw out insinuations unfavorable to the cause of archbishop Carranza; but as soon as he was undeceived, he craved an audience of the inquisitors, at which he did ample justice to that prelate, without asking any mitigation of his own punishment. On the night before his execution he refused the services of the priest appointed to wait on him. When the ceremonies of the auto were finished, and the secular judge had pronounced sentence on the prisoners delivered over to him, De Roxas, in passing the royal box, made an appeal to the mercy of the king. "Canst thou, Sire, thus witness the torments of they innocent subjects? Save us from so cruel a death." "No," replied Philip sternly; "I would myself carry wood to burn my own son, were he such a wretch as thou."[72] De Roxas was about to say something in defence of himself and his fellow-sufferers, when, the unrelenting despot waving his hand, the officers instantly thrust the gag into the martyr's mouth. It remained, contrary to the usual custom, after he was bound to the stake; so much were his judges irritated at his boldness, or afraid of the liberties he would use. Yet   297 we are told, that when the fire was about to be applied to the pile, his courage failed, he begged a confessor, and having received absolution, was strangled. Such appears to be the account of his last moments inserted in the records of the Inquisition;[73] but private letters, written from Spain at the time, give a different representation: "They carried him from the scaffold accompanied with a number of monks, about a hundred, flocking about him, railing and making exclamations against him, and some of them urging him to recant; but he, notwithstanding, answered them with a bold spirit, that he would never renounce the doctrine of Christ."[74]

---

72. Colmenares, in his *Historia de Segovia*, quoted by Puigblanch, (ii. 142) represents Don Carlos de Seso as making a similar address to Philip, and receiving a similar reply; but, according to Llorente's account, that nobleman wore the gag during the whole of the auto-de-fe.

73. Llorente, ii. 239.

74. Register appended to *Skinner's translation of Montanus*, sig. E. ij. b. Sepulveda mentions De Roxas among those who were "thrown

Juan Sanchez, at the commencement of the persecution of the protestants in Valladolid, had made his escape to the Low Countries, under the assumed name of Juan de Vibar. Thinking himself safe, he wrote letters, dated from Castrourdiales in the month of May 1558, and addressed to Dona Catalina Hortega, in whose family he had formerly resided. That lady having been seized as a suspected Lutheran, the letters fell into the hands of the inquisitors, who sent information to Philip, then at Brussels. Sanchez was apprehended at Turlingen, conveyed to Valladolid, and delivered over to the secular magistrate as a dogmatising and impenitent heretic. The gag was taken from his mouth at the place of execution, but as he did not ask for a confessor, the pile was kindled. When the fire had consumed the ropes by which he was bound, he darted from the stake and unconsciously leaped on the scaffold used for receiving the confessions of those who recanted in their last moments. The friars instantly collected to the spot, and urged him to retract his errors. Recovering from his momentary delirium, and looking around him, he saw on the one side some of his fellow-prisoners on their knees doing penance, and on the other Don Carlos de Seso standing unmoved in the midst of the flames, upon which he walked deliberately back to the stake, and calling for more fuel, said, "I will die like De Seso." Incensed at what they considered as a proof of audacious impiety, the archers and executioners strove who should first comply with his request. He died in the thirty-third year of his age.

298

---

alive into the flames, because they persevered in error." (*De Rebus gestis Philippi II.* lib. ii. cap. xxvii. p. 60: Opera, tom. iii.)

The case of Dona Marina Guevara, a nun of St. Belen, presents some singular features which are worthy of observation. When first denounced to the Inquisition, she owned that she had given entertainment to certain Lutheran opinions, but with hesitation, and in ignorance of their import and tendency. Her petition to be reconciled to the church was refused, because she would not acknowledge some things which the witnesses had deponed against her, and because she persisted in her assertion, that she had not yielded a cordial and complete assent to the heresies with 299 which her mind had been tainted. When the depositions were communicated to her by order of the inquisitors, she replied, that it seemed as if they wished to instil into her mind errors of which she was ignorant, rather than induce her to abandon those to which she had incautiously given ear; and that the oath she had taken would not permit her to add to her confession, or to acknowledge crimes of which she was not conscious, and facts which she did not recollect. The whole of the proceedings, while they display the honorable feelings of Marina, and the firmness of her character, depict, in strong colors, the sternness with which the Holy Office adhered to its tyrannical principles. She was connected with persons of high rank, including Valdes the grand inquisitor, who used every means for her deliverance. But the ordinary judges lent a deaf ear to the applications made by their superior in her behalf, which they resisted as an interference with their jurisdiction, and a proof of partiality and weakness, unworthy of one whose office required him to be insensible to the calls of nature and friendship. Valdes was obliged to procure an order from the council of the Supreme, authorizing Don Tellez

Giron de Montalban, the cousin of the prisoner, to have a final interview with her, in the presence of the leading members of the tribunal, with the view of inducing her to yield to their demands. But the attempt was unsuccessful. Dona Marina resisted all the entreaties of her noble relative, and refused to purchase her life by telling a falsehood. The inquisitors, inflexible to their former purpose, proceeded to pronounce sentence against her; and on the day of the auto she was delivered to the secular arm, and being strangled at the place of execution, her body was given to the flames. This act proclaimed, more decidedly than even the reply made by Philip to the son of the marquis de Poza, that there was no safety in Spain for any one who harbored a thought at variance with the Roman faith, or who was not prepared to yield the most implicit and absolute obedience to the dictates of the Inquisition.[75]

300

The autos-de-fe celebrated at Seville were still more memorable than those at Valladolid, if not for the rank of the spectators, at least for the number of prisoners exhibited on the scaffold. The first of these was solemnized on the 24th of September 1559, in the square of St. Francis. It was attended by four bishops, the members of the royal court of justice, the chapter of the cathedral, and a great assemblage of nobility and gentry. Twenty-one persons were delivered over to the secular arm, and eighty were condemned to lesser punishments.

The most distinguished individual, in point of rank,

---

75. *Sepulveda de Rebus gestis Philippi II.* p. 59, 60. Register appended to *Skinner's translation of Montanus*, sig. E. ij. E. iij. Llorente, tom. ii. chap. xx. art. 2.

who suffered death on the present occasion, was Don Juan 301
Ponce de Leon,[76] son of the count of Baylen, and a near
relation of the duchess de Bejar, who was present at the
spectacle. None had given more decided proofs of attachment to the reformed cause, and none had more diligently
prepared himself for suffering martyrdom for it than this
nobleman. For years he had avoided giving countenance
to the superstitions of the country, and had made it a practice to visit the spot where the confessors of the truth suffered, with the view of habituating his mind to its horrors,
and abating the terror which it was calculated to inspire.
But the stoutest heart will sometimes faint in the hour of
trial. The rank of Don Juan inspired the inquisitors with a
strong desire to triumph over his constancy. After extorting from him, by means of the rack, a confession of some
of the articles laid to his charge, they employed their secret
emissaries to persuade him that he would consult his own
safety, and that of his brethren, by confessing the whole.
He had scarcely given his consent to this when he repented. On the night before his execution he complained bitterly of the deceit which had been practised towards him,
and having made an undisguised profession of his faith,
rejected the services of the priest appointed to wait upon
him. De Montes asserts that he preserved his constancy to
the last, and, in support of this statement, appeals to the
official account of the auto, and to his sanbenito which
was hunt up in one of the churches, with the inscription
"Juan Ponce de Leon, burnt as an obstinate Lutheran heretic." But Llorente says, that this epithet was applied to 302
all who were sentenced to capital punishment, and that

76. See before, p. 218.

Don Juan, after he was bound to the stake and saw the fire about to be kindled, confessed himself to one of the attendant priests, and was strangled. His doom entailed infamy, and the forfeiture of every civil right, on his posterity; but the issue of his elder brother failing, Don Pedro, his son, after great opposition, obtained a decision from the royal chancery of Granada in favor of his claims, and was restored by letters from Philip III., to the earldom of Baylen.[77]

No such doubt hangs over the constancy of the persons to be named. Doctor Juan Gonzalez was descended of Moorish ancestors, and at twelve years of age had been imprisoned on suspicion of Mahometanism. He afterwards became one of the most celebrated preachers in Andalusia, and a protestant. In the mist of the torture, which he bore with unshrinking fortitude, he told the inquisitors, that his sentiments, though opposite to those of the church of Rome, rested on plain and express declarations of the word of God, and that nothing would induce him to inform against his brethren. When brought out on the morning of the auto, he appeared with a cheerful and undaunted air, though he had left his mother and two brothers behind him in prison, and was accompanied by two sisters, who, like himself, were doomed to the flames. At the door of the Triana he began to sing the hundred and ninth psalm; and on the scaffold he addressed a few words of consolation to one of his sisters, who seemed to him to wear a look of dejection; upon which the gag was instantly thrust into his mouth. With unaltered mien he listened to

303

---

77. *Cronica de los Ponces de Leon*, apud Llorente, ii. 260.

the sentence adjudging him to the flames, and submitted to the humiliating ceremonies by which he was degraded from the priesthood. When they were brought to the place of execution, the friars urged the females, in repeating the creed, to insert the word Roman in the clause relating to the catholic church. Wishing to procure liberty to him to bear his dying testimony, they said they would do as their brother did. The gag being removed, Juan Gonzalez exhorted them to add nothing to the good confession which they had already made. Instantly the executioners were ordered to strangle them, and one of the friars, turning to the crowd, exclaimed that they had died in the Roman faith; a falsehood which the inquisitors did not choose to repeat in their narrative of the proceedings.

The same constancy was evinced by four monks of the convent of San Isidro. Among these was the celebrated Garcia de Arias,[78] whose character had undergone a complete revolution. From the moment of his imprisonment 304 he renounced that system of cautiousness and tergiversation on which he had formerly acted. He made an explicit profession of his faith, agreeing, in every point, with the sentiments of the reformers; expressed his sorrow that he had concealed it so long; and offered to prove that the opposite opinions were grossly erroneous and superstitious. On his trial he mocked the inquisitors, as persons who presumed to give judgment on matters of which they were utterly ignorant, and reminded them of instances in which they, as well as the qualificators whom they called to their assistance, were forced to confess their incapacity

78. See before, p. 219-221.

to interpret the scriptures. The priests, as a necessary point of form, visited his cell, but none of them durst enter the lists in argument with him. Being advanced in years, he ascended the scaffold, on the day of the auto, leaning on his staff, but went to the stake with a countenance expressive of joy and readiness to meet the flames.

Christobal d'Arellano, a member of the same convent, was distinguished by his learning, the inquisitors themselves being judges. Among the articles in his process, read in the auto, he was charged with having said, "that the mother of God was no more a virgin than he was." At hearing this, D'Arellano, rising from his seat, exclaimed, "It is a falsehood; I never advanced such a blasphemy; I have always maintained the contrary, and at this moment am ready to prove, with the gospel in my hand, the virginity of Mary." The inquisitors were so confounded at this public contradiction, and the tone in which it was uttered, that they did not even order him to be gagged. On arriving at the stake, he was thrown into some degree of perturbation at seeing one of the monks of his convent who had come there to insult over his fate; but he soon recovered his former serenity of mind, and expired amidst the flames, encouraging Juan Chrisostomo, who had been his pupil, and was now his fellow-sufferer.

The fate of Juan de Leon was peculiarly hard. He had resided for some time as an artisan at Mexico, and on his return to Spain was led, under the influence of a superstitious feeling general among his countrymen, to take the vow in the convent of San Isidro, near Seville. This happened about the time that the knowledge of the truth began to be introduced into that monastery. Having imbibed the protestant doctrine, Juan lost his relish for the monastic life, and quitted the convent on the pretext of bad health; but the regret which he felt at losing the religious instructions of the good fathers determined him to rejoin their society. On his return to San Isidro he found it deserted by its principal inhabitants, whom he followed to Geneva. During his residence in this city, intelligence came that Elizabeth had succeeded to the throne of England; and Juan de Leon, with some of his countrymen resolved to accompany the English exiles who were preparing to return home. The Spanish court, in concert with the Inquisition, had planted spies on the road from Milan to Geneva, and at Frankfort, Cologne, and Antwerp, to 306 waylay such Italians or Spaniards as left their native country for the sake of religion. Aware of this fact, Juan de Leon and another Spaniard took a different road, but at Strasburg they were betrayed to a spy, who pursued their route to a port in Zealand, and having procured a warrant, seized them as they were stepping on board a vessel for England. As soon as the officers presented themselves, Juan, aware of their intentions, turned to his companion, and said, "Let us go; God will be with us." After being severely tortured to make them discover their fellow-exiles, they were sent to Spain. During the voyage and the journey by land, they were not only heavily chained like felons, but each of them had his head and face covered with a species of helmet, made of iron, having a piece of the same metal, shapen like a tongue, which was inserted into his mouth, to prevent him from speaking. While his companion was sent to Valladolid,[79] Juan was delivered to the inquisitors

---

79. De Montes calls this person Joannes Ferdinandus; Llorente says

at Seville. The sufferings which he endured, from torture and imprisonment, had brought on a consumption; and

307   his appearance, on the day of the auto, was such as would have melted the heart of any human being but an inquisitor. He was attended at the stake by a monk who had passed his noviciate along with him, and who disturbed his last moments, by reminding him of those things of which he was now ashamed. His mouth being relieved from the gag, he, with much composure and graveness, made a declaration of his faith in few but emphatic words, and then welcomed the flames which were to put an end to his sufferings, and to convey him to the spirits of just men made perfect.[80]

Fernando de San Juan, master of the college of Doctrine, and Doctor Christobal Losada, pastor to the protestant church in Seville, suffered with the same fortitude and constancy. The latter, after he had reached the place of burning, was engaged in a theological dispute by the importunity of the friars, who flattered themselves with being able to convince him of his errors; but perceiving that the people listened eagerly to what was said, they began to speak in Latin, and were followed by Losada, who

---

his name was Juan Sanches. (See before, p. 297.) According to the statement of another author, these were different names of the same individual. "Juan Sanches, otherwise called Juan Fernandez, sometime servant to Doct. Caçalla; the same partie that was taken in Zeland, with Juan de Leon, as they were taking passage into England." (Register appended to *Skinner's translation of Montanus*, sig. E. ij. b.)

80. *Montanus*, p. 223-228.

continued for a considerable time to carry on the conversation with propriety and elegance in a foreign tongue, at
the foot of that stake which was about to consume him to
ashes.[81]

This auto-de-fe furnished examples of Christian heroism, equally noble, in those of the tender sex, several of
whom "were tortured, not accepting deliverance, that they
might obtain a better resurrection." Among these were 308
Dona Isabel de Baena, Maria de Virves, Maria de Cor-
nel, and Maria de Bohorques. The first was a rich matron
of Seville, who had permitted the protestants to meet for
worship in her house, which on that account was laid under the same sentence of execration as that of Leanor de
Vibero at Valladolid.[82] The rest were young ladies, and
connected with the most distinguished families in Spain.
The story of Maria de Bohorques became celebrated,
both from its interesting circumstances, and from its having been made the foundation of an historical novel by
a Spanish writer.[83] She was a natural daughter of Don

---

81. *Montanus*, p. 214-216.

82. Cypriano de Valera, *Dos Tratados*, p. 251. Montanus, p. 223. See
before, p. 291.

83. It is entitled *Cornelia Bororquia*, and was printed at Bayonne.
The author asserts that it is rather a history than a romance. But
Llorente says it is neither the one nor the other, but a tissue of
ill-conceived scenes, which outrage both nature and fact; and he
complains that this and similar works have contributed to support the cause of the Inquisition, by throwing the air of fiction
around its atrocities, and imputing to its agents words and actions which are ridiculous and destitute of verisimilitude. (ii.

Pedro Garcia de Xeres y Bohorques, a Spanish grandee of the first class, and had not completed her twenty-first year when she fell into the hands of the Inquisition. Great care had been bestowed on her education, and being able to read the Bible, and expositions of it, in the Latin tongue, she acquired a knowledge of the scriptures which was possessed by few men, or even clergymen, in her native country. Egidio, whose pupil she was, used to say he always felt himself wiser from an interview with Maria de Bohorques.

309 When brought before the inquisitors she avowed her faith; defended it as the ancient truth, which Luther and his associates had recovered from the rubbish by which it had been hid for ages; and told her judges, that it was their duty to embrace it, instead of punishing her and others for maintaining it. She was severely tortured, in consequence of her refusal to answer certain questions calculated to implicate her friends. From deference to the intercession of her relations, or from the desire of making a convert of one so accomplished, the inquisitors, contrary to their usual custom, sent first two Jesuits, and afterwards two Dominicans, to her cell, to persuade her to relinquish her heretical opinions. They returned full of chagrin at their ill success, but of admiration at the dexterity with which she repelled their arguments. On the night before the auto at which she was to suffer, they repeated their visit, in company with two other priests. She received them with great politeness, but at the same time told them very plainly, that they might have saved themselves the trouble which they had taken, for she felt more concern about her salvation than they could possibly feel; she would have renounced

267.)

her sentiments if she had entertained any doubt of their truth, but was more confirmed in them than she was when first thrown into prison, inasmuch as the popish divines, after many attempts, had opposed nothing to them but what she had anticipated, and to which she was able to 310 return an easy and satisfactory answer. On the morning of the auto-de-fe she made her appearance with a cheerful countenance. During the time that the line of the procession was forming, she comforted her female companions, and engaged them to join with her in singing a psalm suitable to the occasion, upon which a gag was put into her mouth. It was taken out after her sentence was read, and she was asked, if she would now confess those errors to which she had hitherto adhered with such obstinacy. She replied with a distinct and audible voice, "I neither can nor will recant." When the prisoners arrived at the place of execution, Don Juan Ponce, who began to waver at the sight of the preparations for the fiery trial, admonished her not to be too confident in the new doctrines, but to weigh the arguments of those who attended to give them advice. Dona Maria upbraided him for his irresolution and cowardice; adding that it was not a time for reasoning, but that all of them ought to employ their few remaining moments in meditating on the death of that Redeemer for whom they were about to suffer. Her constancy was yet put to a further trial. After she was bound to the stake, the attending priests, having prevailed on the presiding magistrate to delay the lighting of the pile, and professing to feel for her youth and talents, requested her merely to repeat the creed. This she did not refuse, but immediately began to explain some of its articles in the Lutheran sense.

She was not permitted to finish her commentary, and the
311 executioner having received orders to strangle her, she was
consumed in the fire.[84]

The effigy of the licentiate Zafra, whose providential
escape has been mentioned, was burnt at this auto-de-
fe.[85] Among the penitents who appeared on the present
occasion, one deserves to be mentioned as a specimen of
the lenity with which the inquisitors punished a crime
which, in Spain, ought to have been visited with the most
exemplary vengeance. The servant of a gentleman in Puer-
to de Santa Maria having fastened a rope to a crucifix,
concealed it, along with a whip, in the bottom of a chest,
and going to the Triana, informed the holy fathers that
his master was in the habit of scourging the image every

---

84. *Montanus*, p. 210-213. *Geddes, Miscel. Tracts.* vol. i. p. 574.
Llorente, ii. 268-271.

85. See before, p. 244. Llorente, ii. 256. Skinner mentions, among
those "burned in Sivil in the yeare of our Lord 1559, Juan de
Cafra, father to him that escaped out of prison, whereof mention is made fol. 4, whose picture notwithstanding was burned
at the same tyme." If this last is the person referred to in the
text, he must have been privately married; for the individual next
mentioned in Skinner's list, is "Francisca Lopez de Texeda de
Mancanilla, wyfe unto the same partie that so escaped." (Register
appended to the translation of Montanus, sig. Dd. iij. b.) The
same list contains the following names: "Medel de Espinosa, an
embroderer condemned onely for receyving into his house cer-
tayne of Luthers workes that were brought out of Germany. Luys
de Abrego, a man that was wont to get his living by writing of
missals and such other church-bookes."

day. The crucifix was found in the place and situation described by the informer, and the gentleman was thrown into the secret prisons. Happily for him, he recollected a quarrel which he had had with his servant, and succeeded in proving that the accusation had its origin in personal revenge. According to the regulations of the Holy Office the servant ought to have suffered death; but he was merely sentenced to receive four hundred strokes with the whip, and to be confined six years in the galleys. The execution appears to have been confined to the first part of the sentence, which, upon a principle of retaliation worthy of the ingenuity of the Inquisition, was considered as expiatory of the supposed indignity done the crucifix.[86]

312

The second grand auto-de-fe in Seville took place on the 22d of December 1560, after it had been delayed in the hopes of the arrival of the monarch. It was on this occasion that the effigies of the deceased doctors Egidius and Constantine, together with that of Juan Perez,[87] who had fled, were produced and burnt. Fourteen persons were delivered to the secular arm, and thirty-four were sentenced to inferior punishments.[88]

Julian[89] Hernandez was in the first class, and the clos-

---

86. Llorente, ii. 271.

87. See before, p. 199.

88. According to the narrative of John Frampton, thirty persons were burnt, and forty condemned to other punishments, on this occasion; but being himself one of the prisoners, he might easily mistake in computing their numbers. (*Strype's Annals*, vol. i. p. 244.)

89. In page 240 he is by mistake called Juan, instead of Julian.

ing scene of his life did not disgrace his former daring and fortitude. When brought out to the court of the Triana on the morning of the auto, he said to his fellow-prisoners, "Courage, comrades! This is the hour in which we must show ourselves valiant soldiers of Jesus Christ. Let us now bear faithful testimony to his truth before men, and within a few hours we shall receive the testimony of his approbation before angels, and triumph with him in heaven." He was silenced by the gag, but continued to encourage his companions by his gestures, during the whole of the spectacle. On arriving at the stake he knelt down and kissed the stone on which it was erected; then rising he thrust his naked head once and again among the faggots, in token of his welcoming that death which was so dreadful to others. Being bound to the stake, he composed himself to prayer, when Doctor Fernando Rodriguez, one of the attending priests, interpreting his attitude as a mark of abated courage, prevailed with the judge to remove the gag from his mouth. Having delivered a succinct confession of his belief, Julian began to accuse Rodriguez, with whom he had been formerly acquainted, of hypocrisy in concealing his real sentiments through fear of man. The galled priest exclaimed, "Shall Spain, the conqueror and mistress of nations, have her peace disturbed by a dwarf? Executioner, do your office." The pile was instantly kindled; and the guards, envying the unshaken firmness of the martyr, terminated his sufferings by plunging their lances into his body.[90]

313

---

90. *Montanus*, p. 220-222. *Histoire des Martyrs*, f. 497, b. Geddes, *Miscel. Tracts.* vol. i. p. 570. Llorente, ii. 282.

No fewer than eight females, of irreproachable char- 314
acter, and some of them distinguished by their rank and
education, suffered the most cruel of deaths at this auto-
de-fe. Among these was Maria Gomez, who, having recovered from the mental disorder by which she was overtaken
had been received back into the protestant fellowship, and
fell into the hands of the Inquisition.[91] She appeared at
the scaffold along with her three daughters and a sister.
After the reading of the sentence which doomed them to
the flames, one of the young women went up to her aunt,
from whom she had imbibed the protestant doctrine, and,
on her knees, thanked her for all the religious instructions
she had received from her, implored her forgiveness for
any offence she might have given her, and begged her dying blessing. Raising her up, and assuring her that she had
never given her a moment's uneasiness, the old woman
proceeded to encourage her dutiful niece, by reminder her
of that support which their divine Redeemer had promised them in the hour of trial, and of those joys which
awaited them at the termination of their momentary sufferings. The five friends then took leave of one another
with tender embraces and words of mutual comfort. The
interview between these devoted females was beheld by the
members of the Holy Tribunal with a rigid composure of
countenance, undisturbed even by a glance of displeasure;
and so completely had superstition and habit subdued the 315
strongest emotions of the human breast, that not a single expression of sympathy escaped from the multitude at
witnessing a scene which, in other circumstances, would
have harrowed up the feelings of the spectators, and driven

91. See before, p. 215, 270.

them into mutiny.[92]

Three foreigners, two of whom were Englishmen, perished in this auto. Nicolas Burton, a merchant of London, having visited Spain with a vessel laden with goods, fell into the hands of the Inquisition, and refusing to abjure the protestant faith, was burnt alive.[93] The remarks of Llorente on this transaction are extremely just. "Let it be granted, if you will have it so, that Burton was guilty of an imprudence, by posting up his religious sentiments at San Lucar de Barrameda, and at Seville, in contempt of the faith of the Spaniards; it is no less true that both charity and justice required, that in the case of a stranger who had not fixed his abode in Spain, they should have contented themselves with warning him to abstain from all marks of disrespect to the religion and laws of the country, and threatening him with punishment if he repeated the offence. The Holy Office had nothing to do with his private sentiments; having been established, not for strangers, but solely for the people of Spain."[94] That the charge against Burton was a mere pretext, if not a fabrication, is evident from the fact that William Burke, a mariner of Southampton, and a Frenchman of Bayonne, named Fabianne, who had come to Spain in the course of trade, were burnt at the same stake with him, although not accused of any insult on the religion of the country.[95]

Part of the goods in Burton's ship, which was confis-

316

---

92. *Montanus*, p. 85, 86. Llorente, ii. 185-187.

93. *Montanus*, p. 175. Strype's Annals, vol. i. p. 238.

94. Llorente, ii. 283, 284.

95. *Strype's Annals*, i. 238. Llorente, ii. 285.

cated by the inquisitors, belonged to a merchant in London, who sent John Frampton of Bristol to Seville, with a power of attorney, to reclaim his property. The Holy Office had recourse to every obstacle in opposing his claim, and after fruitless labor during four months he found it necessary to repair to England to obtain ampler powers. Upon his landing the second time in Spain, he was seized by two familiars, and conveyed in chains to Seville, where he was thrown into the secret prisons of the Triana. The only pretext for his apprehension was, that a book of Cato in English was found in his portmanteau. Being unable to substantiate a charge on this ground, the inquisitors interrogated him on his religious opinions, and insisted that he should clear himself of the suspicion of heresy by repeating the Ave Maria. In doing this, he omitted the words, "Mother of God, pray for us;" upon which he was put to the torture. After enduring three shocks of the pulley, and while he "lay flat on the ground, half-dead and half-alive," he agreed to confess whatever his tormentors chose to dictate. In consequence of this, he was found violently 317 suspected of Lutheranism, and the property which he had come to recover was confiscated. He appeared among the penitents at the auto at which Burton suffered, and after being kept in prison for more than two years was set at liberty.[96]

Among those who appeared as penitents were several ladies of family and monks of different orders. Others

---

96. Frampton's Narrative, in *Strype's Annals*, i. 239-245. This narrative agrees substantially with the accounts given by *Montanus*, p. 175-179, and by Llorente, ii. 287-289.

were severely punished on the most trivial grounds. Diego de Virves, a member of the municipality of Seville, was fined in a hundred ducats for having said, on occasion of the preparations for Maunday-Thursday, "Would it not be more acceptable to God to expend the money lavished on this ceremony in relieving poor families?" Bartolomé Fuentes having received an injury from a certain priest, exclaimed, "I cannot believe that God will descend from heaven into the hands of such a worthless person;" for which offence he appeared on the scaffold with a gag in his mouth. Two young students were punished for "Lutheran acts," in having copied into their album some anonymous verses, which contained either a eulogium or a satire on Luther, according to the manner in which they were read.[97]

318   Gaspar de Benavides, alcayde, or head jailer, of the inquisition at Seville, was convicted of a course of malversation in his office. There was no species of oppression which this miscreant had not committed in his treatment of the prisoners, before a riot excited by his insufferable cruelties led to a discovery of his guilt. He was merely declared "to have failed in zeal and attention to his charge," and condemned to lose his situation, to appear in the auto with a torch in his hand, and be banished from Seville. Compare this sentence with the punishments inflicted on those who were the means of bringing his knavery to light. For conspiring against him, and inflicting a wound on one of his assistants which proved mortal, Melchior del Salto was burnt alive. A mulatto of fourteen years of age, named

---

97. *Montanus*, p. 192-196. Llorente, ii. 289-291.

Luis, suspected of being an accomplice in the riot, received two hundred lashes, and was condemned to hard labor in the galleys for life; while Maria Gonzalez and Pedro Herrera, servants of the alcayde, were sentenced to the same number of lashes, and confinement in the galleys for ten years, merely because they had treated the prisoners with kindness, and permitted such of them as were relations to see one another occasionally for a few minutes.[98]

The treatment of one individual, who was pronounced 319 innocent in this auto-de-fe, affords more damning evidence against the inquisitors than that of any whom they devoted quick to the flames. Dona Juana de Bohorques was a daughter of Don Pedro Garcia de Xeres y Bohorques, and

---

98. *Montanus*, p. 108-114. Llorente, ii. 289, 291-293. Herrera, at the earnest request of a mother and her daughter, who were confined in separate cells, had humanely permitted them to converse together for half an hour. On their being summoned soon after to the torture-room, he became alarmed lest they should mention this indulgence, and going to the inquisitors confessed what he had done. He was instantly ordered into close confinement, which, together with the grief which he conceived, brought on mental derangement. Having recovered, he appeared in the auto with a rope about his neck. Being led out next day to be publicly whipped, he was seized with a fit of insanity, and throwing himself from the ass on which he was borne, wrested a sword from the attending alguazil, and would have killed him, had not the crowd interposed. For this offence, four years were added to his confinement in the galleys. "The holy fathers (says the historian who relates these facts) will not permit people even to be insane with impunity." (*Montanus*, p. 111.)

the wife of Don Francisco de Vargas, baron of Higuera. She had been apprehended in consequence of a confession extorted by the rack from her sister Maria de Bohorques, who owned that she had conversed with her on the Lutheran tenets without exciting any marks of disapprobation. Being six months gone in pregnancy, Dona Juana was permitted to occupy one of the public prisons until the time of her delivery; but eight days after that event the child was taken from her, and she was thrust into a secret cell. A young female, who was afterwards brought to the stake as a Lutheran, was confined along with her, and did every thing in her power to promote her recovery. Dona Juana was permitted to occupy one of the public prisons until the time of her delivery; but eight days after that event the child was taken from her, and she was thrust into a secret cell. A young female, who was afterwards brought to the stake as a Lutheran, was confined along with her, and did every thing in her power to promote her recovery.

320 Dona Juana had soon an opportunity of repaying the kind attentions of her fellow-prisoner, who, having been called before the inquisitors, was brought back into her dungeon faint and mangled. Scarcely had the latter acquired sufficient strength to rise from her bed of flags, when Dona Juana was conducted in her turn to the place of torture. Refusing to confess, she was put into the engine del burro, which was applied with such violence, that the cords penetrated to the bone of her arms and legs; and some of the internal vessels being burst, the blood flowed in streams from her mouth and nostrils. She was conveyed to her cell in a state of insensibility, and expired in the course of a few days. The inquisitors would fain have concealed the cause

of her death, but it was impossible; and they thought to expiate the crime of this execrable murder, in the eyes of men at least, by pronouncing Juana de Bohorques innocent on the day of the auto-de-fe, vindicating her reputation, and restoring her property to her heirs. "Under what an overwhelming responsibility (exclaims one of their countrymen) must these cannibals appear one day before the tribunal of the Deity!" But may we not hesitate in deciding the question, Whose was the greatest responsibility? that of the cannibals, or of those who permitted them thus to gorge themselves with human blood? Surely the spirit of chivalry had fled from the breasts of the Spanish nobility, else they never would have suffered their wives and daughters to be abused in this manner by an ignoble junto of priests and friars, supported by a monarch equally 321 base and unprincipled.[99]

Having discharged the painful task of describing the four great autos in Valladolid and Seville, it may be proper, before proceeding with the narrative of the extermination of the protestants, to advert to the severe measures adopted against certain dignified ecclesiastics who fell under the suspicion of favoring heresy.

We have had occasion repeatedly to mention the name, and allude to the trial of Bartolomé de Carranza y Miranda, archbishop of Toledo. After sitting in the council of Trent, and accompanying Philip II. to England, where he took an active part in the examination of the protestants who were led to the stake, this learned man was reward-

---

99. *Montanus*, p. 181-184. Cypriano de Valera, *Dos Tratados*, p. 250. Llorente, ii. 293-295.

ed in 1558 with the primacy; but he had not been many months in his diocese when he was denounced to the Inquisition and thrown into prison at Valladolid. Some historians have ascribed this prosecution entirely to the envy and personal hatred of his brethren, particularly Melchior Cano, bishop of the Canaries, and the inquisitor general Valdes.[100] It is unquestionable that the proceedings were exasperated by such base motives; but there were grounds of jealousy, distinct from these, which operated against the primate. Several of the leading persons among the Spanish protestants had received their education under Carranza, who continued to maintain a friendly correspondence with them, and, though he signified his disapprobation of their sentiments in private, did not give information against them to the Holy Office. His theological ideas were more enlarged than those of his brethren, and he appears to have agreed with the reformers on justification and several collateral points of doctrine. In these respects his mode of thinking resembled that of Marco Antonio Flaminio, cardinals Pole and Morone, and other learned Italians.[101] Indeed his intimacy with these distinguished individuals formed part of the evidence against him.[102] His Catechism, which was made the primary article of charge against him, besides its presumed leaning on some points to Lutheranism, was offensive to the Inquisition, because it was published in the vulgar tongue, and incul-

322

100. Llorente, iii. 195.

101. *History of the Progress and Suppression of the Reformation in Italy*, p. 166-188.

102. Llorente, iii. 246.

cated the doctrines of the Bible more than the traditions of the church. At the end of seven years, the cause was transferred to Rome, whither the primate was conveyed; and after various intrigues and delays, pope Gregory XIII. pronounced a definitive sentence on the 14th of April 1576, finding Carranza violently suspected of heresy, confirming the prohibition of his Catechism, and ordaining him to abjure sixteen Lutheran propositions, and to be suspended for five years from the exercise of his archiepiscopal functions. The sentence had scarcely passed when the primate sickened and died, having been eighteen years under process and in a state of confinement.[103]

323

The prosecution of the primate gave rise to others. Eight bishops, the most of whom had assisted at the council of Trent, and twenty-five doctors of theology, including the men of greatest learning in Spain, were denounced to the Holy Office; and few of them escaped without making some humiliating acknowledgement or retractation.[104] Mancio de Corpus Christi, professor of theology at Alcala, had given a favorable opinion of the Catechism of Carranza, to which he had procured the subscriptions of the divines of his university; but hearing that a prosecution was commenced against him, he saved himself from being thrown into the secret prisons by transmitting to the inquisitors another opinion, in which he condemned three hundred and thirty-one propositions in the works of that prelate, whom he had a little before pronounced most

103.   Llorente, tom. iii. chap. xxxii. Bayle, Dict. art. Carranza.

104.   Llorente, ii. 427-480; iii. 62-90.

orthodox.[105] Luis de la Cruz, a favorite disciple of Carranza, was thrown into the secret prisons, in consequence of certain papers of his master being found in his possession, and the intercourse which he had held with Doctor Cazalla and other reformers. Confinement and anxiety produced a tendency of blood to his head, accompanied with fits of delirium, which rendered it necessary, for the preservation of his life, to remove him to the episcopal

324 prison. Notwithstanding this and the failure of the proof brought against him, La Cruz was kept in confinement for five years, in the hopes that he would purchase his liberty by blasting the reputation and betraying the life of his patron.[106] Before Carranza was formally accused, the inquisitors had extracted a number of propositions from his Catechism, and without naming the author, submitted them to the judgment of Juan de Pegna, professor at Salamanca, who pronounced them all catholic, or at least susceptible of a good sense. De Pegna became alarmed, and sent an apology to the Holy Office, in which he acknowledged himself guilty of concealing the favorable opinion which Carranza had entertained of Don Carlos de Seso. This did not pacify the holy fathers, who condemned him to undergo different penances for his faults, among which they reckoned the following: that he did not censure the proposition, "that we cannot say that a person falls from a state of grace by committing a mortal sin;" and that he had given it as his private opinion, "that even though the primate was a heretic, the Holy Office should wink at the

---

105.   Ibid. ii. 442.

106.   Llorente, ii. 443-4.

fact, lest the Lutherans of Germany should canonize him as a martyr, as they had done others who had been punished."[107]

In the mean time the persecution against the Lutherans in Valladolid and Seville had not relaxed. Every means was used to excite the popular odium against them. The abominable calumnies propagated by the pagans of Rome against the primitive Christians were revived; and it was believed by the credulous vulgar, that the protestants, in their nightly assemblies, extinguished the candles and abandoned themselves to the grossest vices.[108] On the feast of St. Matthew, in the year 1561, a destructive fire broke out at Valladolid, which consumed upwards of four hundred houses, including some of the richest manufactories and stores in the city. This was ascribed to a conspiracy of the Lutherans; and every year afterwards, on the day of St. Matthew, the inhabitants observed a solemn procession, accompanied with prayers to our Lord, through the intervention of his holy apostle, to preserve them from this plague and calamity.[109] In the course of the same year, the pope sent Spain a bull, authorizing a jubilee, with plenary indulgences. Among other things, it gave authority to confessors to absolve those who had involved themselves in the Lutheran heresy, upon their professing sorrow for their errors. Though the object of the court of Rome was to amass money, this measure tended to mitigate the persecution which had raged for some years; but the inquis-

325

---

107.   Ibid, ii. 463-4.

108.   Cypriano de Valera, *Dos Tratados*, p. 252.

109.   Illescas, *Hist. Pontif.* tom. ii. f. 451, b. 452, a.

itors, determined that their prey should not escape them, prohibited the bull from being published within the kingdom.[110]

326   The four autos-de-fe which we have already described, although the most celebrated, were not the only spectacles at which the protestants suffered at Valladolid and Seville. It required many years to empty their prisons, from which adherents to the reformed faith continued, at short intervals, to be brought out to the scaffold and the stake. On the 10th of July 1563, a public auto was celebrated in Seville, at which six persons were committed to the flames as Lutherans. Domingo de Guzman[111] appeared among the penitents on this occasion. The hope of an archbishopric had been held out to induce him to recant; and his brother, the duke of Medina Sidonia, exerted himself to procure his release, upon undergoing such a slight penance as would not interfere with his future prospects. But the inquisitors were resolved to prevent the advancement of one who had embraced the reformed tenets; and after causing his books, which exceeded a thousand volumes, to be burnt before his eyes, they condemned him to perpetual imprisonment.[112]

An occurrence which took place at Seville in 1564 diverted for a little the attention of the public, and even of the inquisitors, from the adherents of the reformed doctrine. In consequence of complaints that the confessional

---

110.   *Montanus*, p. 188-9.

111.   See before, p. 218, 262.

112.   Register appended to the translation of *Montanus*, sig. D d. iiij. b. E. i. a.

was abused to lewd purposes, edicts were repeatedly pro- 327
cured from Rome to correct the evil. Several scandalous
discoveries having been made by private investigations,
and the public clamor increasing, the inquisition of Seville came to a resolution, of which they had reason to
repent, that an edict of denunciation should be published
in all the churches of the province, requiring, under a severe penalty, those who had been solicited by priests in
the confessional to criminal intercourse, or who knew of
this having been done, to give information to the Holy
Office within thirty days. In consequence of this intimation, such numbers flocked to the Triana, that the inquisitors were forced once and again to prolong the period of
denunciation, until it extended to a hundred and twenty days. Among the informers were women of illustrious
birth and excellent character, who repaired to the inquisitors with their veils, and under disguise, for fear of being
met and recognized by their husbands. The priests were
thrown into the greatest alarm;[113] the peace of families was
broken; and the whole city rang with scandal. At last, the
council of the Supreme, perceiving the odium which it
brought on the church, and its tendency to prejudice the

---

113. "On the other side it was a joly sport to see the monkes and
      friers and priestes go up and downe hanging downe theyr
      heads, all in dumpe and a melancholy, by meanes of theyr
      guilty consciences, quaking and trembling, and looking every
      hower when some of the familiars should take them by the
      sleve, and call them *coram* for these matters. In so much that
      a number feared lest as great a plague were come among them
      as the persecution that was so hote about that time against the
      Lutherans." (*Skinner's translation of Montanus*, sig. R. iij.)

people against auricular confession, interposed their au-
328 thority, by quashing the investigation, and prohibiting the
edict of denunciation from being repeated.[114]

Valladolid and Seville were not the only cities whose
prisons were crowded with friends to the reformed doctrine. From 1560 to 1570, one public auto-de-fe at least
was celebrated annually in all the twelve cities in which
provincial tribunals of the Inquisition were then established; and at each of these, adherents to the new faith
made their appearance. On the 8th of September 1560,
the inquisition of Murcia solemnized an auto, at which
five persons were sentenced to different punishments for
embracing Lutheranism; and three years after, eleven appeared as penitents in that city on the same charge.[115] It was
in the last-mentioned auto, that a son of the emperor of
Morocco, who had submitted to baptism in his youth, was

---

114.   *Montanus*, p. 184-188. Llorente does not deny the facts stated
by the protestant historian, but contents himself with saying
that he has mistaken the year 1563 for 1564, and that "the
denunciations were much fewer than he pretends." (Tom. iii.
p. 29.) The documents which enabled the ex-secretary of the
Inquisition to correct the exaggeration, must have put it in his
power to state the exact number. There is reason in what he
says on this subject, that while in some instances the priests
were guilty, in others they might be falsely accused from malice or from mistake on the part of the penitents; but did it not
occur to him, that, on either supposition, auricular confession
and the celibacy of the clergy are calculated to have the most
pernicious influence on public morals?

115.   Llorente, ii. 338, 340, 344.

brought on the scaffold for relapsing to Mahometanism, and was condemned to confinement for three years, and 329 to banishment from the kingdoms of Valencia, Aragon, Murcia, and Granada. On the 25th of February 1560, the inquisition of Toledo prepared a grand auto-de-fe for the entertainment of their young queen, Elizabeth de Valois, the daughter of Henry II. of France. To render it the more solemn, a general assembly of the cortes of the kingdom was held there at the same time, to take the oath of fidelity to Don Carlos, the heir apparent to the throne. Several Lutherans appeared among these who were condemned to the flames and to other punishments. On this occasion the duke of Brunswick delivered up one of his retinue to the flames, to testify his hatred of the reformed cause, and to strike terror into the minds of the Germans, Flemings, and French, who were present, and were greatly suspected of heresy.[116] At the same place in the subsequent year, four priests, Spanish and French, were burnt alive for Lutheranism, and nineteen persons of the same persuasion were reconciled. Among the latter was one of the royal pages, whose release was granted by Philip and Valdes, at the intercession of the queen. In 1565, the same inquisition celebrated another auto, at which a number of protestants 330 were condemned to the fire and to penances, under the sev-

116. Cabrera, *Cronica de Don Filipe Segundo, Rey de Espana*, p. 248. Madrid, 1619, folio. The house of Brunswick Lunenburg was at that time divided into three branches. The person referred to in the text, Henry X., duke of Brunswick, was a determined foe to the Reformation. On the other hand, Ernest, duke of Lunenburg-Zell, whose descendants afterwards became electors of Hanover and kings of England, was a zealous reformer.

eral designations of Lutherans, faithful, and huguenaos, or hugonots. The metropolitan city of Spain was so eager to signalize its zeal against heresy, that in 1571, not to mention other examples, an auto was held in it, at which two persons were burnt alive, and one in effigy, while no fewer than thirty-one were sentenced to different punishments, as Lutherans. One of the two who perished in the flames was Doctor Sigismond Archel, a native of Cagliari in Sardinia. He had been arrested at Madrid in 1562, and after suffering for many years in the prisons of Toledo, had contrived to make his escape; but his portrait having been sent to the principal passes of the frontier, he was seized before he got out of the kingdom, and delivered again into the hands of his judges. When the depositions of the witnesses were communicated to him, Sigismond acknowledged all that was laid to his charge, but pleaded, that so far from being a heretic he was a better catholic than the papists; in proof of which he read, to the great mortification of the court, a long apology which he had composed in prison. He derided the ignorance of the priests who were sent to convert him, in consequence of which he was condemned to wear the gag on the scaffold and at the stake; and the guards, envying him the glory of a protracted martyrdom, pierced his body with their lances, while the executioners were kindling the pile, so that he perished at the same time by fire and sword.[117] Though the greater part of the prisoners exhibited in the autos-de-fe of Granada and Valencia were Jews or Mohametans, yet protestants suffered along with them from time to time; among whom our attention is particularly fixed upon Don Miguel de Vera y Santan-

331

---

117.   Llorente, ii. 284, 386, 389.

gel, a Carthusian monk of Portaceli, as belonging to the convent in which the first translation of the Bible into the Spanish language was composed.[118]

None of the provincial tribunals was so much occupied in suppressing the Reformation as those of Logrono, Saragossa, and Barcelona. In the numerous autos celebrated in these cities, a great part of those who appeared on the scaffolds were protestants. But the chief employment of the inquisitors in the eastern provinces consisted in searching for and seizing heretical books, which were introduced from the frontiers of France or by sea. In 1568 the council of the Supreme addressed letters to them, communicating alarming information received from England and France. Don Diego de Guzman, the Spanish ambassador at London, had written that the English were boasting of the converts which their doctrine was making in Spain, and particularly at Navarre. At the same advertisement was given by the ambassador at Vienne, that the Calvinists of France 332 were felicitating themselves on the signing of the treaty of peace between the French and Spanish monarchs, and entertained hopes that their religion would make as great progress in Spain as it had done in Flanders, England and other countries, because the Spaniards, who had already embraced it secretly, would now have an easy communication through Aragon with the protestants of Bearn. From Castres and from Paris the inquisitor general had received certain information that large quantities of books, in the Castilian tongue, were destined for Spain. These were in some instances put into casks of Champagne and Burgun-

118. Ibid. ii. 401, 411. See before, p. 191.

dy wine, with such address that they passed through the hands of the custom-house officers without detection. In this way many copies of the Spanish Bible, published by Cassiodoro de Reyna at Basle in 1569, made their way into Spain, notwithstanding the severest denunciations of the Holy Office, and the utmost vigilance of the familiars.[119]

But the Inquisition was not satisfied with preventing heretical men and books from coming into Spain; it exerted itself with equal zeal in preventing orthodox horses from being exported out of the kingdom. Incredible or ludicrous as this may appear to the reader, nothing can be more unquestionable than the fact, and nothing demonstrates more decidedly the unprincipled character of the inquisitors, as well of those who had recourse to its agency to promote their political schemes. As early as the fourteenth century it had been declared illegal to transport horses from Spain to France. This prohibition originated entirely in the views of political economy, and it was the business of the officers of the customs to prevent the contraband trade. But on occasion of the wars which arose between the papists and hugonots of France, and the increase of the latter on the Spanish borders, it occurred to Philip, as an excellent expedient for putting down the prohibited commerce, to commit the task to the Inquisition, whose services would be more effective than those of a hundred thousand frontier guards. With this view he procured a bull from the pope, which, with a special reference to the hugonots of France, and the inhabitants of Bearn in particular, declared all to be suspected of heresy who should

333

119.   Llorente, i. 477; ii. 392-394, 407.

furnish arms, munitions, or other instruments of war to heretics. In consequence of this, the council of the Supreme in 1569 added to the annual edict of denunciations a clause obliging all, under the pain of excommunication, to inform against any who had brought or transported horses for the use of the French protestants; which was afterwards extended to all who sent them across the Pyrenees. For this offence numbers were fined, whipped, and condemned to the galleys, by the inquisitorial tribunals on the frontiers. Always bent on extending their jurisdiction, the inquisitors sought to bring under their cognizance all questions respecting the contraband trade in saltpetre, sulphur, and powder.[120] Philip, however, diverted their attention from this encroachment on the civil administration, by engaging them in the pursuit of royal game. Ferdinand the catholic, availing himself of favorable circumstances, had added the greater part of the kingdom of Navarre to his dominions; and Charles V., in a fit of devotion, had, by his testament, enjoined his son to examine the claim which the Spanish monarchy had to these territories, and, if it should be found invalid, to restore them to the original proprietor.[121] So far from doing this act of justice, Philip intended to annex the whole of that kingdom to his crown. At his instigation pope Pius IV. in 1563 issued a bull, excommunicating Jeanne d'Albret, the hereditary queen of Navarre, and offering her dominions to the first catholic prince who should undertake to clear them of heresy. With characteristic duplicity Philip professed to

334

120.   Llorente, ii. 394-400.

121.   Sandoval, *Vida del Emperador Don Carlos V.* tom. ii. p. 876.

the French court his disapprobation of the step taken by his Holiness, while, in concert with the inquisitor general Espinosa and the house of Guise, he was concerting measures to seize the person of the queen of Navarre, and of her son, afterwards Henry IV. of France, with the view of carrying them by force into Spain, and delivering them to the Inquisition. This disgraceful conspiracy, formed in 1565, was defeated only by the sudden illness of the officer in whom its execution had been intrusted.[122]

335

The public is not unacquainted with the cruelties perpetrated by the inquisition of Goa, within the settlements of the Portuguese in the East Indies.[123] Similar atrocities were committed by the Spaniards in the New World, in which the tribunal of the Inquisition was erected at Mexico, Lima, and Carthagena. At Mexico, in the year 1574, an Englishman and a Frenchman were burnt alive as impenitent Lutherans, while others were subjected to penances for embracing the opinions of Luther and Calvin.[124] In the close of the seventeenth century, Louis Ramé, French protestant, was detained as a prisoner for four years by the inquisitors of Mexico; and several natives of England and its colonies were forced to abjure their religion, and submit to rebaptization.[125] A splendid auto-de-fe was celebrated at

---

122. Recueil des choses mémorables avenues en France, depuis l'an 1547, jusques à 1597, p. 292. *Mémoires Secrets de M. de Villeroi.* Llorente, chap. xxvii. art. 4.

123. *Dellon's Account of the Inquisition at Goa.* Lond. 1815. *Buchanan's Christian Researches in Asia,* p. 140-165.

124. Llorente, ii. 199.

125. Relation de Mons. Louis Ramé: *Baker's History of the*

the same place in 1659, at which William Lamport, an Irishman, was condemned to the flames, "for being infected with the errors of Luther, Calvin, Pelagius, Wicliff, and John Huss; in a word, because he was guilty of all imaginable heresies." He was the author of two writings, in one of which, to use the language of the indictment, "things were said against the Holy Office, its erection, style, mode of process, &c. in such a manner, that in the whole of it not a word was to be found that was not deserving of reprehension, not only as being injurious, but also insulting to our holy catholic faith." Of the other writing the procurator fiscal says, "that it contained detestable bitterness of language, and contumelies so filled with poison, as to manifest the heretical spirit of the author, and his bitter hatred against the Holy Office." On the day of execution, being desirous of testifying the readiness with which he met death, he was no sooner seated at the foot of the stake, and his neck placed in the ring, than he let himself fall and broke his neck. According to the official report of the auto-de-fe, Lamport trusted "that the devil, his familiar, would relieve him," and as he walked through the streets to the place of execution, continued looking up to the clouds to see if the superior power he expected was coming; but finding all his hopes in vain, he strangled himself.[126]

The year 1570 may be fixed upon as the period of the suppression of the reformed religion in Spain. After that date, protestants were still discovered at intervals by the

336

Inquisition, p. 368-394.

126. Auto General de la Fe, celebrado en Mexico, en 1659: Puig-blanch, tom. i. p. 85-87, 190-192.

Inquisition, and brought out in the autos-de-fe; but they were "as the gleaning grapes when the vintage is done." Several of these were foreigners, and especially Englishmen. The punishment of Burton and others produced remonstrances from foreign powers, which were long disregarded by the Spanish government. All that Mann, the English ambassador at the court of Madrid, could obtain, was a personal protection on the head of religion, while those of his retinue were compelled to go to mass;[127] and having caused the English service to be performed in his house, he was for some time excluded from the court, and obliged to quit Madrid. The circumstances in which Elizabeth was then placed, obliged her to act cautiously; but she wrote to Mann, desiring him to remonstrate with his catholic majesty against treatment so dishonorable to her crown, and so opposite to that which the Spanish ambassador received at London; and intimating that she would recall him, unless the privilege of private worship, according to the rites of their country, were granted to his servants.[128] At a subsequent period, the injury done to commerce by persecution obliged the government to issue orders, that strangers visiting Spain for the purpose of trade should not be molested on account of their religion. The inquisitors, however, made no scruple of transgressing the ordinances of the court on this point, by proceeding from time to time against foreigners, under the pretext that they propagated heresy by books or conversation.

337

---

127. Epistola Jo. Manni, Madr. 4 Nov. 1566: MSS. Bibl. Corpus Christi, No. cxiv. 252.

128. *Strype's Annals*, vol. i. p. 543-4.

Among many others, William Lithgow, the well-known traveller, was in 1620 imprisoned and put to the torture at 338 Malaga;[129] and in 1714 Isaac martin was subjected to the same treatment at Granada.[130]

Of fifty-seven persons, whose sentences were read at an auto held in Cuenca in 1654, one only was charged with Lutheranism.[131] In 1680, an auto-de-fe was celebrated at Madrid, in honor of the marriage of the Spanish monarch, Don Carlos II., to Marie Louise de Bourbon, the niece of Louis XIV. of France; and as a proof of the taste of the nation, a minute account of the whole procedure on that occasion was published to the world, with the approbation of all the authorities, civil and ecclesiastical. Among a hundred and eighteen victims produced on the scaffold, we meet with the name of only one protestant, whose effigy and bones were given to the flames. This was Marcos de Segura, a native of Villa de Ubrique, in Granada, whose sentence bears, that he had formerly been 'reconciled' by the inquisition of Llerena, as a heretic who denied purgatory, but who, having relapsed into this and other errors, was again thrown into prison, where he died in a state of impenitence and contumacy.[132]

Although upwards of sixteen hundred victims were 339

---

129. *Lithgow's Travels*, part x.

130. *The Narrative of Martin's Sufferings* was published in English, and translated into French, under the title of *"le Procès et les Souffrances de Mons. Isaac Martin*. Londres, 1723."

131. Llorente, iii. 470.

132. Joseph del Olmo, *Relacion Historica del Auto General de Fe*, que se celebró en Madrid este ano de 1680, p. 248.

burnt alive in the course of the eighteenth century, we do not perceive that any of them were protestants.[133] But the reformed faith can number among its confessors a Spaniard who suffered in the nineteenth century. Don Miguel Juan Antonio Solano, a native of Verdun in Aragon, was vicar of Esco in the diocese of Jaca. He was educated according to the Aristotelian system of philosophy and scholastic divinity; but the natural strength of his mind enabled him to throw off his early prejudices, and he made great proficiency in mathematics and mechanics. His benevolence led him to employ his inventive powers for the benefit of his parishioners, by improving their implements of husbandry, and fertilizing their soil. A long and severe illness, which made him a cripple for life, withdrew the good vicar of Esco from active pursuits, and induced him to apply himself to theological studies more closely than he had hitherto done. His small library happened to contain

---

133.   The last person who was committed to the flames, was a *beata*, burnt alive at Seville, on the 7th of November 1781. (Llorente, iv. 270.) "I myself (says Mr. Blanco White) saw the pile on which the last victim was sacrificed to human infallibility. It was an unhappy woman, whom the inquisition of Seville committed to the flames, under the charge of heresy, about forty years ago. She perished on a spot where thousands had met the same fate. I lament from my heart, that the structure which supported their melting limbs was destroyed during the late convulsions. It should have been preserved with the infallible and immutable canon of the Council of Trent over it, for the detestation of future ages." (*Practical and Internal Evidence against Catholicism*, p. 122-3.)

a Bible; and by perusing this with impartiality and attention, he gradually formed for himself a system of doctrine, 340
which agreed in the main with the leading doctrines of the
protestant churches. The candid and honorable mind of
Solano would not permit him either to conceal his sentiments, or to disseminate them covertly among his people.
Having drawn up a statement of his new views, he laid it
before the bishop of the diocese for his judgment, and receiving no answer from him, submitted it to the theological faculty of the university of Saragossa. The consequence
was, that he was seized and thrown into the prison of the
holy tribunal at Saragossa, which, in the infirm state of his
health, was the same as sending him to the grave. He contrived, however, by the assistance of some kind friends, to
make his escape, and to reach Oleron, the nearest French
town; but after seriously deliberating on the course which
he should pursue, he came to the resolution of asserting
the truth in the very face of death, and actually returned
of his own accord to the inquisitorial prison. On appearing before the tribunal, he acknowledged the opinions laid
to his charge, but pleaded in his defence, that after long
meditation, with the utmost desire to discover the truth,
and without any other help than the Bible, he had come
to these conclusions. He avowed his conviction, that all
saving truth was contained in the holy scriptures; that
whatever the church of Rome had decreed to the contrary,
by departing from the proper and literal sense of the sacred text, was false; that the idea of a purgatory and *limbus* 341
patrum was a mere human invention; that it was a sin to
receive money for saying mass; that tithes were fraudu-
lently introduced into the Christian church by the priests;

that the exaction of them was as dishonorable on their part, as it was impolitic and injurious to the cultivators of the soil; and that the ministers of religion should be paid by the state for their labors, in the same manner as judges were. The tribunal, after going through the ordinary forms, decided that Solano should be delivered over to the secular arm. The inquisitor general at that time was Arce, archbishop of Saragossa, the intimate friend of the Prince of Peace, and suspected of secret infidelity. Averse to the idea of an execution by fire during his administration, he prevailed on the council of the Supreme to order a fresh examination of the witnesses. This was carried into execution, and the inquisitors renewed their former sentence. Arce next ordered an inquiry into the mental sanity of the prisoner. A physician was found to give an opinion favorable to the known wishes of the grand inquisitor; but the sole ground on which it rested was, that the prisoner had vented opinions different from those of his brethren. The only thing that remained was, to endeavor to persuade Solano to retract those opinions which had been condemned by so many popes and general councils. But this attempt was altogether fruitless. To all the arguments drawn from such topics, he replied, that money was the god wor-

342 shipped at Rome, and that, in all the councils which had been held of late, the papal influence had decided theological questions, and rendered useless the good intentions of some respectable men. In the mean time, his confinement brought on a fever, during which the inquisitors redoubled their efforts for his conversion. He expressed himself thankful for their attention, but told them, that he could

not retract his sentiments without offending God and betraying the truth. On the twentieth day of his sickness, the physician informed him of his danger, and exhorted him to avail himself of the few moments which remained. "I am in the hands of God," said Solano, "and have nothing more to do." Thus died, in 1805, the vicar of Esco. He was refused ecclesiastical sepulture, and his body was privately interred within the enclosure of the Inquisition, near the back gate, towards the Ebro. His death was reported to the council of the Supreme, who stopped further proceedings, to avoid the necessity of burning him in effigy.[134]

Such are the details of the unsuccessful, but interesting, attempt to reform religion in Spain during the sixteenth century. Melancholy as the results were, they present nothing which reflects discredit on the cause, or on those by whom it was espoused. It did not miscarry through the imprudence or the infidelity of its leading friends. On the contrary, we have met with examples of the power of religion, of enlightened and pure love to truth, and of invincible fortitude, combined with meekness, scarcely inferior to any which are to be found in the annals of Christianity. To fall by such weapons as we have described, can be disgraceful to no cause. The fate of the Reformation in Spain, as well as in Italy, teaches us not to form hasty and rash conclusions respecting the course of proceedings on which Providence, for inscrutable reasons, may sometimes

343

134.   Llorente, iv. 127-133. *Blanco White's Practical and Internal Evidence against Catholicism*, p. 239-242.

344 be pleased to frown.[135] The common maxim, that "the

---

135. The following words of a writer, whose knowledge of facts was not equal to his strong natural sense, express an opinion which is not now uncommon:

"I believe it will be found, that when Christians have resorted to the sword, in order to resist persecution for the gospel's sake, as did the Albigenses, the Bohemians, the French Protestants, and some others, within the last 600 years, the issue has commonly been, that they have perished by it, that is, they have been overcome by their enemies, and exterminated; whereas, in cases where their only weapons have been 'the blood of the Lamb, and the word of their testimony, loving not their lives unto death,' they have overcome." (Christian Patriotism, by Andrew Fuller.) The facts which have been laid before the reader will enable him to judge of the truth of the last part of this assertion. Nor is the first part less incorrect and objectionable. The truth is, that the Albigenses, &c. who resisted, were not exterminated; while the Italian and Spanish protestants, who did not resist, met with that fate.

If the defensive wars of the Albigenses, &c. were unsuccessful, it ought to be remembered that those of the protestants in Germany, Switzerland, Scotland, and the Low Countries, were crowned with success. The French protestants were suppressed, not when they had arms in their hands, but when they were living peaceably under the protection of the public faith pledged to them in edicts which had been repeatedly and solemnly ratified. It is to be hoped that the public mind in Britain, much as has been done to mislead it, is not yet prepared for adopting principles which lead to a condemnation of the famous Waldenses and Bohemians, for standing to the defence of their lives, when proscribed and violently attacked on account of their religion. They lived during the

blood of the martyrs is the seed of the church," was re-
markably verified in the primitive ages of Christianity; but
we must distinguish what is effected by the special interposition and extraordinary blessing of heaven, from what
will happen according to the ordinary course of events. In
the nature of things, it cannot but operate as a great, and
with multitudes as an insuperable, obstacle to the reception of the truth, that, in following the dictates of their
conscience, they must expose themselves to every species
of worldly evil; and persecution may be carried to such a
pitch as will, without a miracle, crush the best of causes;
for, though it cannot eradicate the truth from the minds of
those by whom it has been cordially embraced, it may cut
off all the ordinary means of communication by which it
is propagated. Accordingly history shows that true religion
has been not only excluded, but banished for ages from
extensive regions of the globe, by oppressive laws and a
tyrannical administration.

345

---

period of Antichrist's power, and, according to the adorable plan
of providence, were allowed to fall a sacrifice to his rage; but while
the scriptures foretell this, they mention it to their honor, and not
in the way of fixing blame on them. "It was given unto the beast to
make war with the saints, and to overcome them." Instead of being
ranked with those who perished in consequence of their having
taken the sword without a just reason, these Christian patriots deserve rather to be numbered with those who "through faith waxed
valiant in fight, turned to flight the armies of the aliens, and others
were slain with the sword," all of whom, "having obtained a good
report through faith, received not the promises, God having provided some better thing for us."

But we are not on this account to conclude that the Spanish martyrs threw away their lives, and spilt their blood in vain. They offered to God a sacrifice of a sweet-smelling savour. Their blood is precious in his sight; he has avenged it, and may yet more signally avenge it. They left their testimony for truth in a country where it had been eminently opposed and outraged. That testimony has not altogether perished. Who knows what effects the record of what they dared and suffered may yet, through the divine blessing, produce upon that unhappy nation, which counted them as the filth and offscouring of all things, but was not worthy of them? Though hitherto lost on Spain, it has not been without all fruit elsewhere. The knowledge of the exertions made by Spaniards, and of the barbarous measures adopted to put them down, provoked many in other countries to throw off the Roman yoke, and to secure themselves against similar cruelties. In particular, it inspired their fellow-subjects in the Low Countries with a determination not to permit their soil to be polluted by the odious tribunal of the Inquisition, and consolidated that resistance which terminated in the establishment of civil liberty, in connection with the reformed religion, in the United Provinces. While we bow with reverence to those providential arrangements which permitted the standard of truth to fall in one part of the 346 world, we cannot but reflect with gratitude on the signal success vouchsafed to it in others. It was during the years 1559 and 1569 that the death-blow was given to the reformed religion in Spain; and during the same period the religious liberties of the protestants of Germany were finally secured, the reformed church was regularly organized in the kingdom of France, England was freed from popery by the accession of Elizabeth, and the cause of the Reformation, after struggling long for existence, attained to a happy and permanent establishment in Scotland.

VIII

Protestant Exiles from Spain

THOSE WHO HAVE TAKEN an interest in the preceding narrative will feel a desire to know something of the fate of those Spaniards who escaped the horrors of the dungeon and the stake by abandoning their native country. 347

From the time that violent measures were first adopted to put down the new opinions, individuals who had incurred the suspicions of the clergy, or whose attachment to their country yielded to their fears or to their passion for religious liberty, began to quit the Peninsula. As the persecution grew hotter, the emigration increased; nor had it altogether ceased at the close of the sixteenth century. Some of the emigrants crossed the Pyrenees, after which they sought out abodes in France and Switzerland; others, escaping by sea, took refuge in the Low Countries and in England.

Antwerp was the first place in which the refugees were formed into a church. The reformed opinions had been early introduced into this great mart of Europe, in consequence of the multitude of strangers who continually 348 resorted to it, and the superior freedom which is enjoyed wherever commerce flourishes. It was to the merchants of Antwerp that the Spaniards were first indebted for the means of their illumination;[1] and they continued long to promote the good work which they had begun, by encouraging translations of the scriptures and other books into the Spanish language.[2] Antonio de Corran, or Corranus, a learned native of Seville, was pastor of the Spanish church in Antwerp before the year 1568, when that city fell into the hands of the duke of Alva, of sanguinary memory.[3] After it recovered its liberty, the exiles returned to their former asylum, and enjoyed the pastoral labours of another native of Seville, Cassiodoro de Reyna, the translator of the Bible, who appears to have continued with them until 1585, when the city was again brought under the Spanish yoke, after a memorable siege by the duke of Parma. During his residence there, he drew up, for the use of his hearers, the Antwerp Catechism, which he published both in Spanish and French.[4]

349   Previously to his settling at Antwerp, De Reyna had

---

1.   See before, p. 124.

2.   Testimony is borne to the zealous liberality of the merchants of Antwerp, both by De Reyna and De Valera, in the prefaces to their translations into Spanish.

3.   MSS. of Archbishop Parker in the University Library of Cambridge, No. cxiv. 334. *Strype's Life of Grindal*, p. 148.

4.   *Walchiii Bibliotheca Theologia*, tom. i. p. 463-4. De Reyna also published at Antwerp, in 1483, a French translation of *Chytræus's History of the Augsburg Confession*. (Ib. p. 328. Ukert, Luther's Leben, tom. i. p. 282.)

resided at Strasburg, Frankfort, and other imperial cities, where he found a number of his countrymen, whom he would willingly have served as a preacher. But the German divines received him coldly, on account of his leaning to the sentiments of Calvin and the Swiss churches, on the subject of the eucharist.[5] On this account, he retired to Basle, and meeting with a kind reception in that seat of literature, he finished his translation of the Bible, which had been his chief employment for several years.[6]

The Palatinate, and the dominions of the landgrave of Hesse-Cassel, opened a more hospitable retreat to the refugees than any other part of Germany. It was in Heidelberg that De Montes published that work which first laid open to the eyes of Europe the mysteries of the Spanish inquisition, and the sufferings which his protestant coun-   350

---

5. *Fechtii Apparatus ad Hist. Eccles.* Sec. XVI. p. 305. Iin 1573, De Reyna published at Frankfort the Greek text of the Gospel according to John, with Tremellius's Latin translation of it from the Syriac; to which he added notes of his own. (*Le Long, Bibl. Sacra,* part. ii. vol. iii. cap. iv. sect. iv. § 11. edit. Masch.)

6. A copy of this Bible, preserved in the public library of Basle, has the following inscription in the handwriting of the translator: "*Cassiodorus Reinius Hispanus Hispalensis, inclytæ hujus Academiæ alumnus, hujus sacrorum librorum versionis Hispanicæ author, quam per integrum decennium elaboravit, et auxilio pientissimorum ministrorum hujus Ecclesiæ Basileensis ex decreto prudentissimi Senatus typis ab honesto viro Thoma Guarino cive Basileensi excusam demum emisit in lucem, in perpetuum gratitudininis et observantiæ monumentum huc librum inclytæ huic Academiæ supplex dicabat A. 1570, mense Junio.*" (*Miscellanea Groningana,* tom. iii. p. 99, 100.)

trymen had endured from that inhuman tribunal;[7] while a confession of faith in the name of the exiles from Spain, along with an account of their persecution, came from the press of Cassel.[8]

France was happily in such a state as to offer a refuge to the Spanish protestants, when driven from their native country. Many of them repaired to the city of Lyons, where means of religious instruction had been provided for them, as well as for their brethren who had fled from Italy.[9] The French protestants showed themselves uniformly disposed to sympathize with the Spanish refugees, contributed to their support, shared with them that degree of religious liberty which they happened at the time to enjoy, and admitted several of them to be pastors of their

351

---

7. The Heidelberg Catechism was also translated into Spanish, for their use. (*Gerdesii Florilegium Libr. Rar.* p. 77. edit. 1763.)

8. The Confession of the Spanish exiles was published in Spanish and German at Cassel in 1601. And at the same time was printed a *Brief History of the Spanish Inquisition*, with an *Account of the Spectackel (auto-de-fe)* at Valladolid, 21 May 1558. (Freytag, Adparatus Litterarius, tom. iii. p. 196-200.) The Confession was printed in German at Amberg in 1611, by Joachim Ursin, who published at the same time *Hispanicæ Inquisitionis et Carnificinæ Secretiora.* (*Gerdesii Florilegium Libr. Rar.* p. 86-7.) Learned men differ as to the real author, who concealed himself under this fictitious name; some fixing on Innocent Gentillet, the author of Anti-Machiavel, and others on Michael Beringer. The materials of the work are chiefly borrowed from that of Montanus.

9. See before, p. 200, note §. *History of the Reformation in Italy*, p. 405-6.

churches.[10] It is gratifying to find the French synods also receiving into their communion Moors, who had escaped, along with the protestants, from the inquisition of Spain, and now abjured Mahometanism under circumstances which rendered their change of religion less obnoxious to suspicion.[11]

But it was in Geneva and England that the greater part of Spanish refugees found a safe harbour and permanent abode. As they were intimately connected with the Italian refugees who settled in these places, we shall, according to a former promise,[12] combine the affairs of both in the following narrative.

As early as 1542, there was formed at Geneva a congregation of Italian refugees, which had the chapel of the cardinal d'Ostie assigned to it by the council, and was un-   352

---

10. Gaspar Olaxa, a Spaniard, was minister of Castres, but deposed for fomenting dissensions in that church, before the year 1594. (*Quick's Synodicon*, vol. i. p. 172, 188.) At a subsequent period, Vincente Solera was minister of St. Lo, in Normandy. (Ibid. i. 509; ii. 241.) In 1614, Juan de Luna and Lorenzo Fernandez, Spaniards who had abjured monachism and popery, obtained, on the recommendation of the church of Montauban, pecuniary relief from the National Synod of Tonneins. (Ibid. i. 413-4.) And in 1620, Geronimo Quevedo, who had escaped from the Inquisition, received a pension from the Synod of Alex, to be continued at the discretion of the church of Montpellier. (Ibid. ii. 43.)

11. Ibid. i. 491-2.

12. *History of the Progress and Suppression of the Reformation in Italy*, p. 408.

der the pastoral inspection of Bernardino de Sesvaz.[13] Its meetings were, however, discontinued after a short time, probably by the removal of some of its principal members; and they were not resumed until the year 1551.

The person to whom its revival was chiefly owing was Galeazzo Carroccioli, whose life presents incidents which would excite deep interest in a romance.[14] He was the eldest son of Nicol-Antonio Carraccioli, marquis of Vico, one of the grandees of Naples. His mother was of the noble family of the Caraffi, and sister to the cardinal of that name who was raised to the pontifical chair. At the age of twenty, he married Vittoria, daughter to the duke of Nuceria, who brought him a large fortune, and bore him six children. The emperor Charles V., who was under obligations to the marquis, conferred on his son the office of gentleman-sewer; and the personal accomplishments of Galeazzo, the uniform correctness of his manners, his affability, and the talents which he discovered for public business, led all who knew him to anticipate his gradual and certain advancement in worldly honors. Serious impres-

353 sions, accompanied with a conviction of the errors of the

---

13. *Spon, Histoire de Geneve*, tom. i. p. 290, note; 4to edition. I have not met with the name of Sesvaz among the Italian reformers, and am inclined to suppose that Ochino, who arrived at Geneva in the course of the year 1542, assumed that appellation for the purpose of concealment at the beginning of his exile.

14. *The Life of Carraccioli* was written in his native tongue, by Nicola Balbani, minister of the Italian church in Geneva. It was translated into Latin by Beza; into French by Minutoli, and by Sieur de Lestan; and into English by William Crashaw.

church of Rome, were made on his mind by Valdes and
Martyr, at the time that the protestant tenets were secretly
embraced by many individuals in Naples; and his religious
dispositions were cherished by the advices of that pious
and elegant scholar, Marc-Antonio Flaminio.[15] Having
accompanied the emperor to Germany, his acquaintance
with the reformed doctrine was enlarged by conversation
with some of the leading protestants, and the perusal of
their writings; and his attachment to it was confirmed by
an interview which, on his way home, he had at Strasburg
with Martyr, who had lately forsaken his native country
for the sake of religion. After his return to Naples, he endeavored to prevail on such of his countrymen as held the
same views with himself to meet together in private for
their mutual edification; but he found that the severe measures lately resorted to had struck terror into their minds,
and that they were resolved, not only to conceal their sentiments, but also to practice occasional conformation to
the rites of popish worship. He now entered into serious
deliberation with himself on one of the most delicate and
painful questions which can be forced on a person in his
circumstances.

What was he to do? Was he to spend his whole life in 354
the midst of idolatry, in the way of concealing that faith

---

15. Giannone says that Flaminio wrote a letter to Caraccioli, exhorting him to adhere to the Reformation, which had been embraced
by the marchioness of Pescara and others. The letter, rich with the
unction of true piety, is inserted in the *Life of Caraccioli*, chap. v.
and in *Schelhorn's Amœnitates Ecclesiasticæ*, tom. ii. p. 122-132; but
it makes no mention of the Reformation.

which was dearer to his heart than life, and incurring the threatening, "Him that confesseth me not before men, I will not confess before my Father and his angels?" Or, was it his duty to leave father, and wife, and children, and houses, and lands, for Christ's sake and the gospel's? The sacrifice of his secular dignities and possessions did not cost him a sigh; but as often as he reflected on the distress which his departure would inflict on his aged father, who, with parental pride, regarded him as the heir of his titles, and the stay of his family,— on his wife whom he loved and by whom he was loved tenderly,— and on the dear pledges of their union, he was thrown into a state of unutterable anguish, and started back with horror from the resolution to which conscience had brought him. At length, by an heroic effort of zeal, which few can imitate, and many will condemn, he came to the determination of bursting the tenderest ties which perhaps ever bound man to country and kindred. His nearest relations, so far from being reconcilable to the idea of his abandoning the church of Rome, had signified their displeasure at the pious life which he had led for some years, and at his evident disrelish for the gaieties of the court. Having no hope of procuring their consent, he concealed his design from them, and, availing himself of the pretext of business which he had to transact with the emperor, set out for Augsburg, whence he speedily repaired to Geneva.[16] The intelligence of his arrival at that place, and his abjuration of the Roman religion, while it filled the imperial court with astonishment, plunged his family into the deepest

355

16. His arrival in that city, in June 1551, excited such surprise that he was at first suspected by some as a spy. (*Spon*, i. 290.)

distress. One of his cousins, who had been his intimate friend, was despatched from Naples to represent the grief which his conduct had caused, and urge him to return. As soon as his refusal was known, sentence was passed against him, and he was deprived of all the property which he inherited from his mother. At the risk of his life, he went to Italy and met his father at Verona, where he remained until the marquis went to the emperor, and obtained, as a special favor, that the sentence pronounced against his son should not extend to his grandson. During his father's absence, Galeazzo was waited upon by the celebrated Fracastoro, who used his great eloquence to persuade him to comply with the wishes of his friends. In the following year he met his father a second time at Mantua, when an offer was made to him, in the name of his uncle, now pope Paul IV., that he should have a protection against the Inquisition, provided he would take up his residence within the Venetian states; a proposal to which neither his safety nor the dictates of his conscience would permit him to accede. All this time he had been refused the privilege of seeing his family; and it was not until the end of the year 1557 that he received a letter from his wife Vittoria, earnestly requesting an interview with him, and fixing the place of the meeting. Having obtained a safe-conduct from the government of the Grisons, he immediately set out for Lesina, an island on the coast of Dalmatia, over against his paternal castle of Vico; but, on his arrival at the appointed place, Vittoria, instead of making her appearance, sent two of her sons to meet their father. He had scarcely returned to Geneva from this fatiguing and dangerous journey, when he received another packet from his 356 wife, apologizing for her breach of engagement, and begging him to come without delay to the same place, where she would not fail to meet him, along with his father and children. On his reaching Lesina the second time, none of the family had arrived; and unable to brook further delay, he crossed the Gulf of Venice, and presented himself at his father's gate. He was received with every demonstration of joy, and for some days the castle was thronged with friends who came to welcome him. But it behoved the parties to come at last to an explanation. Taking Vittoria aside, Galeazzo apologized for not having imparted to her the secret of his departure, gave a full account of the reasons of his conduct, and begged her to accompany him to Geneva; promising that no constraint should be laid upon her conscience, and that she should be at liberty to practice her religion under his roof. After many protestations of affection, she finally replied, that she could not reside out of Italy, nor in a place where any other religion than that of the church of Rome was professed; and further, that she could not live with him as her husband, so long as he was infected with heresy. Her confessor had inculcated upon her that it was a damnable sin to cohabit with a heretic, and dreading the influence which her husband might exert over her mind, had prevented her from keeping her first appointment. The day fixed for his departure being come, Galeazzo went to take leave of his father, who, laying aside the affection with which he had hitherto treated him, and giving way to his passion, loaded him with reproaches and curses. On quitting his father's apartment, he had to undergo a still severer trial of his sensibility. He found his wife and children, with a number

357

of his friends, waiting for him in the hall. Bursting into tears, and embracing her husband, Vittoria besought him not to leave her a widow, and her babes fatherless. The children joined in the entreaties of their mother; and the eldest daughter, a fine girl of thirteen, grasping his knees, refused to part with him. How he disengaged himself, he knew not; for the first thing which brought him to recollection was the noise made by the sailors on reaching the opposite shore of the Gulf. He used often to relate to his intimate friends, that the parting scene continued long to haunt his mind; and that, not only in dreams, but also in reveries into which he fell during the day, he thought he heard the angry voice of his father, saw Vittoria in tears, and felt his daughter dragging at his heels. His return gave great joy to his friends at Geneva, who, in proportion to 358 the confidence which they reposed in his constancy, were alarmed for the safety of his person.

Painful as this visit had been to his feelings, it contributed to restore his peace of mind, by convincing him that he could entertain no hope of enjoying the society of his family except on the condition of renouncing his religion. After he had remained nine years in exile, he consulted Calvin on the propriety of contracting a second marriage. That reformer, who took a deep interest in the character of his noble friend, felt great scruples as to the expediency of this step, but ultimately gave his approbation to it, after he had consulted the divines of Switzerland and the Grisons. Accordingly, the courts of Geneva having legally pronounced a sentence of divorce against Vittoria, on the ground of her obstinate refusal to live with her husband, he married Anne Fremejere, the widow of a French refugee from Rouen, with whom he continued to live happily in a state of dignified frugality. On being informed of this part of his conduct, we feel as if it detracted from the high unsullied virtue which Galeazzo had hitherto displayed. His second nuptials, though contracted according to the rules of the canon law, gave occasion of reproach to the keen adversaries of the Reformation; but they did not lower him in the estimation of his acquaintance of either religious persuasion. By the citizens of Geneva he was all along held in the highest respect; the freedom of the city had been conferred on him soon after his arrival

359 among them; a house was allotted to him by the public; and he was admitted a member both of the great and small council. Princes, ambassadors, and learned men, popish as well as protestant, who visited the city, regularly paid their respects to the marquis; a title which was always given him, though he refused to assume it even after the death of his father. Nothing gave greater offence to the papal court, and the government of Naples, than his choosing the see of heresy for his residence. It was probably with the view of removing this prejudice, and thereby procuring remittances from his patrimonial estate, that he consented, in the spring of 1572, to a proposal made by Admiral Coligni to take up his abode with him;[17] but providentially he was prevented from removing to France so soon

---

17. On that occasion the Council of Geneva testified the strongest reluctance to consent to his departure. They promised to release him from all public charges, and to supply him with every thing which he needed; while the Sieurs Roset and Franc offered him the use of their country houses. (*Fragmens, extraits des Registres de Genève*, p. 44.)

as he had intended, and thus escaped the massacre of St. Bartholomew, which took place in August that year. After residing five years at Nion and Lausanne for the sake of economy in his living, he returned to Geneva, which he did not again leave until his death, which happened in 1586, in the sixty-eighth year of his age.[18]

The first thing which engaged the attention of Caracci-   360 oli, after his settlement in Geneva, was the re-organizing of the Italian congregation. Lattantio Ragnoni, a gentleman of Sienna, whom he had known at Naples, having arrived a few days after him, and given proofs of his orthodoxy and qualifications for public teaching, was persuaded by him to undertake the office of pastor to his countrymen.[19] They accordingly recommenced their public exercises in the Magdalene church, which was assigned to them by the council.[20] Caraccioli himself became one of their elders, and by the respectability of his character, and the wisdom of his counsels, contributed more than any other individual to the permanent prosperity of that church. In the close of the year 1553, they obtained a preacher of greater abilities in Celso Massimiliano, usually called Martinengo, because he was the son of a count of that name, in the territories of Brescia. He had entered into the order of canons regular, and having imbibed the reformed doctrine from Peter Martyr, preached it for some time with great bold-

---

18. *Life of Galeachius Caracciolus, Marsuis of Vico, passim. Giannone, Hist. de Naples,* live. xxxii. chap. 5. *Gerdesii Italia Reformata,* p. 104-112. *Spon,* i. 290. *Fragmens,* ut supra, p. 16, 22, 24, 50.

19. Ibid., chap. xi.

20. *Spon, Hist. de Genève,* tom. i. p. 290.

ness and eloquence; but understanding that snares were laid for his life, he fled to the Valteline, whence he came to Basle, with the intention of proceeding to England. By the importunities of Caraccioli he was induced to abandon his intended journey, and to undertake the pastoral charge of the Italian church at Geneva.[21] On his death in 1557, Calvin exerted himself to procure for them the services of Martyr and Zanchi, who excused themselves on account of their engagements; and the church appears to have remained under the sole inspection of Ragnoni[22] until 1559, when the procured Nicola Balbani, who continued to serve them with much approbation nearly to the close of the sixteenth century.[23] It would seem that this situation was also held by Jean Baptiste Rotan, a learned man, who, on removing to France, incurred the suspicion of seeking to betray the reformed church by reconciling it to Rome.[24]

361

The peace of the Italian church was for some time disturbed by the antitrinitarian controversy. Alciati, a military officer from Milan, and Blandrata, a physician from

---

21. *Zanchii Epist. ad Landgravium: Opera*, tom. vii. p. 3. *Spon*, i. 299, 300. *Life of Caracciolus*, chap. xvii.

22. It appears from a letter of Calvin, that Lattantio Ragnoni survived Martinengo. (*Calvini Epist.* p. 128: Opera, tom. ix.)

23. Senebier, *Hist. Lit. de Genève*, tom. i. p. 115-6. "The Italian minister of Geneva, Balbani, (says Joseph Scaliger) carried a barrette (a leather cap or cowl) in his breast, which he wore in the pulpit, and put his hat over it when he preached; as all the other Genovese pastors wear small flat bonnets." (*Secunda Scaligerana*, voc. Barrette.)

24. Bock, *Hist. Antitrin.* tom. ii. p. 665. *Conf. Gerdesii Ital. Ref.* p. 327-329, Senebier, i. 395.

Piedmont, in the visits which they made to Geneva, privately disseminated their sentiments, which were adopted by Valentinus Gentilis, a native of Cosenza in Calabria, who had joined the Italian congregation. The celebrated lawyer Gribaldo, after differing with Calvin, had taken up his residence at Fargias, a villa which he purchased in the neighbouring district of Gex, within the jurisdiction of Bern, from which he kept up an intercourse with the secret agitators in Geneva. They had caused great uneasiness 362 to Martinengo, who, in recommending his church to the care of Calvin, when he was on his death-bed, adjured that reformer to guard them against the arts of these restless spirits.[25] In concert with Ragnoni, their surviving pastor, Calvin exerted himself in allaying these dissensions, and, in 1558, drew up a confession of faith for the use of the Italian congregation. This was subscribed by Gentilis, under the pain of perjury if he should afterwards contradict it; but, encouraged by Gribaldo, he began again to spread the opinions which he had renounced, upon which a process was commenced against him, which issued in his expulsion from the city.[26]

The internal peace of the Italian church being restored, it continued to flourish, and gained fresh accessions every year by the arrival of persons from the different parts of Italy. All classes in Geneva, the magistrates, the ministers, and the citizens, vied with each other in their kind attention to the exiles from Italy, who were admitted to privi-

---

25. *Calvini Epistolæ*, p. 128: *Opera*, tom. ix.

26. Bock, *Hist. Antitrin.* tom. ii. p. 427-443, 466-472. *Calvini Epist.* p. 160-162. *Spon*, i. 301-304.

leges, and advanced to offices, in common with the native inhabitants of the city. Nor had the republic any reason to repent of this liberal policy. The adopted strangers transferred their loyalty and affections to Geneva; and among those who have served her most honorably in the senate, the academy, and the field, from that time to the present, we recognize with pleasure Italian refugees and their descendants. It is sufficient here to mention the names of Diodati, Turretini, Calandrini, Burlamaqui, Micheli, Minutoli, Butini, and Offredi.

363

Individual Spaniards, who found it necessary to fly from the Inquisition, had taken refuge in Geneva from the time that Egidio was thrown into prison at Seville.[27] In 1557, additions were made to their number;[28] and the persecution increasing during the two subsequent years, emigrants poured in from all parts of the Peninsula.[29] The council extended to them the privileges which had been already granted to the emigrants from Italy. It was Juan Perez, to whom his countrymen were otherwise so much indebted,[30] who first formed a Spanish church in Geneva.[31]

---

27. See before, p. 199.

28. "*Oct. 14, 1557. On recoit 300 habitans le même matin; savoir, 200 Francois, 50 Anglois, 25 Italiens, 4 Espagnols, &c.; tellement que l'antichambre du conseil ne les pouvoit tous contenir.*" (*Fragmens Biographiques et Historiques, extraits des Registres de Genève*, p. 24.)

29. In a letter, dated Zurich, 10 June 1558, Martyr writes to Utenhovius, "*Quin et Hispani, ac ii docti et probi viri, turmatim Genevam confluunt.*" (*Gerdesii Scrinium Antiq.* tom. ii. p. 673.)

30. See before, p. 199.

31. *Bezæ Icones*, sig. Ii. iij.; comp. Spon, i. 299.

After his departure to France, they enjoyed the pastoral labors of De Reyna and others of their learned country-men; but, as many of their members removed to England and other places, and as most of them understood Italian, 364 they adjoined themselves, before the close of the century, to the church which was placed under the charge of Balba-ni.[32] One of the most distinguished of their number, both in point of learning and piety, was Pedro Gales. While he taught Greek and jurisprudence in Italy, he had fallen un-der the suspicion of heresy, and being put to the torture at Rome, lost one of his eyes. Escaping from prison, he came to Geneva about the year 1580, and was appointed joint professor of philosophy with Julio Paci, an Italian lawyer.[33] During an interruption of the academical exercises caused by the attempts of the duke of Savoy on Geneva, Gales was persuaded to accept the rectorship of the college of Guienne at Bordeaux. But finding his situation unpleas-ant, in consequence of the civil wars which then raged in France, and the envy of one of his colleagues, he left it, with the intention of repairing to the Netherlands. On his journey he was seized by some of the partisans of the League, and delivered first to his countrymen, and after-wards to the Spanish Inquisition, by whose sentence he

32. In the epistle dedicatory to his edition of the Spanish confession of faith, Eberhardt von Retrodt says that, when he was at Geneva in 1581, he heard "Sign Balbado" (Balbani) preach to a large congre-gation of Italians and Spaniards, "in their own church."

33. Paci was the intimate friend of the learned Peiresc. Tiraboschi la-bours to show that he returned to the Roman faith in his latter days; but his arguments are inconclusive.

was committed to the flames, after making an undaunted
365 profession of his faith.[34] He had made a large collection of
ancient manuscripts, with annotations of his own, part of
which was preserved, and has been highly prized by the
learned.[35]

England had the honor of opening a harbour to protestants of every country who fled from persecution at the
beginning of the Reformation. The first congregation of
strangers formed in London was the Dutch or German,
which met in the church of Austin Friars, under the super-
intendence of the learned Polish nobleman John a Lasco.
It was followed by the erection of the French and Italian
congregations. As early as 1551 there was an Italian church
in London, of which Michael Angelo Florio was pastor.[36]

---

34. *Meursii Athenæ Batavæ*, p. 333. The Jesuit Andreas Schottus,
unwilling to have it thought that a person of such erudition was put
to death by the Inquisition, says, "It is reported that he was seized
along with his wife by a military band, and expired in the Pyrenees."
(*Schotti Bibliotheca Hispanica*, p. 612.)

35. Cujas, Casaubon, and Father Labbe have all extolled the learning of
Gales. (*Colomesiana, Collection par Des Maizeaux*, tom. i. p. 612-
3. Bayle, *Dict. art. Gales, Pierre.*) The person whom I have called
Pedro Gales in p. 181 was, I am satisfied on reflection, Nicolaus
Gallasius, or De Gallars, one of the ministers of Geneva.

36. *Scrinium Antiquarium*, tom. ii. p. 674; tom. iv. p. 478. Florio is the
author of an extremely rare work: "*Historia de la Vita e de la Morte
de l'illustriss. Signora Giovanna Graia, gia Regina eletta e publicata
d'Inghilterra. Con l'aggiunto d'una doctiss. disputa...e nel' Proemio de
l'Authore, M. Michelangelo Florio Fiorentino, gia Predicatore famoso
de' Sant' Evangelo in piu cita d'Italia, et in Londra. Stampato appres-*

On its restoration after the death of queen Mary, Florio re- 366
turned; but, owing to some irregularity of conduct, he was
not admitted to his former place, which was conferred on
Jeronimo Jerlito.[37] The most distinguished of its members
were Jacomo Contio, better known as an author by the
name of Acontius, who was suspended for some time from
communion, on suspicion of his being infected with Arian
and Pelagian tenets;[38] his friend Battista Castiglioni, who
had a place at court, and taught Italian to Queen Elizabeth;[39] Julio Borgarusci, physician to the earl of Leices-
ter;[40] Camillo Cardoini, a Neapolitan nobleman, whose
son was afterwards made governor of Calabria, as a reward
for abjuring the protestant religion,[41] and Albericus Gentilis, who became professor of civil law at Oxford.[42] The

so Rechardo Pittore, ne l'anno di Christo 1607."

37. *Strype's Life of Grindal*, p. 108, 135. *History of the Reformation in
Italy*, p. 374.

38. Bayle, *Dict. art. Acontius; addition in Eng. Trans. Gerdesii Hist. Ref.*
tom. iii. Append. No. xvi. *Scrin. Antiqu.* tom. vii. p. 123. *Strype's
Life of Grindal*, p. 45.

39. Bayle, ut supra. *Gerdesii Italia Reformata*, p. 166.

40. *Strype's Life of Grindal*, p. 225.

41. *Wood's Fasti Oxon.* col. 228. edit. Bliss. Senebier, *Hist. Lit de Genève*,
tom. ii. p. 181.

42. Matteo Gentile, a physician of Ancona, left his native country for
religion, accompanied by his two sons, Alberico and Scipio. The
latter settled with his father in Germany, and became as eminent
a civilian as his brother. (*Wood's Athenæ Oxon.* vol. ii. p. 90. *Fasti
Oxon.* p. 217. edit. Bliss. *Gerdesii Ital. Ref.* p. 271-274.)

foreign Italian congregation appears to have been united to the French in the course of the sixteenth century; but in 1618 the noted Antonio de Dominis, archbishop of Spalatro, preached in Italian at London, and had one of the family of Calandrini appointed as his colleague.[43]

367

There had been Spaniards in England from the time of Henry VIII., whose first queen belonged to that nation. Her daughter Mary entertained them about her person, and their number greatly increased after her marriage to Philip II. of Spain. As several of them were converted to protestantism, some writers are of opinion that they must have heard the gospel preached in their native tongue during the reign of Edward VI.[44] But it does not appear that the Spanish protestants were formed into a congregation until the accession of Elizabeth. During the year 1559 they met for worship in a private house in London, and had one Cassiodorio for their preacher. In the course of the following year they presented a petition to Cecil and Grindal bishop of London, for liberty to meet in public. They had hitherto refrained, they said, from taking this step, by the advice of persons whom they greatly respected, and from fear of giving offence; but they were convinced that their continuing to do so was no less discreditable to the religion which they professed, than it was incommodious to themselves. Their adversaries took occasion to say, that they must surely harbour some monstrous tenets, detested even by Lutherans, when they were not permitted, or did

368

---

43. *Woodrow's Life of Robert Boyd of Trochrig*, p. 260; MS. in the Library of the College of Glasgow.

44. *Strype's Life of Cranmer*, p. 246.

not venture, to assemble publicly in a city where protestants from every country were allowed this privilege. Some of their countrymen had withdrawn from their assembly, and others had declined to join it, lest they should suffer in the trade which they carried on with Spain, from their attendance on a private and unauthorized conventicle. They added, that if the king of Spain complained of the liberty granted to them, they would desist from the exercise of it, and quit the kingdom rather than involve it in a quarrel with foreign states.[45] The government was favourable to their application, and it would seem that they met soon after in one of the city churches, whose ministers, as stated in their petition, were willing to accommodate them. London was not the only place which furnished them with an asylum; but in other towns both they and the Italians generally assembled for worship along with the French emigrants.[46] With the view of countering the invidious and unfounded reports circulated against their orthodoxy, the Spanish protestants in England drew up 369 and published a confession of their faith, which was ad-

---

45. *Strype's Life of Grindal*, p. 47-8. *Strype's Annals of the Reformation*, vol. i. p. 237.

46. Besides the metropolis, the Dutch and French exiles settled, and for some time had churches, in Southwar, Canterbury, Norwich, Colchester, Maidstone, Sandwich, and Southampton. (*Strype's Annals*, i. 554.) In 1575, John Migrode was pastor of the Dutch church in Norwich. (*Bibl. Bremensis, class.* vi. p. 518.P And in 1583, Mons. Mary was pastor of the French church in that city. (*Aymon, Synodes Nationaux des Eglises Reformées de France*, tom. i. p. 169.)

opted by their brethren scattered in other countries.[47] This document proves that the Spanish exiles, while they held the doctrines common to all protestants, were favourable to the views which the reformed churches maintained in their controversy with the Lutherans respecting the eucharist.[48]

The countenance granted by the government of England to protestant exiles, and particularly to Spaniards, gave great offense to the pope and to the king of Spain. It was specified as one of the charges against Elizabeth, in the bull of Pius V. excommunicating that princess. This drew from bishop Jewel the following triumphant reply.

---

47. Gerdesius says it was published at London in 1559. (*Florilegium Libr. Rar.* p. 87. edit. an. 1763. *Scrinium Antiq.* tom. i. p. 151.) The following is its title, as given in an edition with a German translation: "*Confession de Fe Christiana hecha por ciertos Fieles Espannoles, los quales huyendo los abusos de la Iglesia Romana, y la crueldad de la Inquisition de Espanna, dexaron su patria, para ser recibidos de la Iglesia de los Fieles por hermanos in Christo. Anfenglick in Hispanischer Sprachen beschrieben jetzt aber allen frommen Christen zu Nutz und Trost verteuchet, durch Eberhardten von Redrodt Fürstl. Hessischen bestalten Hauptman über I.F.G. Leibguardia im Schlos und Vestung Cassel. Gedruckt zu Cassel durch Willem Wessel, 1601.*" 8vo folior. 69. (Freytag, *Adparatus Litter.* tom. iii. p. 196-200.)

48. See the extracts from the Spanish confession given by Gerdesius, in his *Scrinium Antiquarium*, tom. i. p. 149, 150. The same fact is confirmed by another publication: "*Anton. Corrani, dicti Benerive, Epistola ad Fratres Augustanæ Confessionis, data Antwerpiæ, d. 21 Januarii 1567;*" which was printed in Latin, French, German, and English.

Having mentioned that they had either lost or left behind 370
their all, goods, lands, and houses, he goes on to say: "Not
for adultery, or theft, or treason, but for the profession of
the gospel. It pleased God here to cast them on land. The
queen, of her gracious pity, granted them harbour. Is it
become a heinous thing to show mercy? God willed the
children of Israel to love the stranger, because they were
strangers in the land of Egypt. He that showeth mercy
shall find mercy. But what was the number of such who
came to us? Three or four thousand. Thanks be to God,
this realm is able to receive them, if the number be greater.
And why may not queen Elizabeth receive a few afflicted
members of Christ, which are compelled to carry his cross?
Whom, when he thought good to bring safely by the dangers of the sea, and to set in at our havens, should we
cruelly have driven them back again, or drowned them, or
hanged them, or starved them? Would the vicar of Christ
give this counsel? Or, if a king receive such, and give them
succor, must he therefore be deprived? They are our brethren; they live not idly. If they take houses of us, they pay
rent for them; they hold not our grounds, but by making
due recompense. They beg not in our streets, nor crave any
thing at our hands, but to breathe our air, and to see our
sun. They labour truly, they live sparefully; they are good
examples of virtue, travail, faith, and patience. The towns
in which they abide are happy, for God doth follow them
with his blessings." Referring to the Spaniards who came
to England in the reign of queen Mary, the bishop thus
contrasts them with their protestant countrymen. "These 371
are few, those were many; these are poor and miserable,
those were lofty and proud; these are naked, those were

armed; these are spoiled by others, those came to spoil us; these are driven from their country, those came to drive us from our country; these came to save their lives, those came to have our lives. If we were content to bear those then, let us not grieve now to bear these."[49]

The Spanish monarch was not less indignant than his Holiness at the asylum granted to his protestant subjects. Not contented while persecuting them at home, he hunted them in every country to which they were driven. Large sums of money were appropriated to the maintaining of spies, and defraying other expenses incurred by that disgraceful traffic. In France and Germany, individuals were from time to time carried off, and delivered over to the Inquisition. Not daring to make such attempts on the free soil of England, the emissaries of Spain had recourse to methods equally infamous. They required the English government to deliver up the refugees as traitors and criminals who had fled from justice. Francisco Farias and Nicolas Molino, two respectable members of the Spanish congregation, who had resided eight years in this country, were denounced by one of their countrymen who acted as a spy in London. In consequence of this, the Spanish ambassador received instructions from his court to demand of Elizabeth, that they should be sent home to be tried for crimes which were laid to their charge; and to induce her to comply with the request, their names were coupled with that of a notorious malefactor who had lately escaped from Flanders. If these innocent men had not had friends at court who knew from experience to sympathize with

372

---

49. View of a Seditious Bull, in *Bishop Jewel's Works*.

the exile, they might have been delivered up to a cruel death.[50] To enable it to meet any future demand of this kind, the English government adopted measures to obtain an exact account of all the members of the foreign congregations who had come from any part of the king of Spain's dominions.[51]

In the year 1568, Corranus came from Antwerp, and undertook the pastoral charge of the Spanish congregation in London. Having been involved in a quarrel with Jerlito and Cousin, the ministers of the Italian and French congregations, who accused him of error and defamation, the parties appealed to Beza, who referred the controversy to bishop Grindal. The commissioners named by the bishop to try the cause suspended Corranus from preaching.[52] He appears to have been a man of a hot temper;[53] but his learning recommended him to secretary Cecil, by whose 373 influence the suspension was taken off, and he was made reader of divinity in the Temple. When he went to Oxford at a subsequent period, some of the heads of colleges scrupled to receive him, on account of the suspicions formerly entertained as to his orthodoxy; but their objections were

---

50. *Strype's Life of Grindal*, p. 109; Append. No. xiii.

51. Ibid. p. 110, 111. In the year 1568, the Spaniards and the Italians who had been subjects of the king of Spain, amounted to about 57 in London alone. (Ibid. p. 135.)

52. Ibid. p. 125-127, 147-149.

53. When the sentence was intimated to him, he exclaimed, "It seems you English are determined to wage both a civil and ecclesiastical war against the Spaniards; a civil war by taking their ships, an ecclesiastical in my person."

overcome, and he was admitted to read lectures on theology in the university, as well as to hold a living in the church of England.[54] Though there is no evidence that Cypriano de Valera ever acted as a preacher in England, yet he took an active part in the affairs of the foreign churches.[55] But his labors were chiefly by means of the press, in which respect he was more extensively beneficial to his countrymen than any of the exiles. He arrived in England soon after the accession of Elizabeth, and appears to have spent the remainder of his life chiefly in this country. After studying for some time at both universities,[56] he devoted himself to the writing of original works in Spanish, and the translating of others into that language. The most of these were published in England, where also his translation of the Bible, though printed abroad, was prepared for the press. It would seem that the circulation of the last-mentioned work in Spain was much more extensive than we could have expected.[57]

374

---

54. *Strype's Life of Grindal*, p. 149. *Wood's Athenæ Oxon.* vol. i. p. 578-581; *Fasti*, vol. i. p. 203. edit. Bliss. He died in 1591, aged 64.

55. Riederer, *Nachrichten*, tom. iii. p. 482.

56. The act of his incorporation at Oxford, 21 Feb. 1565, bears, that he was M. A. of Cambridge, of three years' standing. He had obtained the degree of B. a. Cantab. in 1559-60. (*Wood's Fasti Oxon.* vol. i. p. 169.)

57. To his works already mentioned, the following may be added. "*El Catholico Reformado.*" (*Antonii Bibl. Hisp. Nov.* tom. i. p. 261.) "*Catecismo, que signifa, forma de instrucion, &c. En casa de Ricardo del Campo, 1596.*" This is a translation of Calvin's Catechism, and was printed at the same press, and in the same year, with Valera's

The influx of Spanish refugees into England ceased with the sixteenth century, though a solitary individual, who had found the means of illumination in his native country, flying from the awakened suspicions of the inquisitors, occasionally reached its hospitable shores after that period.[58]

Spanish New Testament. (Riederer, *Nachrichten*, tom. iii. p. 475-484.) His Spanish translation of Calvin's Institutions appeared in 1597. (*Gerdesii Florilegium Libr. Rar.* p. 55.) The celebrated Diodati, in a letter to the Synod of Alençon, dated 1 May 1637, says: "The new Spanish translation of Cyprian de Vallera hath produced incredible effects in Spain; no less than three thousand copies having penetrated, by secret ways and conveyances, into the very bowels of that kingdom. Let others publish the fruit of my Italian version, both in Italy and elsewhere." (*Quick's Syndicon*, vol. ii. p. 418.)

58. Ferdinando Texeda, B. D. of the university of Salamanca, having embraced the protestant religion, came to England about the year 1623. (*Wood's Fasti*, p. 413.)

Effects which the Suppression of the Reformation Produced on Spain

TYRANNY, WHILE IT SUBJECTS those against whom it is im- 375
mediately directed to great sufferings, entails still greater
misery on the willing instruments of its vengeance. Spain
boasts of having extirpated the reformed opinions from
her territory; but she has little reason to congratulate herself on the consequences of her blind and infatuated policy. She has paid, and is still paying, the forfeit of her folly
and crimes, by the loss of civil and religious liberty, and
by the degradation into which she has sunk among the
nations.

Other causes, no doubt, contributed to produce this
melancholy issue; but that it is to be traced chiefly to a
corrupt religion, will appear from a general comparison of
the condition of Spain with other European nations, and
from an examination of her internal state.

It is a fact now admitted on all hands, that the Reformation has ameliorated the state of government and society in 376 all the countries into which it was received. By exciting inquiry and diffusing knowledge, it led to the discovery and correction of abuses; imposed a check, by public opinion, if not by statute, on the arbitrary will of princes; generated a spirit of liberty among the people; gave a higher tone to morals; and imparted a strong impulse to the human mind in the career of invention and improvement. These benefits have been felt to a certain degree in countries into which the reformed religion was only partially introduced, or whose inhabitants, from local situation and other causes, were brought into close contact with protestants. But while these nations were advancing with different degrees of rapidity in improvement,—acquiring free governments, cultivating literature and science, or extending their commerce and increasing their resources,—Spain, though possessed of equal or greater advantages, became stationary, and soon began to retrograde. It is impossible to account for this phenomenon from any peculiarity in her political condition at the middle of the sixteenth century. Italy was in very different circumstances in this respect, and yet we find the two countries nearly in the same condition, owing to their having pursued the same measures in regard to religion. On the other hand, the political state of France, at the era referred to, was very similar to that of Spain. The nobles had been stripped of their feudal power in both countries; the French parliaments had become as passive instruments in the hands of the sovereign as the Spanish 377 cortes; and both kingdoms were equally exhausted by the wars which for more than half a century they had waged against one another. But the bulls of the Vatican had not the same free course in France as in the Peninsula. The Reformation deposited a seed in that country which all the violence and craft of Louis XIV., a despot as powerful as Philip II., could not eradicate; and though persecution drove from its soil thousands of its most industrious citizens, yet, as there was no Inquisition there, literature and the arts survived the shock. The consequence has been, that, after coming out of the storms of a revolution which long raged with the most destructive fury, and being subjected to a military government of unparalleled strength, France still holds a place among the great powers of Europe, nor has she been entirely stripped of her liberties, though she has received back that family which formerly reigned over her with unlimited authority; while Spain, after being long subject to a branch of the same family, and participating of all the effects of the revolutionary period, is now lying prostrate and in chains at the feet of a despot and his ghostly ministers.

But the evils which Spain has brought upon herself, by her bigoted and intolerant zeal for the Roman catholic religion, will appear in a more striking light from an examination of her internal state.

The unsuccessful attempt to reform religion in Spain led to the perpetuation of the tribunal of the Inquisition, not only by affording a pretext for arming it with new 378 powers, but by increasing the influence which it already exerted over the public mind. It became the boast of that tribunal that it had extirpated the northern heresy, and henceforth all true Spaniards were taught to regard it as the palladium of their religion. This, if it did not entail the miseries of tyranny and ignorance in Spain, at least sealed the entail. To the superficial and egotistical philosophy, which is too often to be met with in the present day, we owe the discovery, that the Inquisition was no cause of the decline of the Spanish nation, inasmuch as it was merely the organ of the government. That the Spanish monarchs employed it as an engine of state, we have seen, and that it could not have tortured the bodies, or invaded the property of the subjects, without power conveyed to it by the state, is self-evident; but it is equally true that it was in itself a moral power, and exerted its authority over the minds of both princes and subjects. When Macanaz persuaded Philip V. to lay restraints on the transmission of money to Rome, his Holiness, by means of the Inquisition, not only drove the minister into exile, but forced his master to retract the law which he had passed, and, in a letter addressed to the council of the Supreme, to confess, that, led astray by evil council, he had rashly put his hand into the sanctuary. And to complete its triumph, the enlightened Macanaz, while in France, was induced to write a defence of the Holy Office, which is appealed to by its apologists in Spain to this day.[1] When at a recent period the cortes wished to abolish that tribunal, they were made to feel that it had an existence independently of their authority, and a foundation deeper than that which mere laws had given it.

But civil and religious despotism are natural allies. Though the Inquisition exalted the power of the pope above that of the king, and its advocates have sometimes

379

---

1.   Puigblanch, ii. 12-21.

had recourse to the principles of civil liberty to vindicate the restraint and dethronement of princes who proved refractory to the church,[2] yet it all along yielded the most effective support to the arbitrary measures of the government, and exerted its influence in crushing every proposal to correct abuses in the state, and stifling the voice of complaint. Under other forms of despotism, actions, or the external manifestations of liberal opinions, have been visited with punishment; but in Spain every reflection on politics was denounced by the monks as damnable heresy, 380 and proscribed in the sanctuary of conscience.

Every since the suppression of the Reformation it has been the great object of the inquisitors and ruling clergy to arrest the progress of knowledge. With this view they have exercised the most rigid and vigilant inspection of the press and the seminaries of education. Lists of prohibited books have been published from time to time, including

---

2.   The treatise of the Jesuit Mariana, *De Rege, et Regis Institutione,* which was burnt at Paris by the hands of the common hangman, is well known to the learned. In the library of Lambeth there is a copy of the Works of Charles I. with the corrections made on it by order of the inquisition of Lisbon. Furious dashes of the pen appear across those passages in the prayers which refer to the protestant religion. Describing a "right monarchy," the British monarch had said, "where counsel may be in many, as the senses, but the supreme power can be but in one, as the head." The inquisitors have allowed this passage to stand; but over against it on the margin, they have written, "If king, false; if pope, true." (*Catal. of Archiepiscopal Library at Lambeth,* No. cccxxii.)

vernacular translations of the Bible,[3] and the writings not
only of the reformers, but also of Roman catholics who
discovered the slightest degree of liberality in their sentiments, or who treated their subjects in such a way as to
encourage a spirit of inquiry. A commentary on the Pentateuch by Oleaster, a member of the council of Trent, and
a Portuguese inquisitor, which had been several years in
circulation, was ordered to be called in and corrected, because the author had ventured to depart from the Vulgate
and the interpretations of the fathers.[4] The commentaries
of Jean Ferus, a French monk, who had availed himself
of the learning of the protestants, were censured as containing "the heretical sentiments of Luther;" and for reprinting them in Spain, Michael de Medina, guardian of
the Franciscans at Toledo, was thrown into the secret prisons of the Inquisition, and was saved from the disgrace of
making a public recantation, only by a premature death.[5]
Arias Montanus was under the necessity of defending
himself against the charges which the inquisitorial censors

381

---

3. The prohibition of Bibles in the Spanish language was erased from
the index by an edict dated 20 Dec. 1782; and yet the inquisition
of Seville, by a general edict promulgated 1 Feb. 1790, commanded
all such Bibles to be denounced. This might be an oversight; but it
is certain that the index still contains a prohibition of two books,
upon this ground, that they point out the advantages of reading the
scriptures. Nor was it the intention of the Inquisition to give the
Bible to the common people; and accordingly it is printed in such
a form as to confine it to the wealthy.

4. Simon, *Lettres Choisies*, tom. i. p. 193-197.

5. Simon, ut supra, p. 148-152. Llorente, iii. 86-88.

brought against his polyglot Bible, published under the patronage of Philip II.[6] Luis de Leon, professor of divinity at Salamanca, having written a translation of the Song of Solomon in Spanish, to which he added short explanatory notes, was confined for five years in the dungeons of the Inquisition; and his poetical paraphrases of the book of Job and other parts of scripture, distinguished for their elegance and purity, were long suppressed.[7]

The taste for theological studies, which had been produced by the revival of letters in Spain, survived for some time the suppression of the Reformation. It was cherished in secret by individuals, who, convinced that the protestants excelled in the interpretation of scripture, appropriated their writings in whole or in part, and published them as their own. The Latin Bible, with notes, by Leo Juda, and other Swiss divines, after undergoing certain corrections, was printed at Salamanca with the approbation of the censors of the press; but the real authors being discovered, it was subsequently put into the index of prohibited books.[8] Hyperius, a reformed divine, was the author of an excellent book on the method of interpreting the scriptures. Having removed from it every thing which appeared to contradict the tenets of the church of Rome, Lorenzo de Villavicencio, an Augustinian monk of Xeres in Andalusia, published that work as his own, not even excepting the preface; and in consequence of the little in-

382

---

6. Rodriguez de Castro, *Biblioteca Espanola*, tom. i. p. 649-666.

7. *Antonii Bibl. Hisp. Nov.* tom. ii. p. 45-7. *Geddes's Prospectus*, p. 87.

8. *Le Long, Bibl. Sacra*, tom. iii. p. 439-448. edit. *Masch. Carpzovii Critica Sacra*, p. 739.

tercourse which subsisted between Spain and the north of Europe, nearly half a century elapsed before the plagiarism was detected.[9] Martini Martinez was less fortunate; for publishing a similar work, in which he exalted the originals above the Vulgate, he was subjected to penance, and prohibited from writing for the future.[10] Precluded from every field of inquiry or discussion, the divines of Spain addicted themselves exclusively to the study of scholastic and casuistic theology.

383 The same tyranny was extended to other branches of science, even those which are most remotely connected with religion. All books on general subjects composed by protestants, or translated by them, or containing notes written by them, were strictly interdicted. A papal bull, dated 17 August 1627, took from metropolitans, patriarchs, and all but the inquisitor general, the privilege of reading prohibited books. Nicolas Antonio, the literary historian of Spain, was obliged to remain five years in Rome before he obtained this privilege, with the view of finding materials for his national work.[11] The Pontifical History of Illescas was repeatedly suppressed, and the author constrained at last to put his name to a work containing sentiments and opinions dictated to him by others, and diametrically opposite to those which he had formerly given to the world.[12] While the native historians of Spain

---

9. Carl. Friedric Staudlin, *Geschichte der Theologischen Wissenschaften*, tom. i. p. 145. *Riveti Opera*, tom. ii. p. 948.

10. *Antonii Bibl. Hisp. Nov.* tom. ii. p. 105.

11. Puigblanch, ii. 366, 434.

12. Llorente, i. 475, 476.

were prevented from speaking the truth, histories written by foreigners were forbidden under the severest pains as satires on the policy and religion of the Peninsula. The consequence has been, that the Spaniards entertain the most erroneous conceptions of their own history, and are profoundly ignorant of the affairs of other countries.[13]

Not satisfied with exerting a rigid censorship over the press, the inquisitors intruded into private houses, ransacked the libraries of the learned and curious, and carried off and retained at their pleasure such books as they, in their ignorance, suspected to be of a dangerous character. So late as the beginning of the eighteenth century, we find Manuel Martini, dean of Alicant, and one of the most enlightened of his countrymen in that age, complaining bitterly, in his confidential correspondence, of what he suffered from such proceedings.[14]   384

Universities and other seminaries of education were watched with the most scrupulous jealousy. The professors in the university of Salamanca, who appear to have shown a stronger predilection for liberal science than their brethren, were forbidden to deliver lectures to their students; and similar orders were issued by Philip II. to those of the Escurial, who were instructed to confine themselves to reading from a printed book.[15] Moral philosophy is too intimately allied both to religion and politics not to have excited the dread of the defenders of superstition and des-

---

13. Sismondi, *Hist. of the Literature of the South*, vol. iv. p. 124.

14. *Martini Epist.* p. 32, 36: Schelhorn, *Ergötzlichkeiten*, tom. i. p. 685-690.

15. Simon, *Lettres Choisies*, tom. i. p. 365.

potism; and, in fact, the feeble attempts made in Spain to throw off the degrading yoke have chiefly proceeded from the teachers of that science. This accordingly gave occasion to repeated interdicts, besides processes carried on against individuals. During the reign of Don Carlos IV., the prime minister, Caballero, sent a circular to all the universities, forbidding the study of moral philosophy, "because what his majesty wanted was, not philosophers, but loyal subjects."[16] Even natural philosophy, in its various branches, was placed under the same trammels, and the Copernican system is still taught in that country as a hypothesis.

385   Medical science is neglected; and surgeons, before entering on practice, are obliged to swear, not that they will exercise the healing art with fidelity, but that they will defend the immaculate conception of the blessed Virgin.[17]

The great events which distinguished the reign of the emperor Charles V., by awakening the enthusiasm, contributed to develop the genius of the Spanish nation; and the impulse thus given to intellect continued to operate long after the cause which had produced it was removed. But the character of the degenerate age in which they lived was impressed even on the towering talents of Cervantes, Lope de Vega, and Calderon, and can be easily traced in the false ideas, childish prejudices, and gross ignorance of facts which disfigure their writings. With these master spirits of literature the genius of Spain sunk; and when it began to recover from the lethargy by which it was long oppressed, it assumed the most unnatural form. Imag-

---

16. *Doblado's Letters*, p. 115, 358.

17. *Townsend's Travels*, ii. 283.

ination being the only field left open to them, Spanish writers, as if they wished to compensate for the restraints under which they were laid, set aside the rules of good taste, and abandoned themselves to all the extravagancies of fancy, which they embodied in the most inflated and pedantic language. Although the natural talents of the inhabitants are excellent, there is at present no taste for literature in Spain. The lectures on experimental philosophy which Solano began to deliver gratis in the capital towards the close of the last century, though distinguished by their 386 simplicity and elegance, were discontinued for want of an audience. Reading is unknown except among a very limited class. Every attempt to establish a literary magazine has failed, through the listlessness of the public mind and the control of the censorship.[18] And the spies of the police and the Inquisition have long ago banished every thing like rational conversation from those places in which the people assemble to spend their leisure hours.[19]

In Italy the same causes produced the same effects. Genius, taste, and learning were crushed under the iron hand of the inquisitorial despotism. The imprisonment of Galileo on the seventeenth, and the burning of the works of Gi-

---

18. It has been wittily said, that in Madrid, provided you avoid saying any thing concerning government, or religion, or politics, or morals, or statesmen, or bodies of reputation, or the opera, or any other public amusement, or any one who is engaged in any business, you may print what you please, under the correction of two or three censors.

19. *Townsend's Travels*, ii. 154, 275. *Doblado's Letters*, p. 377, 380.

annone in the eighteenth century,[20] are sufficient indications of the deplorable state of the Italians, during a period
in which knowledge was advancing with such rapidity in
countries long regarded by them as barbarous. When their
intellectual energies began to recover, they were directed
to a species of composition in which sentiment and poetry
are mere accessories to sensual harmony, and the national
love of pleasure could be gratified without endangering
the authority of the rulers. To ennoble pleasure and render
387 it in some degree sacred; to screen the prince from the
shame of his own indolence and effeminacy; to blind the
people to to every consideration but that of the passing
moment; and to give the author an opportunity to exert
his talents without incurring the vengeance of the Inquisition—is the scope and spirit of the Italian opera.[21] Later
writers in Italy, whose productions breathe a fiery spirit of
liberty, were of the French, or rather revolutionary school,
and afford no criterion for judging of the national feelings
and taste.

In Spain the increase of superstition, and of the numbers and opulence of the clergy, has kept pace with the
growth of ignorance. The country is overrun with clergy,
secular and regular. Towards the close of the last century it
contained nearly nine thousand convents; and the number
of persons who had taken the vow of celibacy approached
to two hundred thousand.[22] The wealth of the church was

---

20. *Anecdotes Ecclésiastiques de l'Histoire de Royaume de Naples brulée a
    Rome en 1726*, pref. p. viii. Amst. 1738.

21. Sismondi, *History of the Literature of the South*, vol. ii. p. 290.

22. *Townsend's Travels*, vol. ii. p. 233. The city of Toledo, which con-

equally disproportionate to that of the nation, as the numbers of the clergy were to its population. The cathedral of Toledo, for example, besides other valuable ornaments, 388 contained four large silver images, standing on globes of the same metal; a grand massive throne of silver, on which was placed an image of the Virgin, wearing a crown valued at upwards of a thousand pounds; and a statue of the infant Jesus, adorned with eight hundred precious stones. Six hundred priests, richly endowed, were attached to it; and the revenues of the archbishop were estimated at nearly a hundred thousand pounds.[23] The sums which are extorted by the mendicant friars, and which are paid for masses and indulgences, cannot be calculated; but the bulls of crusade alone yield a neat yearly income of two hundred thousand pounds to his Catholic Majesty, who purchases them from the pope, and retails them to his loving subjects.[24] Equally

---

tains 25,000 souls, has 26 parish churches, 38 convents, 17 hospitals, 4 colleges, 12 chapels, and 19 hermitages. Medina del Campo consists of 1000 houses, and has 9 parish churches, 70 priests, 17 convents, and 2 hospitals. Salamanca contains 3000 houses, and has 27 parish churches, 15 chapels, 580 priests, and 1509 persons under vows. (Ibid. vol. i. 309-362; ii. 84.)

23. Townsend, i. 309-311. *Conf. Scaligerana Secunda, voc. Espagnols.*

24. For this bull the nobles pay about 6 shillings and 4 pence, the common people about 2 shillings and 4 pence, in Aragon. In Castile it is somewhat cheaper. No confessor will grant absolution to anyone who does not possess it. (Townsend, ii. 171-2. *Doblado's Letters*, p. 214.) Dr. Colbach has given an account of this traffic. In 1709 a privateer belonging to Bristol took a galleon, in which they found 500 bales of these precious goods, containing each 16 reams, and

great are the encroachments which superstition has made on the time of the inhabitants. Benedict XIV. reduced the number of holydays in the states of the church, and recommended a similar reduction in other kingdoms. But in Spain there are still ninety-three general festivals, besides those of particular provinces, parishes, and convents; to 389 which we must add the bull-feasts,[25] and the Mondays claimed by apprentices and journeymen.[26]

Commerce and all the sources of national wealth are obstructed by persecution and intolerance. But the evil is unspeakably aggravated, when the greater part of the property of a nation is locked up, and a large proportion of its inhabitants, and of their time, is withdrawn from useful labor. Holland, with no soil but what she recovered from the ocean, waxed rich and independent, while Spain, with a third part of the world in her possession, has become poor. The city of Toledo is reduced to an eighth part of its former population; the monks remain, but the citizens have fled. Every street in Salamanca swarms with sturdy beggars and vagabonds able to work; and this is the case wherever the clergy, convents, and hospicios are numerous. With a soil which, by its extent and fertility, is capable of supporting an equal number of inhabitants, the population of Spain is not half that of France.

---

amounting in all to 384,000 bulls. Captain Campier says he careened his ship with them.

25. These disgraceful spectacles are countenanced by the clergy, and a priest is always in attendance to administer the sacrament to the *matadors who may be mortally wounded.*

26. Townsend, i. 350; ii. 233-235.

The effects produced on the national character and morals are still more deplorable. Possessing naturally some of the finest qualities by which a people can be distinguished—generous, feeling, devoted, constant—the Spaniards became cruel, proud, reserved and jealous. The revolting spectacles of the auto-de-fe, continued for so long a period, could not fail to have the most hardening influence on their feelings.[27] In Spain, as in Italy, religion is associated with crime, and protected by its sanctions. Thieves and prostitutes have their images of the Virgin, their prayers, their holy water, and their confessors. Murderers find a sanctuary in the churches and convents. Crimes of the blackest character are left unpunished in consequence of the immunities granted to the clergy.[28] Adultery is common, and those who live habitually in this vice find no difficulty in obtaining absolution. The *cortejos*, or male paramours, like the cicisbei in Italy, appear regularly in the family circle. In great cities the canons of cathedrals act in this character, and the monks in villages. The parish priests live almost universally in concubinage, and all that the more correct bishops require of them is,

390

---

27. Cogan mentions that he was one day walking in the streets of London with a young lady from Portugal, about nine years of age, a protestant, and of a mild, compassionate disposition. Seeing a crowd collected around a pile of faggots on fire, he expressed an anxiety to know the cause, upon which the young lady replied without any emotion, "It is only some people going to burn a Jew." (*Philosophical Treatise on the Passions*, note L.)

28. Sismondi, *Hist. of the Lit. of the South*, vol. iii. 404; iv. 6, 7, 18. *Townsend's Travels*, i. 223, 398. *Doblado's Letters*, p. 222.

that they do not keep their children in their own houses. Until they begin to look towards a mitre, few of the clergy think of preserving decorum in this matter.[29]

391   The dramatical pieces composed by their most celebrated writers, and acted on the stage with the greatest applause, demonstrate the extent to which the principles of morality have been injured by fanaticism and bigotry. In one of them,[30] after the hero has plotted the death of his wife, and accomplished that of his parents, Jesus Christ is represented as descending from heaven to effect his salvation by means of a miracle. In another,[31] an incestuous brigand and professed assassin preserves, in the midst of his crimes, his devotion for the cross, at the foot of which he was born, and the impress of which he bears on his breast. He erects a cross over each of his victims; and being at last slain, God restores him to life in order that a saint might hear his confession, and thus secure his admission into heaven. In another piece,[32] Alfonso VI. receives the capitulation of the Moors of Toledo, and, in the midst of his court and knights, swears to maintain their religious liberties, and to leave for their worship the largest mosque in the city. During his absence, Constance his queen violates the treaty, and places the miraculous image of the Virgin in the mosque. Alfonso is highly indignant at this breach of faith, but the Virgin surrounds Constance with a crown of glory, and convinces the king, to the great de-

---

29   *Townsend's Travels,* ii. 147-151. *Doblado's Letters,* p. 220.

30. The *Animal profeta,* by Lope de Vega.

31. The *Devocion de la Cruz,* by Calderon.

32. The *Virgen del Sagrario,* by the same author.

light of the spectators, that it is an unpardonable sin to keep faith with heretics. To give one instance more; in another piece,[33] the hero, while leading the most abandoned 392 life, is represented as adhering to the true faith, and thus meriting the protection of St. Patrick, who follows him as his good genius to inspire him with repentance. When about to commit a murder, in addition to numbers which he had already perpetrated, he is converted by an apparition of himself, who exclaims, "What atonement can be made for a life spent in crime?" to which a voice of celestial music replies, "Purgatory." He is then directed into St. Patrick's Purgatory, and at the end of a few days comes out pardoned and purified. Still more precious specimens of religious absurdity and fanaticism might have been given from the autos sacramentales, a species of composition which continued to be popular till a late period, and has employed the pens of the most celebrated writers in Spain.

The Italians are bound to religion chiefly by the ties of interest and pleasure. The Spaniards are naturally a grave people; their devotional feelings are strong; and had they lived under a free government, they would have welcomed a purer worship, when, after a long period of ignorance, it was unveiled to their eyes, and might have proved its most enthusiastic and constant admirers.[34] But their minds have been subjugated and their feelings perverted by a long course of debasing slavery. As to religion, the inhabitants of Spain are now divided into two classes, bigots and dis- 393

---

33. The *Purgatorio de San Patricio*, by the same author.

34. "*Si l'Espagnol estoit libre, il embrasseroit fort la Religion, au prix de l'Italien.*" (Scaligerana Secunda, voc. *Italiens.*)

semblers. There is no intermediate class. Under such an encroaching system of faith as that of the church of Rome, which claims a right of interference with almost every operation of the human mind, the prohibition of all dissent from the established religion is a restraint sufficiently painful. But this is the least evil. Every Spaniard who disbelieves the public creed is constrained to profess himself to be what he is not, under the pain of losing all that he holds dear on earth. What with masses, and confessions, and festivals, and processions, and bowing to crosses and images, and purchasing pardons, and contributing to deliver souls from purgatory, he is every day, and every hour of the day, under the necessity of giving his countenance to what he detests as a Christian, or loathes as the cause of his country's degradation. It is not enough that he contrives to avoid going to church or chapel: the idol presents itself to him abroad and at home, in the tavern and in the theater. He cannot turn a corner without being in danger of hearing the sound of a hand-bell which summons him to kneel in the mud, till a priest, who is carrying the consecrated host to some dying person, has moved slowly in his sedan chair from one end of the street to the other. If he dine with a friend, the passing bell is no sooner heard than the whole party rise from the table and worship. If he go to the theater, the military guard at the door, by a well-known sound of his drum, announces the approach

394 of a procession, upon which "Su Magestad! Dios, Dios!" resounds through the house; the play is instantly suspended, and the whole assembly, actors and spectators, fall on their knees, in which attitude they remain until the sound of the bell has died away, when the amusement is resumed

with fresh spirit. He has scarcely returned to his inn, when a friar enters, bearing a large lanthorn with painted glass, representing two persons enveloped with flames, and addresses him, "The holy souls, brother! Remember the holy souls."[35]

Religion in its purity is calculated to soothe and support the mind under the unavoidable calamities of life; but when perverted by superstition, it aggravates every evil to which men are exposed, by fostering delusive confidence, and leading to the neglect of those natural means which tend to avert danger, or alleviate distress. In Spain every city, every profession, and every company of artisans, has its tutelary saint, on whose miraculous interposition the utmost reliance is placed. The merchant, when he embarks his goods for a foreign country, instead of insuring them against the dangers of the sea in the ordinary way, seeks for security by paying his devotions to the shrine of the saint under whose protection the vessel sails.. There is scarcely a disease affecting the human body which is not submitted to the healing power of some member of the calendar. So late as 1801, when the yellow fever prevailed 395 in Seville, the civil authorities, instead of adopting precautionary measures for abating the violence of that pestilential malady, applied to the archbishop for the solemn prayers called Rogativas; and not trusting to these, they resolved to carry in procession a fragment of the true cross, preserved in the cathedral of Seville, which had formerly chased away an army of locusts, together with a large wooden crucifix, which, in 1649, had arrested the progress

---

35. *Doblado's Letters*, p. 8-14, 169. *Townsend's Travels*, i. 336.

of the plague. The inhabitants flocked to the church; and the consequence was, that the heat, fatigue, and anxiety of the whole day spent in this ridiculous ceremony, increased the disease in a tenfold proportion.[36]

Popery, by the false light and repulsive form in which it represents Christianity, tends naturally to produce deism and irreligion. In France, where a certain degree of liberty was enjoyed, it led at first to the covert dissemination and afterwards to the bold avowal of infidel opinions, by those who held the greatest influence over the public mind. In countries where a rigid system of police, civil and ecclesiastical, has been kept up, its operation has been different, but not less destructive to national character and the real interests of religion. The great body of the unbelievers, anxious only for present enjoyment, and regarding religion in no other light than as an engine of state, have made no scruple of fostering the popular credulity, that they might share its fruits; while those of a more generous and independent spirit, writhing under the degrading yoke, have given way to irritation of feeling, and, confounding Christianity with an intolerant superstition, cherish the desperate hope that religion, in all its forms, will one day be swept from the earth, as the support of tyranny and the bane of human happiness. it is well known that the Italian clergy have for a long time given the most unequivocal proofs that they disbelieve those doctrines, and feel indifferent to those rites, from which they derive their maintenance and wealth.[37] We were formerly

---

36. Townsend, i. 152-154. *Doblado*, p. 195-199, 316-318.

37. An English gentleman who had resided long in Italy, and obtained

aware that the principles of irreligion were widely diffused among the reading classes in Spain; but more ample information, furnished by recent events, has disclosed the fact, that this evil is not confined to the laity, and that infidelity is as common among the educated Spanish clergy as vice is among the vulgar crowd of priests. There is a lightness attached to the character of the Italians, which, together with the recollection that they have been the chief instruments of enslaving the Christian world, disposes us 397 to turn away from the manifestations of their irreligion with feelings of contempt. But such is the native dignity of the Spanish character, and its depth of feeling, that we dwell with a mixed emotion of pity and awe on the ravages which infidelity is making on so noble a structure. Who can read the following description by a Spaniard without the strongest sympathy for such of his countrymen as are still in that "gall of bitterness and bond of iniquity" from which he was so happily rescued! "Where there is no liberty, there can be no discrimination. The ravenous appetite, raised by a forced abstinence, makes the mind gorge itself with all sorts of food. I suspect I have thus imbibed some

---

lodgings in a convent, was frequently engaged in friendly discussions with the most intelligent individuals of the house on the points of difference between the churches of Rome and England. On the termination of one of these disputes, after the greater part of the company had retired, a young monk, who had supported the tenets of his church with great ability, turning to his English guest, asked him, if he really believed what he had been defending. On his answering seriously in the affirmative, the monk exclaimed, *Allor lei crede piu che tutto il convento.* Then, Sir, you believe more than all the convent. (*Doblado's Letters,* p. 476.)

false and many crude notions from my French masters. But my circumstances preclude the calm and dispassionate examination which the subject deserves. Exasperated by the daily necessity of external submission to doctrines and persons I detest and despise, my soul overflows with bitterness. Though I acknowledge the advantages of moderation, none being used towards me, I practice none, and in spite of my better judgment learn to be a fanatic on my own side. Pretending studious retirement, I have fitted up a small room to which none but confidential friends find admission. There lie my prohibited books in perfect concealment, in a well-contrived nook under a staircase. The Breviary alone, in its black binding, clasps, and gilt leaves, is kept upon the table, to check the doubts of any chance intruder."[38] The same person writes at a subsequent period: "The confession is painful indeed, yet due to religion itself—I was bordering on atheism. If my case were singular, if my knowledge of the most enlightened classes of Spain did not furnish me with a multitude of sudden transitions from sincere faith and piety to the most outrageous infidelity, I would submit to the humbling conviction that either weakness of judgment or fickleness of character had been the only source of my errors. But though I am not at liberty to mention individual cases, I do attest, from the most certain knowledge, that the history of my own mind is, with little variation, that of a great portion of the Spanish clergy. The fact is certain; I make no individual charge; every one who comes within the description may still wear the mask, which no Spaniard can throw off without bid-

398

---

38. *Doblado's Letters*, p. 134; comp. p. 112-3.

ding an eternal farewell to his country."[39]

It is evident from this slight sketch that there are many and powerful obstacles to the regeneration of Spain. Superstition is interwoven with her national habits and feeling; and civil and spiritual despotism are bound together by an indissoluble league, while they find a powerful auxiliary in the depraved morals of the people; for liberty has not a greater enemy than licentiousness, and an immoral people can neither preserve their freedom when they have 399 it, nor regain it after it has been lost. But what augurs worse than perhaps any thing else for Spain is, that it does not possess a class of persons animated by the spirit of that reformation to which the free states of Europe chiefly owe their political privileges. Infidelity and skepticism, besides weakening the moral energies of the human mind, have a tendency to break up the natural alliance which subsists between civil and religious liberty. Those who are inimical or indifferent to religion cannot be expected to prove the firm and uncompromising friends of that liberty which has religion for its object. They love it not for itself, and cannot be prepared to make all sacrifices for its sake. Thus, when tyranny takes the field, brandishing its two swords, the right arm of liberty is found to be palsied. The irreligious or skeptical principles of those who have been called liberals must always excite a strong and well-grounded prejudice against their schemes. If they demand a reform in the state, the defenders of abuse have only to raise against them the cry of impiety. Bigots and

---

39. *Blanco White's Practical and Internal Evidence against Catholicism,* p. 7-12; comp. p. 129-134.

hypocrites are furnished with a plausible pretext for putting them down. And good men, who may be convinced of the corruptions which adhere to both church and state, and might be willing to co-operate in removing them, are deterred from joining in the attempt, by the apprehension that it may lead to the overthrow of all religion. It is not difficult to trace the operation of all these causes in defeating the struggles for liberty which have been made within these few years in Italy and the Peninsula.

400

But may we not cherish better hopes, as the result of those events which have recently induced the more enlightened portion of the Spanish nation to turn their eyes to Britain instead of France, from which they formerly looked for instruction and relief? Let us hope that those individuals who have taken refuge in this country, and whose conduct has sown that they are not unworthy of the reception they have met with, will profit by their residence among us; that any of them who, from the unpropitious circumstances in which they were placed, may have formed an unfavourable opinion of Christianity, will find their prejudices dissipated in the free air which they now breathe; that what is excellent in our religion, as well as our policy, will recommend itself to their esteem; and that, when providence shall open an honorable way for their returning to their native country, they will assist in securing to it a constitution, founded on the basis of rational liberty, in connection with a religion purified from those errors and corruptions which have wrought so much woe to Spain—which have dried up its resources, cramped and debased its genius, lowered its native dignity of character, and poisoned the fountains of its domestic and social happiness.

APPENDIX

No. I

Dedication by Francisco de Enzinas of his Spanish Translation of the New Testament.[1]

To the Puissant Monarch Charles V. ever August Emperor, King of Spain, &c. Francisco de Enzinas wishes Grace, Health and Peace.

Sacred Majesty,—many and various opinions have been broached in our day, as to the expediency of translating the Scriptures into the vulgar tongues: and how opposite soever they are to each other, they argue equal zeal for Christianity, and proceed upon reasonings sufficiently probable. For my own part, without meaning to condemn those of different sentiments, I have espoused the side of them who conceive that such translations, were they executed by learned men of mature judgment and great skill in the several languages, would mightily advance the interest of the Christian Republic, by affording both instruction to the illiterate, and comfort to the well-informed,

---

1. Translated from the original, printed at Antwerp in 1543.

who delight to hear in their own language the discourses of Jesus and his Apostles concerning those mysteries of our redemption from which our souls derive salvation and comfort. But, with the view of at once satisfying those who think differently, and of showing that this undertaking is neither new nor dangerous, I am anxious to state to your Majesty, in a few words, the reasons which have induced me to commence this work. And this I do under a sense of the duty which I owe to your Majesty, who is not

402 only the highest minister of God in temporal things, and the greatest monarch in Christendom, but also my king and lord, to whom I am bound, as a vassal, to give account of my leisure and my busy hours; and who is, to speak the truth, in what regards religion, a diligent overseer, and zealous for the honor of Jesus Christ and the spiritual interests of his kingdom.

First, in reading the Acts of the Apostles, I find that, when the Jews and Gentiles were exerting all their powers against the kingdom of Christ, which then began to prosper, and when they were unable to impede it on account of the great miracles which Peter and the other Apostles performed, and the heavenly doctrines which they taught, they laid hold of St. Peter and St. John, and consulted what measures they should pursue towards them and this new religion. After various opinions had been given, Gamaliel, the teacher of St. Paul, and the most honored of the assembly, arose. He told them, that they ought to be cautious in this affair, as it was one of great importance; and produced several examples of persons who had lately formed sects and taught new doctrines, but had in a short time perished along with the tenets they inculcated. After some discourse, he concluded in this manner: In fine, my opinion is, that you should let these men alone and permit them to do as they please; for if this doctrine of theirs be new, or of the world, or the invention of men pleased with novelty, then it and they will soon perish. But if it be from God, be assured that neither you nor any mortal will be able to stop its progress: the very attempt to do this would be a fighting against God and the determination he has taken. I have often, sacred Majesty, reflected on these words, when reviewing the dispute which has now lasted for twenty years. Certain persons, influenced by good motives, have frequently opposed with great perseverance the printing of such translations; but far from being able to prevail, they have lost ground every day, and new versions are issuing successively from the press in all the kingdoms of Christendom; while those who opposed them at first, have now begun to keep silence on the subject, and even to read and approve of them not a little. In all this, methinks, I see the saying of Gamaliel fulfilled, and that this is an undertaking, which, if well executed, will serve greatly to advance the glory of God. After having waited many years for the end of this dispute, I see that it has at length arrived at a happy termination, and that God has most certainly made use of it for his own purposes. This consideration induces me to try what I can do in the matter, with the view of benefiting my countrymen to the utmost of my power, 403 though I should succeed but in part; for it is a true saying, that in great and difficult achievements, the very wish and attempt are worthy of high commendation.

The second reason, sacred Majesty, which has had weight with me, is the honor of our Spanish nation, which has been calumniated and ridiculed by other nations on this head. Although their opinions differ in many points, yet all of them agree in this, that we are either indolent or scrupulous, or superstitious; and from this charge none of the strangers with whom I have conversed will exculpate us. Although the spiritual advantage of our neighbour and the service of God are no doubt the considerations which ought to influence the Christian, yet, so long as we live in the flesh, and walk by the light of reason, we shall find that honor will often lead us to do at once what no arguments could induce us to perform. Now, not to speak of the Greeks and the other nations who were made acquainted with the salvation of Jesus Christ by reading the Sacred Scriptures in their own language, there is no people, as far as I know, except the Spaniards, who are not permitted to read the Bible in their native tongue. In Italy there are many versions, the greater part of which has issued from Naples, the patrimony of your Majesty. In France they are innumerable. In that quarter, I have myself seen many, while new ones are published daily in its principal towns. In Germany, they are as plentiful as water, not only in Protestant, but also in Catholic states. The same may be said of all the realms of the illustrious king Don Fernando, your Majesty's brother; as also of England, Scotland, and Ireland. Spain stands alone as if she were the obscure extremity of Europe. For what reason that privilege has been denied to her which has been conceded to every other country, I know not. Since in every thing we boast, and that not unjustly, that we are the foremost, I cannot see why in this business, which is of the highest moment, we should be the last. We labour under no deficiency in genius, or judgment, or learning; and our language is, in my opinion, the best of the vulgar ones; at least it is inferior to none of them.

The third reason which has induced me to undertake this work is, that were it injurious in itself, or did it lead to bad consequences, I am convinced, that among all the laws which have been enacted since the appearance of these sects, one would have issued from your Majesty or the Pope, forbidding, under great penalties, the composition and printing of such books. As this has not been done to my knowledge, notwithstanding the many laws passed, and the great diligence (thank God) used since that time, 404 I am persuaded that no evil can attach to the undertaking, and that it is in perfect consistency with the laws of your Majesty, and of the supreme pontiff. Nor do I want examples to countenance me, seeing that similar works have been published in all languages and nations. It is a mark of little prudence, says the comic poet, when I reckon nothing well done, except that which I myself do, and suppose I alone hit the mark, and every other person errs. So it happens in the present case. For, not to speak of the European nations, whose sentiments on this subject I have already shown, if we consult the history of the ancients we shall find that all of them held the same opinion. The Jews, though they were an illiterate and hardened race, as Christ remarks, had their law delivered to them in their own language, difficult as it was to be understood on account of the types of the Messiah which it contained. After their return from Babylon, as they were better acquainted with the Syriac than the Hebrew, they made use of the Chaldee paraphrases, which they called the Targums. The

Christians, succeeding them, possessed the Scriptures in Greek, which, at that period, was the common language of the East. The other nations translated them into their own tongues, viz. Egyptian, Arabian, Persian, Ethiopian, and Latin; and in these languages also they had their Psalmody, as St. Jerome affirms in his epitaph upon Paula. This father likewise translated the Bible into Hungarian, for the benefit of his own countrymen. The Latins henceforth employed the Latin version,—a custom which remained in their church for more than 600 years, till the time of the Emperors Phocas and Heraclius, and Pope Gregory the Great. The practice of reading the Holy Scriptures in a language which all could understand, was abandoned, not from a conviction of its being wrong, but because at the irruption of foreign nations into Europe the Latin tongue ceased to be spoken among the common people, while the church continued to employ it as formerly, and has continued to do so at the present day. This, however, is the case only in these parts of Europe. In Greece, the modern Christians preserve the old practice; as also in Africa, Egypt, Ethiopia, Syria, Palestine, Persia, the East Indies, and throughout all the world. It would appear, then, that I am not singular in my sentiments on this subject; that this undertaking is not novel; and that that cannot be an evil which has existed for such a length of time in the Church of God, which so many nations have approved of, and which the Catholic Church esteems to be good. If any one should be inclined to think it injurious on account of the danger there is at present of heresy, let such a one know that heresies do not arise from the reading of the Scriptures

405 in the vulgar tongues, but from their being ill understood,

and explained contrary to the interpretation and doctrine of the Church, which is the pillar and foundation of the truth, and from their being treated of by ill-disposed men, who pervert them to suit their own wicked opinions. The same thing was remarked by St. Peter concerning the epistles of St. Paul, which heretics in that age, as well as this, were in the practice of abusing in order to confirm their false tenets.

These reasons, sacred Majesty, have induced me to undertake this work. Not to say that it is a most just and holy cause, it is certainly worthy of your Majesty's royal dignity, worthy of your knowledge, worthy of your judgment, worthy of your approbation, and worthy of your protection. And since I am well assured, with Solomon, that the hearts of good princes are governed by God, I trust in Heaven that your Majesty will take this my work in good part; that you will encourage and defend it by your authority; and that you will employ all means to procure it a favourable reception by others. This ought to be done the more on this account, that the good which may be expected to result from it throughout the kingdom, is neither wealth, nor honor, nor worldly advantages, but spiritual blessings, and the glory of Christ Jesus. May he prosper your Majesty in the journey and enterprise you have undertaken, and in all others of a like nature; and after you have reigned long upon the earth, may he receive you to reign with himself in heaven. Amen.

From Antwerp, 1 October, 1543

No. II

Extracts from a Preface by Juan Perez to his Spanish Translation of the New Testament.[1]

Two reasons have induced me to undertake the important task of translating the New Testament, from the language in which it was originally composed, into our common and native Romance language. The one is, that when I found myself lying under great obligations to my countrymen on account of the vocation which the Lord had given me to preach the gospel, I could discover no method by which I could better fulfil, if not wholly, at least in part, my desire and obligation, than by bestowing on them a faithful version of the New Testament in their own language. In this respect I have obeyed the will of the Lord, and followed the example of his holy Apostles. * * * The holy Apostles, instructed in the will and intention of their master, with the view of discharging their ministry, and publishing more extensively that which was committed to their care, did not write in Hebrew, which was then understood only by a few persons already skilled in the Holy Scriptures, nor yet in the Syriac and Latin tongues. Nearly all of them wrote the gospel in Greek, as it was then employed and understood not only in Greece, but also among the Jews and Romans, and generally by all those who inhabited Asia and such parts of Europe as were subject to the Roman empire; for neither the Latin nor any

406

---

1. Translated from the original Spanish, as given by Riderer, *Nachrichten zur Kirchen-Gelehrgen und Bucher-Geschichte*, vol. ii. p. 147-149. Altdorf, 1765.

other language was at that time so generally known or so common as the Greek. * * * The other reason to which I referred as urging me to the present undertaking, is the advancement of my nation's glory, famed as it has always been in every quarter for its bravery and victories, and inclined to boast that it is freer than all other nations from those errors which have arisen in the world against the Christian religion. To overcome others is a thing which is esteemed glorious and desirable among men; but to overcome one's self is much more glorious and honourable in the sight of God; for to subdue our domestic enemies is the way to subject ourselves entirely to his government, and the victory obtained over them is the more illustrious and the more to be desired, as an intestine war is of all others the most dangerous, and as the reward here held out to the conquerors is the most precious and the most lasting. That which accomplishes the greatest of all victories is the reading and understanding of the contents of this sacred volume. In order that it may be understood and improved, I have translated it into the Romance. It is certainly honorable and glorious that we should be exempt from errors and all their consequences. Every one in the nation ought to labour as much as in him lies that this glory may accrue to us. For my part I have endeavored to provide a defence by which our country may always be protected from evil and from the entrance of error, by providing it with the New Testament, wherein is a summary of all the laws and advices we have received from heaven; so that we may not only be enabled to detect infallibly every error, but also to avoid it with certainty. It is impossible that our glory can 407 be lasting and permanent, unless we call in the aid of this volume, by habitually reading its statutes and meditating on its counsels.

No. III

Extracts from the Confession of a Sinner, by Constantine Ponce dela Fuente, Chaplain to the Emperor Charles V.[1]

O thou Son of God, whom the eternal Father hath sent to be the Saviour of men, that though mightest offer thyself a sacrifice as a satisfaction for sin, I would present myself before the throne of they mercy, beseeching thee to listen while I speak, not of my own righteousness and merits, but of the transgressions and grievous errors which I have committed against me, and more especially against the majesty, the goodness, and the compassion of thy Father. Draw me forcibly by a discovery of that everlasting punishment with which my sins inwardly menace me. But O thy compassion draws me by a very different cord; making me to know, though not so quickly as I ought, all that thou has been to me, and all that I have been to thee. I present myself before thy sacred majesty, accused and condemned by my own conscience, and constrained by its torture to speak out and confess, in the presence of earth and heaven, before men and angels, and in the audience of thy sovereign and divine justice, that I deserve to be banished for ever from the kingdom of heaven, and to live in perpetual misery under the chains and tyranny of Satan. O my Lord and Saviour, my cause would be lost, I would

---

1.   Translated from a French version in *Histoire des Martyrs*, p. 503-506. Anno 1597.

be utterly undone, wert not thou a judge to deliver from condemnation those whom their sins have handed over to eternal death. * * * * Blessed and praised for ever be thy name by all those who know thee, because thou camest into this world not to comdemn but to save sinners; because being thyself just, thou hast become the advocate of the guilty, even of thine enemies and accusers, and hast been afflicted and tempted in all things, in order to give us a surer proof of thy compassion. Thou art holiness for the polluted, satisfaction for the guilty, payment for the insolvent, knowledge for the erring, and a surety for him that has no help. What I know of thee, O my Saviour, draws me unto thee, and I have begun to know thee in a manner which makes me see that I am a wretch unworthy 408 to approach thy presence.

How shall I begin, O Lord, to render an account of my transgressions? What direction shall I take, the better to discover the error of my ways? Lord, give me eyes to look upon myself, and strengthen me to bear that look; for my sins are so great that I am ashamed to recognize them as mine, and try to remedy them by other sins—belying and disowning myself, if by any means I may find in me something not so exceedingly culpable. In all this, Lord, I mark the greatness of thy compassion; for when I shut my own eyes lest I be confounded at the sight of my sins, thou openest thine, that thou mayest observe and watch over me. Thou hast put it beyond doubt, O Redeemer of the world, that thou examinest wounds with the intention of healing them, and that how disgusting soever they may be, they are not an eyesore to thee, nor art thou ashamed to cleanse them with thine own hand. Guide me, Lord, and lead me along with thee; for if I walk alone, I shall wander from the right path. Thy company shall strengthen me to bear the presence of myself. Sustain me, that I may not lose courage. Hold me firmly, that I may not fly from myself. Command the devil to be silent when thou speakest with me.

There was a time, Lord, when I was nothing; thou gavest me existence and formedst me in my mother's womb. There thou didst impress on me thy image and resemblance, and gave me the capacity of enjoying thy blessings. There is nothing in me so minute or so delicate but what was conducted by thy wisdom and singular design to its full perfection. I entered the world by a great miracle and under the power of thy hand. I was nursed and invigorated by thy providence. I was naked and thou clothedst me, weak and thou strengthenedst me; in short thou has made me to feel that I live by leaning on thy mercy which will never fail me. Before that I knew myself to be miserable, I was undone; I contracted sin even in coming out of my mother's womb; this was my inheritance in being in the line of Adam. Behold the fortune which I heir from my father; it is to know myself miserable and sinful. Notwithstanding this, thy compassion has embraced me, thou hast helped me in my poverty, and delivered me from my evils. Thou hast enriched and adorned me, thou hast divorced me from my own heart on which I leaned for support, and hast washed me as with pure water in thy precious blood. Thou hast intrusted me with those favours which I most needed, which made me thine, which delivered me from mine enemy, and gave me an assured pledge of eternal 409 happiness. If thy wisdom had not imposed silence, if I had not confided in thee, seeing my true nature and condition, what could I have said but, in the words of Job, "Would that they had carried me from the womb to the grave, for surely that life which ought to prove a blessing is only for my evil and for my transgression, and it were better that I had never been!" Yet would I not be the judge of thy glory, seeing I have so little advanced it, nor of thy will, seeing it is the right rule of all justice. I am thy servant, Thou hast preserved my privileges, though I myself took no charge of them. My innocence endured only so long as I had not eyes to look with delight on vanity and malice. I may say that when asleep I was thine, but no sooner did I awaken to the knowledge of thee than I discovered my aversion to look upon thee; and the greater my obligations were to follow thee, the faster did I fly from thy presence. I was in love with my own ruin and gave it full reign; and in this manner did I allow it to dissipate thy benefits. I joined myself to thine enemies, as if my happiness consisted in being traitor to thee. I closed my eyes, I shut up all my senses that I might not perceive that I was in thy house, that thou wast the Lord of the heavens whose rain descends upon me, and of the earth which sustains me in life. I was a sacrilegious person, a despiser of thy bounty, ungrateful, a contemner of thy mercy, an audacious man, fearing not thy justice. Nevertheless I slept as soundly as if I were one of thy servants, and appropriated every thing to myself without considering that it came from thee. * * * *

Such has been the pride of man, that he aimed at being God; but so great was thy compassion towards him in his fallen state, that thou abasedst thyself to become not only of the rank of men, but a true man, and the least of men, taking upon thee the form of a servant, that thou mightest set me at liberty, and that by means of thy grace, wisdom, and righteousness, man might obtain more than he had lost by his ignorance and pride. He had thrown himself into the power of the devil, to be formed into his image and remain his prisoner, banished from thy presence, condemned in thy indignation, the slave of him who had seduced him, and whose counsel he chose to follow in contempt of the justice and majesty of the Father. But so completely hast thou retrieved what man had lost, that I may justly say, "Man is true God," since God is true man, since believers have the privilege of being made partakers of the divine nature, since they are all thy brethren, and since the Father joins with thee in calling them to imitate thee, that they may grow daily in thy likeness, and execute thy will, and that thus each of them may be in truth de-410 nominated a son of God, and born of God. O the misery of those who would seek for happiness in any other than thee, seeing that thy compassion can give them more than even their own presumption could demand! Thou knowest, Lord, the return I have made for thy benefits, and whether or not I have merited them. Would that I knew this as well! that flying far from myself, I might come nearer unto thee; for, to complete my misery, all that I know and feel of my heinous sins, forms the least part of them. It is many years, Lord, since thou becamest man for me, and didst abase thyself to such a depth that I might be raised thus high. Having once presumed to equal myself with God, I forsook the path in which thou wouldst have me to walk, and took that which led to my destruction, listening to the voice of thine enemy, and avowedly taking up arms against thee. What was this but my arrogant heart seeking to govern me by its own wisdom, to set me at large in my own ways, and to settle down in the pleasure and satisfaction of its own obstinate disobedience? I was a worm in comparison with others, and all plainly perceived my littleness and insignificance; but as for me, my discourses were my gods; so far had I forgotten what thou wast, and how low thou didst condescend for my sake. Thou hast abased thyself in order to become a man—a new man, of the same line with Adam, and yet without the sin of Adam; for such a nature was suited at once to thy greatness and to the work of our justification. Thou didst take upon thee human flesh, and wast born of a virgin-mother, that thou mightest be every way fitted to our condition, and that thou mightest be entirely such a one as it behoved him to be who is at once God and man. Thou hast called us to be new creatures, that by the privilege of our union with thee we might throw off the depravity which we had inherited from our father, and in thee to receive new life and strength, that as we have borne the image of the old and sinful man, so we may recover the resemblance of the new and innocent man. As for me enamoured of my old nature, and satisfied with my former lusts, as if I did well in pursuing them, I deemed it sufficient to believe that thou wast innocent; I was desirous of remaining guilty, not considering that by this conduct I both ruined my own soul, and egregiously outraged thy goodness by rejecting and forsaking thee, even when thou wast come to seek and to save me.

But notwithstanding all this, thy mercy is so powerful that it draws me unto thee; for if thy hatred against sin has been manifested in divers ways, much more have the workings of thy mercy appeared in the salvation of men. To punish sinners thou hadst only to issue a command; but, Lord, to save them from destruction, thou

411 hadst to lay down thy life; this cost thee thine own blood shed upon the cross, even by the hands of those for whom thou didst offer it. In executing justice, thou hast acted as God; but to display thy marvellous mercy thou hast become man, assuming our infirmities, enduring disgrace and death, that we may be assured of the pardon of our sins. Lord, since it pleases thee that I should not perish, I come unto thee like the prodigal son, desiring to share that kind treatment which all who dwell in thy house receive, having found to my bitter experience that all those for whom I forsook thee are mine enemies. Although the recollection of my sin accuses me bitterly, and I am sorely amazed at the sight of thy throne, yet I cannot but assure myself that thou wilt pardon and bless me, and that thou wilt not banish me for ever from thy presence. Lord, hast not thou said and sworn, that thou hast no pleasure in the death of the sinner, and that thou delightest not in the destruction of me? Hast not thou said, that thou art not come to call the righteous but sinners to repentance, not to cure the whole but them that are sick? Wast not thou chastised for the iniquity of others? Has not thy blood sufficient virtue to wash out the sins of all the human race? Are not thy treasures more able to enrich me, than all the debt of Adam to impoverish me? Lord, although I had been the only person alive, or the only sinner in the world, thou wouldst not have failed to die for me. O my Saviour, I would say, and say it with truth, that I, individually,

stand in need of those blessings which thou hast given to all. What though the guilt of all had been mine, thy death is all mine. Even though I had committed all the sins of all, yet would I continue to trust in thee, and to assure myself that thy sacrifice and pardon is all mine, though it belong to all. Lord, thou wilt show this day who thou art. Here is a work by which thou mayest glorify thyself before the Father and before the host of heaven, even more than by the work of creation. Since thou art a physician, and such a physician, here are wounds which none but thyself is able to heal, inflicted on me by thy enemies and mine. Since thou art the health, and the life, and the salvation, sent from our Father in heaven, look upon my desperate maladies which no earthly physician can cure. Since thou art a Saviour, here is a ruin, by the repairing of which, thou wilt cause both enemies and friends to acknowledge thy hand and power.

Formerly I was amazed at the wickedness of those that crucified thee. So blind was I, that I did not perceive myself among the foremost of that band. Had I attended to the treacheries of my heart and the scandals of my wicked works, in contempt of thy judgment, commandments, 412 and mercy, I must have recognized myself. Yes; I held in my hands the crown of thorns for thy head, the nails to affix thee to the cross, the gall and vinegar to give thee to drink. The indifference with which I treated thy sufferings for me was all these. To have gone farther would have been to put myself beyond the reach of the remedy. But the horror of thy punishment, and the anger of the Father against those who despise thee, impose silence on me, and force me to confess, that truly thou art the Son of God. It is enough that I am the robber and malefactor sought out by thee. It is time to cry for a cure. Lord, remember me now that thou art come to thy kingdom. Having nothing to allege for my justification but an acknowledgement that I am unrighteous, destitute of every thing to move thy compassion but the greatness of my misery, unable to urge any other reason why thou shouldst cure me, but that my case is hopeless from every other hand, for my part I have no other sacrifice than my afflicted spirit and broken heart; and this I would not yet have had, if thou hadst not awakened me to the knowledge of my danger. The sacrifice which I need is that of thy blood and righteousness. * * * Abide with me for my preservation; for the flesh grumbles and resists, the devil will redouble his assaults the nearer I approach thee, and the world is full of gins and snares to entrap me. But such art thou, Lord, and so carefully dost thou watch over my salvation, that I am assured thou wilt never forsake me, and that thou wilt so guard and secure me, that I shall not be permitted to ruin myself.

No. IV

Letter from Francisco Farias and Nicolas Molino to Grindal, Bishop of London.

Most humane and illustrious Bishop,—the request which we have now humbly to present to you is, that you would give us your advice upon an affair of importance, as our father and faithful pastor. We understand, and have ascertained upon the best grounds, that a person inimical to the gospel, who for certain reasons had fled from Spain, has, with the view of regaining the favour of the Span-

413

ish monarch, fabricated a calumnious story, and has been communicating with the ambassador from Spain, and the governess of Flanders. The object of this calumny is, that we two, Spaniards, who have been these eight years exiles in this country for the word of God, should be delivered up and carried back to Spain. Their plan is as follows: that the king of Spain should be advertised to require the Spanish Inquisitors to draw information against us of heinous crimes, to which they should add another information against a Spaniard of infamous character, who has fled from Flanders for robbery and other crimes, and is now living here; that along with these advices, King Philip shall write to the queen, requesting these criminals to be delivered up to his ambassador, with the view of their being sent to Spain; and that the name of the notorious malefactor from Flanders shall be placed first in the list, that so no one may doubt that we are chargeable with as great or even greater crimes.

As to the informations which may be brought hither, we call God to witness, for whose name we suffer exile, that nothing can be laid to our charge which, if true, does not entitle us to praise rather than blame. But knowing that, on account of our religion, we have incurred the great odium of the Spanish Inquisition, and that, from the time we left Spain till the present time, it had expended above six thousand crowns in attempts to discover us and our fellow-exiles, we have no doubt that the Inquisitors will find as many false witnesses as they please, and thus be able to fix upon us whatever crimes they wish. Now, supposing that such informations should be presented to her Majesty the queen, along with letters from King Philip, desiring that we should be delivered up, we desire to know whether or not we shall be exposed to danger. If we should, it is our intention to remove to some other country where such a calumny will not be listened to. On this account, most pious Bishop, we request your advice as speedily as possible, in order that we may provide for our safety in time; for Judas will not sleep till he has betrayed us, and perhaps the informations are already upon the road. Besides, one of our wives is pregnant, and will not be able to bear the fatigues of the journey, if it be delayed much longer. You will see then that delay may be the means of our being delivered up, and taken to a place where we shall suffer the most inhuman tortures. If Providence has assigned this lot to us, we will adore him, and pray that he would confirm us in his faith, and so strengthen us that we may be enabled, for the glory of his name, to remain firm to the end.

No. V

Specimens of early Spanish Translations of the Scriptures.

The fragment of the Translation of the Bible by Bonifacio Ferrer, printed in 1478, but composed about the beginning of the 15th century, is extremely curious, as indicating the state of the Spanish language of that early period. As a specimen of it I shall give the last chapter of the book of Revelation, as reprinted in the Biblioteca Espanola of Rodriguez de Castro. To this I add, for the purpose of comparison, the same chapter in the version of the New Testament by Francisco de Enzinas, taken from the original work, printed in 1543.

Ferrer's Version

Mostra a mi vn riu de aygua viua resplandentaxi com crestall proceint de la seilla de deu [e] del anyell. En lo mig de la plaza de ella: e de la una parte e altra del riu lo fust de vida por tant dotze fruyts: per cascus mesos reten sô fruyt: e les fulles del fust a sanitat de les gêts. E res maleyt no sera pus: e la seilla de deu e del anyel seran en aquella: e los serunents de ell suiran a aquell: e veuran la faç de ell: e lo nom de ell scrit en los fronts de ells. E nit pus no sera: e no hauran fretura de lum de candela ne d'lum de sol: car lo senyor deu illuminara aqlls: e regnaran en los setgles dels setles. E dix a mi: aquestes paules fidellisimes son e verdaderes. E lo senyor deu dels spirits dels prophetes ha trames lo angel seu mostrar als seruêts seus les coses: que côue tost esser fetes. E veus que vinch iuaçosament. Benauenturat es lo qui guarda les paules de lu [sic] pphecia d'aquest libre.

E yo ioan qui oi e viu aquestes coses. E puix que les

Enzinas's Version

Y el me amostro un rio limpio de agua viua, resplandesçiente como Christal, que salia de la silla de Dios y del Cordero. En el medio de la plaça della. Y de la una parte y de la otra del rio el arbor de la vida, que trai doze frutos, dando cada mes su fruto: y las hojas del arbor son para la sanidad de los gentiles. Y toda cosa maldita, no sera mas. Pero el throno de Dios y el Cordero estara en ella, y sus sieruos le seruiran, y veran su rostro, y su nombre estara en sus frentes. Y la noche no esta mas alli, y no tienen neçessidad de lubre de candela ni de la lumbre del Sol. Por que el Senor dios los alumbra, y reinaran para siempre jamas. Y me dixo: Estas palabras son fieles y verdaderas. Y el Senor Dios de los sanctos prophetas ha embiado su angel, para mostrar a sus sieruos las cosas que es neçessario que sean hechas bien presto. Y veis aqui que yo vengo presto. Bienauenturado es aquel que guarda las palabras de la propheçia de este libro. Y yo

415

hagui oides e vistes: caygui per-
queado res dauant los peus del
angel: qui mostraua a mi aquestes
coses. E dix a mi: guarda nou
faces. Seruent so ensemps ab tu
e ab los frares teus prophetes: e
ab aquells qui seruen les paraules
de la prophecia de aquest libre. A
deu adora. E dix a mi: no sagelles
les paraules de la prophecia de
aquest libre. Car lo temps es
prop. Qui nou noga en cara: e
qui en les sutzures es en sutzeeix-
ca en car: e qui iustes sia iustificat
en cara e lo sant sia santificat en
cara. Ueus que vinch tots: e lo
guardo meu es ab mi: retrea cascu
segons les obres sues yo so alpha
e o: prímer e darrer: principi e fi.
Benauenturats son los que lauen
les stoles sues en la sanch del anyell, per que sia la potestat de ells
en en lo fust de vida: e per portes
entren en la ciutat. De fora los
cans a j'ents veri e los luxuriosos
los homicides e los seruint a les
idoles: e tot aquell qui ama e fa
mentira, yo iesus be trames [sic]
lo angel meu a testificar aquestes
coses a uosaltres en les esglesies,
416   yo so rael e linatge de dauid: ste-

Iohan soi aquel que ha oydo, y
visto estas cosas. Y despues que
yo vbe oydo y visto: yo me eche
para adorar delante del los pies
del Angel que me mostraba estas
cosas. Y el me dixo: Mira que to
no lo hagas: por que yo soi con-
sieruo tuyo, y de tus hermanos los
prophetas, y de los que guardan
las palabras de este libro. Adora
a Dios. Y me dixo: No senales las
palabras de la propheçia de esto
libro, por que el tiêpo esta çerca.
El que es injusto, sea injusto mas:
El que es suçio, ensuçiese mas. Y
el que es justo sea justificado mas.
Y el sancto sea sanctificado mas.
Y veis aqui, yo bengo presto. Y mi
galardon esta comigo, para dar a
cada vno, como sera su obra. Yo
soi, Alpha y O, el primero y el
postrero, el prinçipio y el fin.

Bien auenturados son los
que hazen sus mandamientos,
para que so potencia sea en el arbor de la vida, y que entren por
las puertas en las çibdad. Pero
los perros serran de fuera, y los
hecizeros, las rameras y los homi-
cidas, jdolatras, y cada vno que
ama, y haze mentira. Yo Iesus he

la resplandent e matutina. E lo
spos e la sposa di en: vine. E lo
qui ou: diga vine. E qui ha set
vinga. E qui vol prenda de grat
aygua de vida. Car faç testimonia
tot oint les paraules de la prophecia de aquest libre. Si algu haura aiustat aquestes: aiustara deu
sobre aqll les plagues que son
scrites en aquest libre: e si algu
haura diminuit de les paraules
de la prophecia de aquest libre:
tolra deu la part de ell del libre
de vida e de la ciutat sancta: e de
aquestes coses que son scrites en
aquest libre. Diu ho lo qui testimonia dona de aquestes coses.
Encara Uinch tots: amen. Uine
senyor iesus. La gracia del senyor
nostre iesucrist sia ab tots vosal-
tres Amen.

embiado mi Angel, para daros
testimonio de estas dosas en las
yglesias. Yo soi la raiz y el genero
de Dauid, la estrella resplandesçiente de la manana: Y el espirito
y la esposa dizen: Ben. Y el q lo
oy, diga: Ben. Y el que tiene sed:
benga. Y el que quiere, tome del
agua de la vida debalde.

Pues yo protesto a cada vno
que oy las palabras de la propheçia
de este libro: si alguno anadiere a
estas cosas, pondra Dios sobre el
las plagas escritas en este libro. Y
si alguno disminuyere de las palabras del libro de esta propheçia,
Dios quitara su parte del libro de
la vida, y de la santa çibdad, y de
las cosas que estâ escritas en este
libro. El que da testimonio de
estas cosas, dize: Cierto, yo bengo en breve. Amê. Tanbien. Ven
senor Jesus. La graçia de nuestro
Senor Iesu Christo sea con todos
vosotros. Amen.

INDEX

www.ingramcontent.com/pod-product-compliance
Lightning Source LLC
Chambersburg PA
CBHW021658120626
46545CB00004B/1290